RUSSIAN HISTORY ATLAS

Other Atlases in This Series

Russian History Atlas

Martin Gilbert
Fellow of Merton College, Oxford

Cartographic consultant ARTHUR BANKS

Macmillan Publishing Co., Inc.

NEW YORK

Contents

Preface

I have designed this Atlas in the hope that it is possible to present—
within the span of 146 maps—a survey of Russian history from the
earliest times to the present day. In drafting each map, I drew upon
material from a wide range of published works—books, articles, atlases
and single sheet maps—each of which I have listed in the bibliography.

On the maps themselves I have included much factual material not
normally associated with historical geography, such as the text of one of
Stalin's few surviving personal communications—the postcard to his sister-
in-law (printed on map 54), and Lenin's telegram to the Bolsheviks in
Sweden (printed on map 87). I have drafted each map individually, in such
a way as to enable the maximum factual information to be included
without making use of a separate page of text; and I have compiled the
index in order that it may serve as a means of using the Atlas as if it were a
volume of narrative.

I wish to acknowledge the help of many colleagues and friends. In 1962
I began research into Russian history under the supervision of Dr George
Katkov, whose insatiable curiosity about elusive historical facts, and whose
enthusiasm in tracking them down, have influenced all my subsequent
work. I also benefitted from the teaching and encouragement of Mr David
Footman, Mr Max Hayward, Dr Harry Willetts and the late Mr Guy Wint.
When I was preparing the first sketches for this Atlas, the maps I had
drawn and the facts I had incoprorated on them were scrutinized by three
friends—Mr Michael Glenny, Mr Dennis O'Flaherty and Dr Harry
Shukman—to each of whom I am most grateful for many detailed
suggestions, and for giving up much time to help me. At the outset of my
research I received valuable bibliographical advice from Dr J. L. I.
Simmons, and suggestions for specific maps from Mr Norman Davies,
Dr Ronald Hingley, Mr John B. Kingston and Mr Ewald Uustalu.
Jane Cousins helped me with bibliographical and historical research;
Mr Arthur Banks transcribed my sketches into clear, printable maps, and
Kate Fleming kept a vigilant eye on the cartography. Susie Sacher helped
me to compile the index: Sarah Graham, as well as undertaking all the

secretarial work, made many important suggestions, factual and cartographic.

I should welcome any suggestions for new maps which could be incorporated in subsequent editions, and any note of errors or obscurities.

Note on Transliteration

I have tried to adopt a uniform system of transliteration from the Russian. But where a place is familiar to English readers in an anglicized form, I have used the familiar form (thus Archangel, not Arkhangelsk; Caucasus, not Kavkaz; Moscow, not Moskva). Towns in the frontier area between eastern Europe and Russia are in general given their Russian transliteration: I have given alternate spellings in the index. In the case of the Polish towns of Belzec, Bialystok and Przemysl, I have retained the Polish forms (rather than the less familiar Russian, Belzhets, Belostok and Peremyshl.)

List of Maps

Section One

ANCIENT AND EARLY MODERN RUSSIA

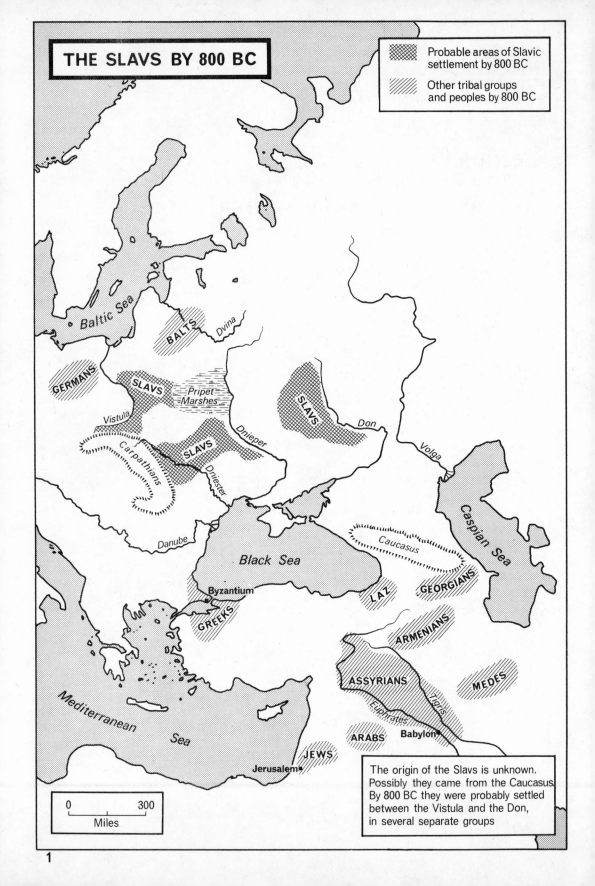

THE SLAVS BY 800 BC

Probable areas of Slavic settlement by 800 BC

Other tribal groups and peoples by 800 BC

Baltic Sea

BALTS

Dvina

GERMANS

SLAVS

Pripet Marshes

Vistula

Carpathians

SLAVS

Dnieper

SLAVS

Don

Volga

Dniester

Danube

Caspian Sea

Caucasus

Black Sea

Byzantium

GREEKS

LAZ

GEORGIANS

ARMENIANS

MEDES

ASSYRIANS

Tigris

Euphrates

Babylon

Mediterranean Sea

ARABS

JEWS

Jerusalem

The origin of the Slavs is unknown. Possibly they came from the Caucasus. By 800 BC they were probably settled between the Vistula and the Don, in several separate groups

0   300
Miles

1

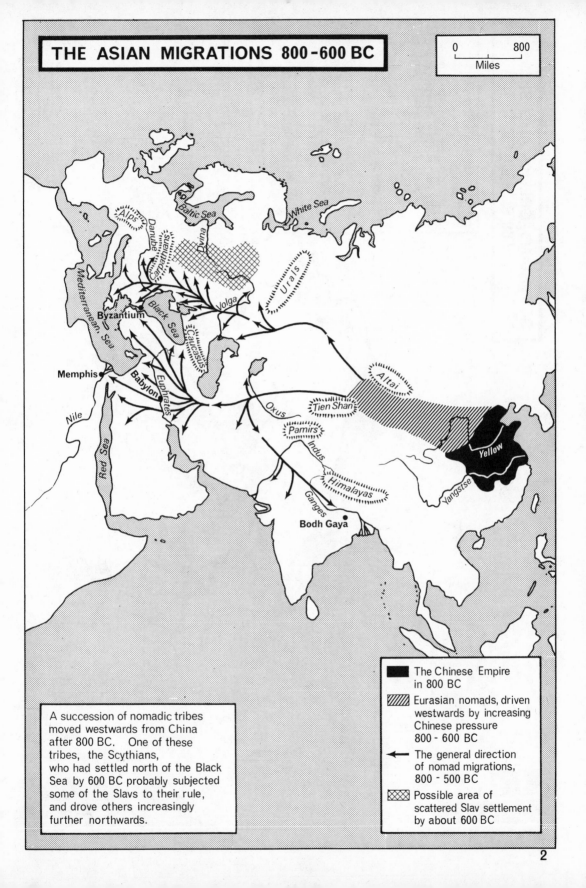

THE ASIAN MIGRATIONS 800-600 BC

0   800
Miles

A succession of nomadic tribes moved westwards from China after 800 BC.   One of these tribes, the Scythians, who had settled north of the Black Sea by 600 BC probably subjected some of the Slavs to their rule, and drove others increasingly further northwards.

The Chinese Empire in 800 BC

Eurasian nomads, driven westwards by increasing Chinese pressure 800 - 600 BC

The general direction of nomad migrations, 800 - 500 BC

Possible area of scattered Slav settlement by about 600 BC

Baltic Sea
White Sea
Alps
Danube
Carpathians
Divina
Urals
Volga
Mediterranean Sea
Byzantium
Black Sea
Caucasus
Altai
Tien Shan
Memphis
Babylon
Euphrates
Oxus
Pamirs
Yellow
Nile
Red Sea
Indus
Himalayas
Ganges
Yangtse
Bodh Gaya

2

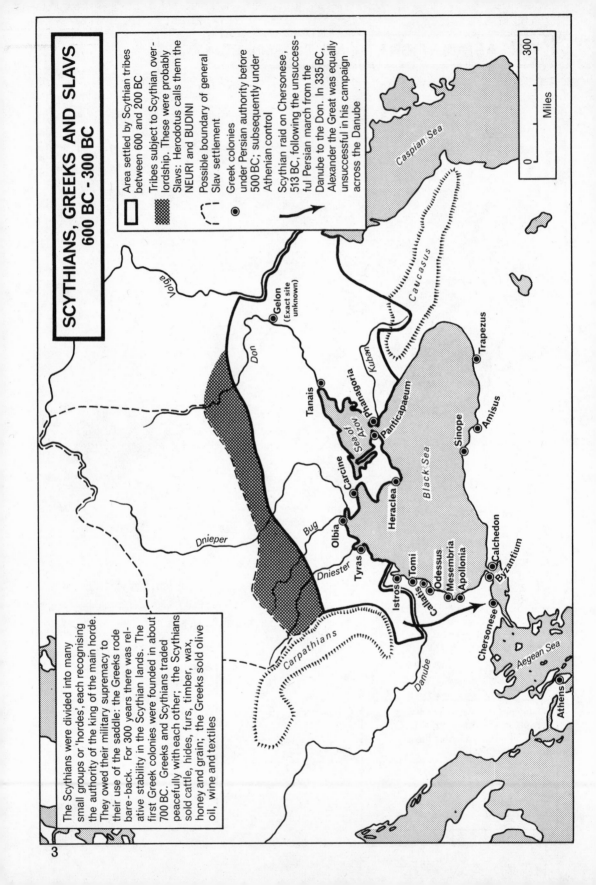

SCYTHIANS, GREEKS AND SLAVS
600 BC - 300 BC

☐ Area settled by Scythian tribes between 600 and 200 BC

▨ Tribes subject to Scythian over-lordship. These were probably Slavs: Herodotus calls them the NEURI and BUDINI

- - - Possible boundary of general Slav settlement

⊙ Greek colonies

Greek colonies under Persian authority before 500 BC; subsequently under Athenian control

→ Scythian raid on Chersonese, 513 BC, following the unsuccess-ful Persian march from the Danube to the Don. In 335 BC, Alexander the Great was equally unsuccessful in his campaign across the Danube

The Scythians were divided into many small groups or 'hordes', each recognising the authority of the king of the main horde. They owed their military supremacy to their use of the saddle: the Greeks rode bare-back. For 300 years there was rel-ative stability in the Scythian lands. The first Greek colonies were founded in about 700 BC. Greeks and Scythians traded peacefully with each other; the Scythians sold cattle, hides, furs, timber, wax, honey and grain; the Greeks sold olive oil, wine and textiles

Miles

Caspian Sea

Volga

Gelon (Exact site unknown)

Don

Caucasus

Kuban

Tanais

Phanagoria

Panticapaeum

Sea of Azov

Trapezus

Amisus

Carcine

Sinope

Heraclea

Black Sea

Bug

Dnieper

Olbia

Dniester

Tyras

Calchedon

Byzantium

Istros

Tomi

Callatis

Odessus

Mesembria

Apollonia

Carpathians

Danube

Chersonese

Aegean Sea

Athens

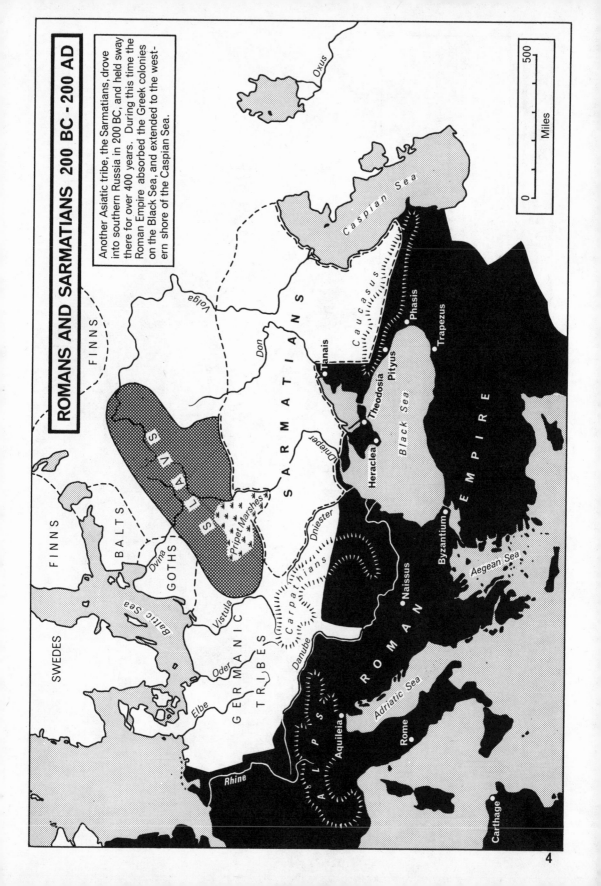

ROMANS AND SARMATIANS 200 BC - 200 AD

Another Asiatic tribe, the Sarmatians, drove into southern Russia in 200 BC, and held sway there for over 400 years. During this time the Roman Empire absorbed the Greek colonies on the Black Sea, and extended to the western shore of the Caspian Sea.

500

0

Miles

Oxus

Caspian Sea

FINNS

Volga

Don

S A R M A T I A N S

Caucasus

Tanais

Dnieper

Phasis

Trapezus

Theodosia

Pityus

Black Sea

Heraclea

SWEDES

FINNS

BALTS

Dvina

S L A V S

Baltic Sea

GOTHS

Pripet Marshes

Dniester

Vistula

GERMANIC

Oder

TRIBES

Carpathians

Danube

Elbe

Byzantium

Aegean Sea

Naissus

R O M A N

Adriatic Sea

A L P S

Rhine

Aquileia

Rome

E M P I R E

Carthage

4

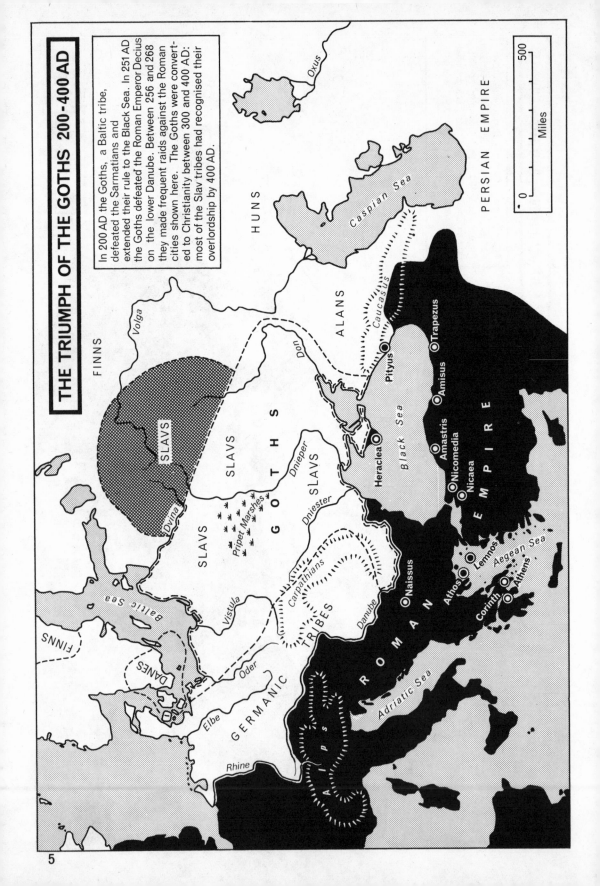

THE TRIUMPH OF THE GOTHS 200-400 AD

In 200 AD the Goths, a Baltic tribe, defeated the Sarmatians and extended their rule to the Black Sea. In 251 AD the Goths defeated the Roman Emperor Decius on the lower Danube. Between 256 and 268 they made frequent raids against the Roman cities shown here. The Goths were converted to Christianity between 300 and 400 AD: most of the Slav tribes had recognised their overlordship by 400 AD.

500

Miles

0

PERSIAN EMPIRE

Oxus

FINNS

Volga

HUNS

Caspian Sea

ALANS

Caucasus

FINNS

SLAVS

SLAVS

Don

Pityus

Trapezus

Dvina

SLAVS

GOTHS

Dnieper

SLAVS

Amisus

Black Sea

Dniester

Heraclea

Amastris

Baltic Sea

Pripet Marshes

Nicomedia

Nicaea

DANES

Vistula

Carpathians

TRIBES

Naissus

Lemnos

Aegean Sea

EMPIRE

Oder

Danube

ROMAN

Athos

Corinth

Athens

GERMANIC

A L P S

Adriatic Sea

Elbe

Rhine

5

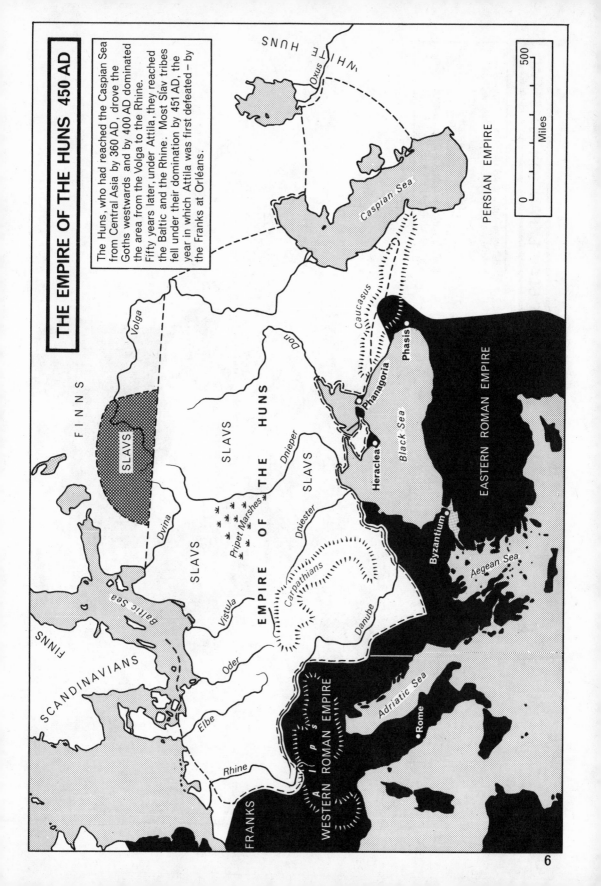

THE EMPIRE OF THE HUNS 450 AD

The Huns, who had reached the Caspian Sea from Central Asia by 360 AD, drove the Goths westwards and by 400 AD dominated the area from the Volga to the Rhine. Fifty years later, under Attila, they reached the Baltic and the Rhine. Most Slav tribes fell under their domination by 451 AD, the year in which Attila was first defeated – by the Franks at Orléans.

WHITE HUNS

PERSIAN EMPIRE

Oxus

Caspian Sea

Miles

0   500

FINNS

Volga

Don

SLAVS

SLAVS

SLAVS

SLAVS

Dnieper

Dvina

Pripet Marshes

Caucasus

Phanagoria

Phasis

EMPIRE OF THE HUNS

Dniester

Heraclea

Black Sea

EASTERN ROMAN EMPIRE

FINNS

Baltic Sea

Vistula

Oder

Carpathians

Danube

Byzantium

Aegean Sea

SCANDINAVIANS

Elbe

Rhine

A l p s

WESTERN ROMAN EMPIRE

Adriatic Sea

• Rome

FRANKS

6

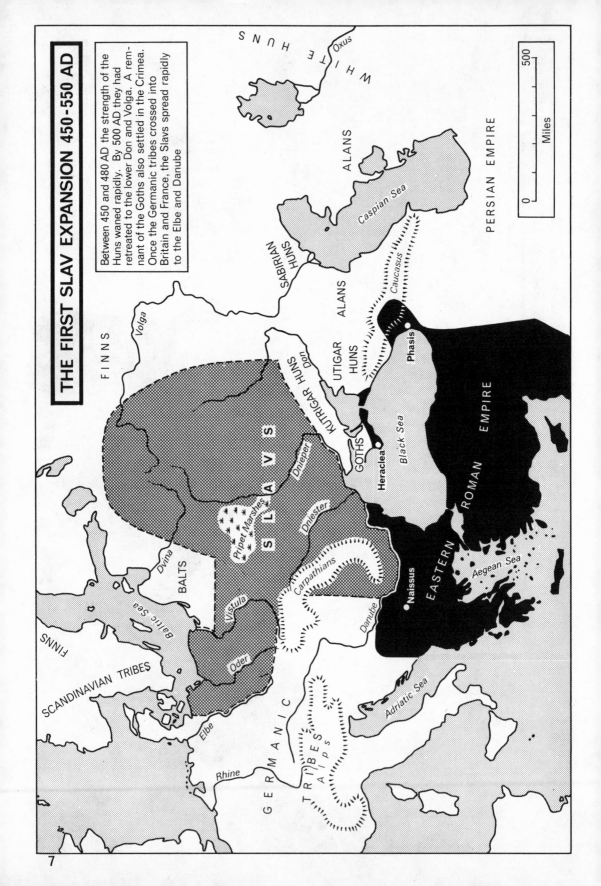

THE FIRST SLAV EXPANSION 450-550 AD

Between 450 and 480 AD the strength of the Huns waned rapidly. By 500 AD they had retreated to the lower Don and Volga. A remnant of the Goths also settled in the Crimea. Once the Germanic tribes crossed into Britain and France, the Slavs spread rapidly to the Elbe and Danube

WHITE HUNS

Oxus

ALANS

Caspian Sea

PERSIAN EMPIRE

SABIRIAN HUNS

ALANS

UTIGAR HUNS

Caucasus

Phasis

FINNS

Volga

Don

KUTRIGAR HUNS

GOTHS

Heraclea

Black Sea

EASTERN ROMAN EMPIRE

Dnieper

SLAVS

Pripet Marshes

Dniester

Aegean Sea

BALTS

Dvina

Carpathians

Naissus

FINNS

Baltic Sea

Vistula

Danube

SCANDINAVIAN TRIBES

Oder

GERMANIC TRIBES

Adriatic Sea

Elbe

Alps

Rhine

500

0

Miles

500

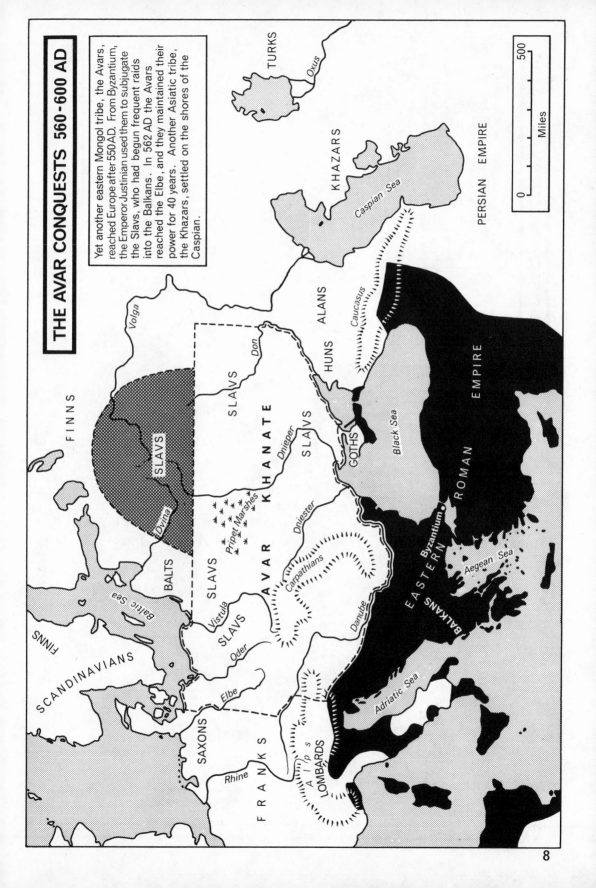

THE AVAR CONQUESTS 560-600 AD

Yet another eastern Mongol tribe, the Avars, reached Europe after 550 AD. From Byzantium, the Emperor Justinian used them to subjugate the Slavs, who had begun frequent raids into the Balkans. In 562 AD the Avars reached the Elbe, and they maintained their power for 40 years. Another Asiatic tribe, the Khazars, settled on the shores of the Caspian.

TURKS

Oxus

KHAZARS

PERSIAN EMPIRE

Caspian Sea

0 500

Miles

FINNS

Volga

SLAVS

Don

SLAVS

ALANS

HUNS

Caucasus

SLAVS

Dvina

SLAVS

BALTS

Dnieper

A V A R   K H A N A T E

SLAVS

GOTHS

Black Sea

R O M A N   E M P I R E

Baltic Sea

Pripet Marshes

Dniester

Carpathians

Byzantium

E A S T E R N

Aegean Sea

FINNS

SCANDINAVIANS

Vistula

SLAVS

Danube

B A L K A N S

SLAVS

Oder

SAXONS

Elbe

Adriatic Sea

F R A N K S

Alps

Rhine

LOMBARDS

8

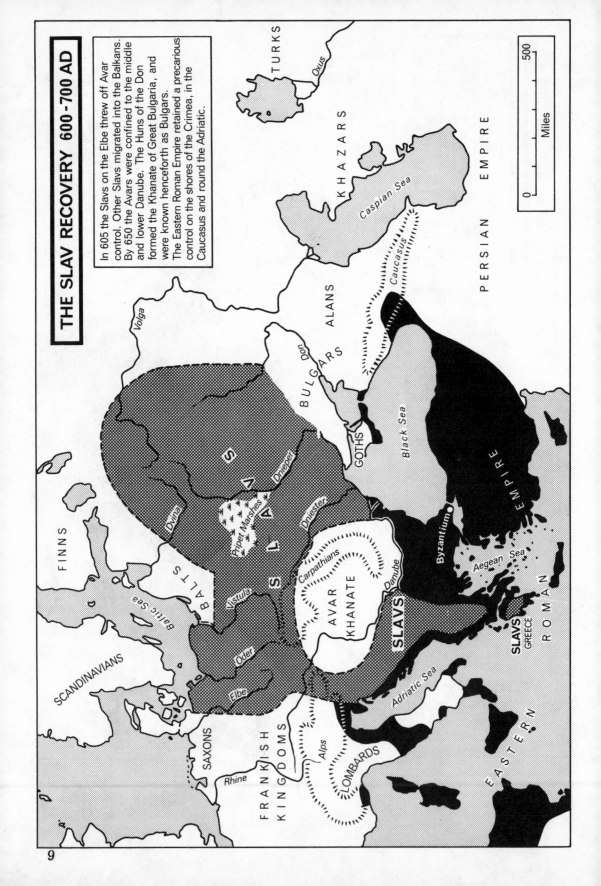

THE SLAV RECOVERY 600-700 AD

In 605 the Slavs on the Elbe threw off Avar control. Other Slavs migrated into the Balkans. By 650 the Avars were confined to the middle and lower Danube. The Huns of the Don formed the Khanate of Great Bulgaria, and were known henceforth as Bulgars. The Eastern Roman Empire retained a precarious control on the shores of the Crimea, in the Caucasus and round the Adriatic.

500

Miles

0

TURKS

Oxus

KHAZARS

Caspian Sea

PERSIAN EMPIRE

Volga

BULGARS

ALANS

Don

Caucasus

FINNS

S L A V S

Dvina

Dnieper

Pripet Marshes

Dniester

GOTHS

Black Sea

EMPIRE

BALTS

Vistula

Carpathians

Danube

Byzantium

Aegean Sea

Baltic Sea

AVAR KHANATE

SLAVS

ROMAN

SCANDINAVIANS

Oder

Alps

Adriatic Sea

SLAVS

GREECE

SAXONS

Elbe

FRANKISH KINGDOMS

LOMBARDS

EASTERN

Rhine

9

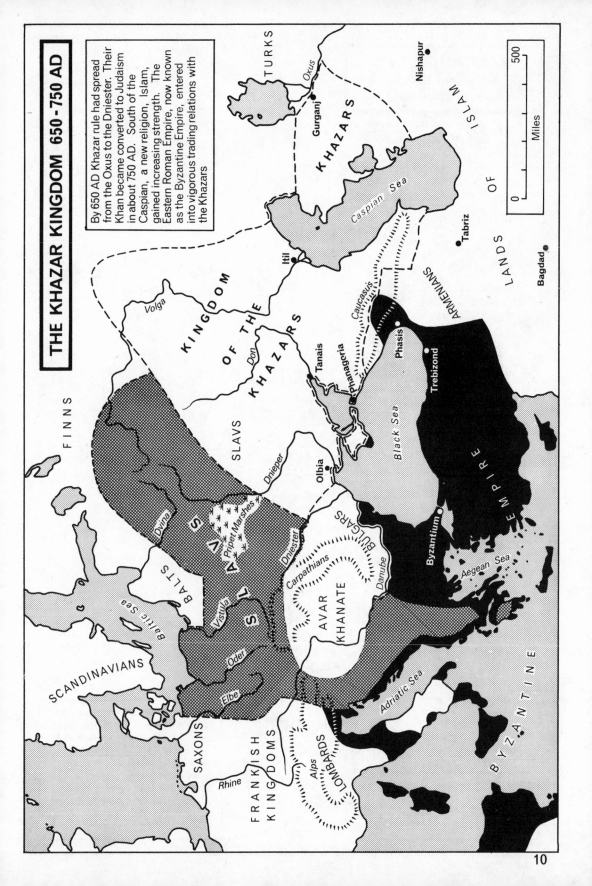

THE KHAZAR KINGDOM 650-750 AD

By 650 AD Khazar rule had spread from the Oxus to the Dniester. Their Khan became converted to Judaism in about 750 AD. South of the Caspian, a new religion, Islam, gained increasing strength. The Eastern Roman Empire, now known as the Byzantine Empire, entered into vigorous trading relations with the Khazars

TURKS

KHAZARS

Nishapur

Oxus

Gurganj

LANDS OF ISLAM

Caspian Sea

Tabriz

Itil

Bagdad

KINGDOM

Volga

OF THE

Don

KHAZARS

Caucasus

ARMENIANS

Tanais

Phanageria

Phasis

FINNS

SLAVS

Dnieper

Trebizond

Black Sea

EMPIRE

Olbia

Duina

Pripet Marshes

S

V

A

L

Dniester

BULGARS

Byzantium

Aegean Sea

BALTS

Vistula

Carpathians

Danube

SCANDINAVIANS

Baltic Sea

Oder

S

L

A

V

S

AVAR KHANATE

Adriatic Sea

BYZANTINE

Elbe

SAXONS

FRANKISH KINGDOMS

Alps

LOMBARDS

Rhine

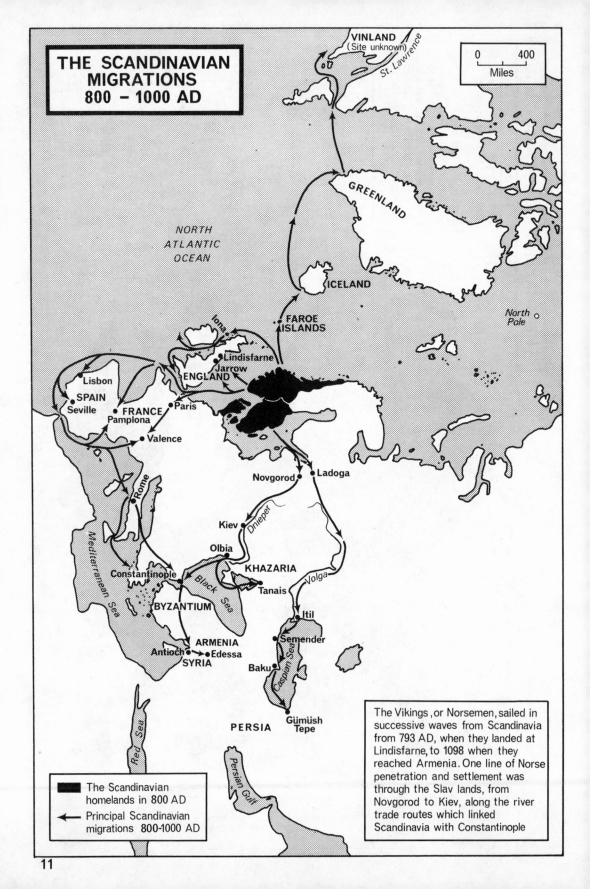

THE SCANDINAVIAN
MIGRATIONS
800 – 1000 AD

0   400
Miles

VINLAND
(Site unknown)

St. Lawrence

GREENLAND

NORTH
ATLANTIC
OCEAN

ICELAND

North
Pole

FAROE
ISLANDS

Iona

Lindisfarne
Jarrow
ENGLAND

Lisbon
SPAIN
Seville
FRANCE   Paris
Pamplona
Valence

Rome

Novgorod   Ladoga

Kiev   Dniepet

Olbia

KHAZARIA   Volga

Constantinople   Black Sea

Tanais

Mediterranean Sea   BYZANTIUM

Itil

Semender

ARMENIA
Antioch   Edessa
SYRIA

Baku

Caspian Sea

Red Sea

Gümüsh
Tepe

PERSIA

Persian Gulf

The Vikings, or Norsemen, sailed in
successive waves from Scandinavia
from 793 AD, when they landed at
Lindisfarne, to 1098 when they
reached Armenia. One line of Norse
penetration and settlement was
through the Slav lands, from
Novgorod to Kiev, along the river
trade routes which linked
Scandinavia with Constantinople

▬▬ The Scandinavian
homelands in 800 AD
◄── Principal Scandinavian
migrations 800-1000 AD

11

Slav settlement by 880 AD

SERB Principal Slav tribes

BALTS Other tribes

'Kievan Rus', ruled by the Norsemen (Varangarians), who took tribute from the neighbouring Slavs, and protected them against Khazar and Pecheneg attacks

NORSE

SWEDES

FINNS

DANES

Visby

OBODRICHI

Baltic Sea

SLOVIANIANS

Novgorod

CHEREMESIANS

Volga

BALTS

VIATCHIANS

MORDVINS

POLOCHANE

Smolensk

GERMANS

POLES

MAZOVIANS

Pripet Marshes

KRIVICHIANS

RADIMICHIANS

SILESIANS

CZECHS

DEREVLIANS

SEVERIANS

Don

MORAVIANS

SLOVAKS

VOLHYNIANS

POLIANIANS

Kiev

KHAZARS

Elbe

SLOVENES

Danube

MAGYARS

PECHENEGS

Venice

CROATS

VLACHS

Tmutorokan

Caucasus

Adriatic Sea

SERBS

Black Sea

ARMENIANS

Preslav

BULGARS

Constantinople

Ægean Sea

Athens

GREEKS

The Norse settlers between Novgorod and Kiev quickly dominated the local Slavs, over whom they established political control. Known as "Varangarians", these Norse overlords moulded the Slavs into a coherent federation, "Kievan Rus". Originally Norse speaking, Kievan Rus, or Russia, saw a close mingling of Scandinavian and Slav culture; and the emergence of a strong Kievan, or Russian national consciousness. The first Varangarian ruler, Rurik, led an expedition against Constantinople in 860 AD. His successor Oleg established his capital at Kiev in about 880 AD.

0   300

Miles

12

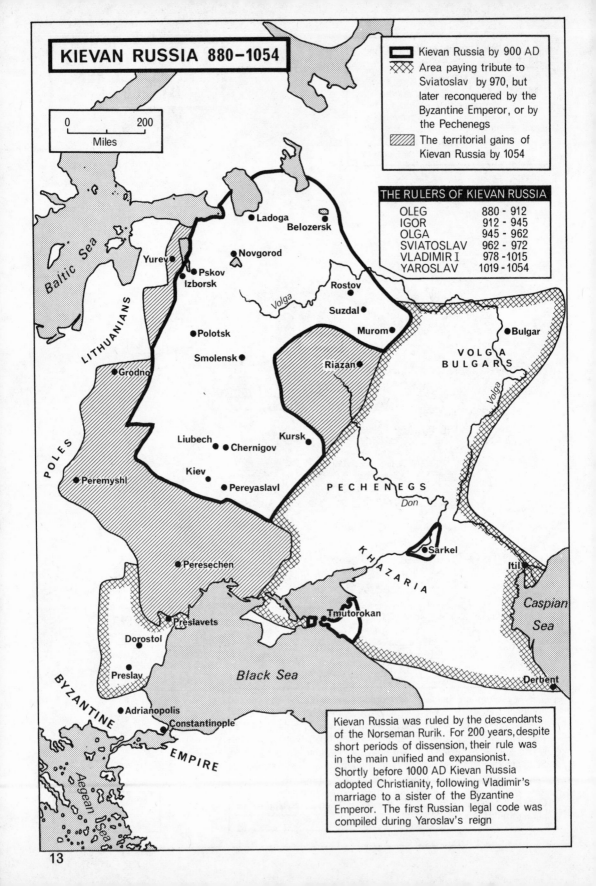

KIEVAN RUSSIA 880–1054

0 — 200
Miles

Kievan Russia by 900 AD

Area paying tribute to Sviatoslav by 970, but later reconquered by the Byzantine Emperor, or by the Pechenegs

The territorial gains of Kievan Russia by 1054

THE RULERS OF KIEVAN RUSSIA

OLEG	880 – 912
IGOR	912 – 945
OLGA	945 – 962
SVIATOSLAV	962 – 972
VLADIMIR I	978 – 1015
YAROSLAV	1019 – 1054

Baltic Sea

Ladoga
Belozersk

Yurev
Novgorod
Pskov
Izborsk

Rostov
Suzdal
Murom
Bulgar

LITHUANIANS

Polotsk
Smolensk
Volga

VOLGA BULGARS

Grodno

Liubech
Chernigov
Kursk

POLES

Kiev
Pereyaslavl

PECHENEGS
Don

Peremyshl

Volga

Peresechen

KHAZARIA

Sarkel

Itil

Caspian Sea

Preslavets
Tmutorokan

Dorostol

Preslav

Black Sea

Derbent

BYZANTINE

Adrianopolis
Constantinople

EMPIRE

Aegean Sea

Kievan Russia was ruled by the descendants of the Norseman Rurik. For 200 years, despite short periods of dissension, their rule was in the main unified and expansionist. Shortly before 1000 AD Kievan Russia adopted Christianity, following Vladimir's marriage to a sister of the Byzantine Emperor. The first Russian legal code was compiled during Yaroslav's reign

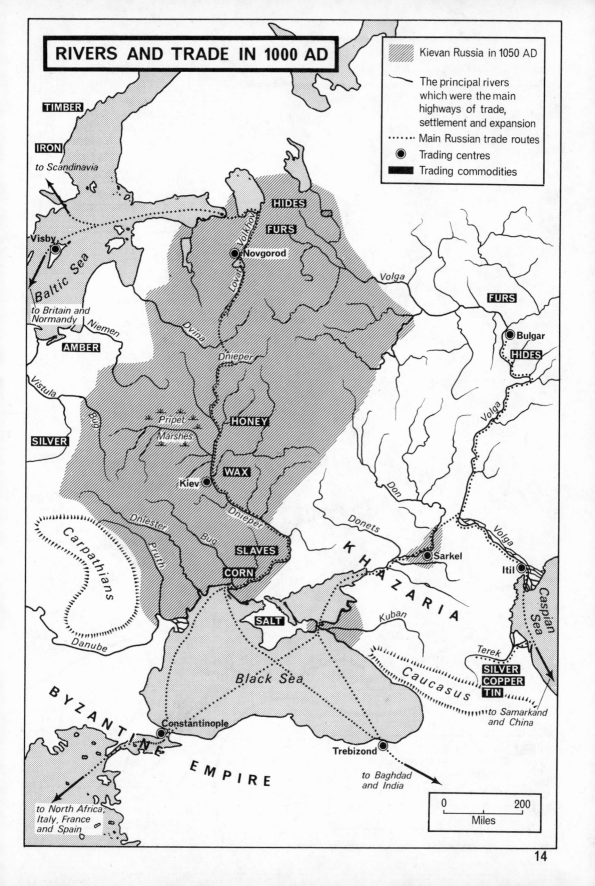

RIVERS AND TRADE IN 1000 AD

Kievan Russia in 1050 AD

The principal rivers
which were the main
highways of trade,
settlement and expansion

Main Russian trade routes

Trading centres

Trading commodities

TIMBER

IRON

to Scandinavia

HIDES

FURS

Visby

Baltic Sea

*to Britain and
Normandy*

Niemen

AMBER

Vistula

Bug

SILVER

Novgorod

Volkhov

Lovat

Dvina

Dnieper

Pripet

Marshes

HONEY

WAX

Kiev

Dniester

Prut

Bug

Dnieper

SLAVES

CORN

Volga

FURS

Bulgar

HIDES

Volga

Don

Donets

K H A Z A R I A

Sarkel

Itil

Volga

*Caspian
Sea*

Carpathians

Danube

SALT

Kuban

Black Sea

Caucasus

Terek

SILVER
COPPER
TIN

*to Samarkand
and China*

B Y Z A N T I N E

E M P I R E

Constantinople

Trebizond

*to Baghdad
and India*

*to North Africa,
Italy, France
and Spain*

0	200

Miles

CHRISTIANITY AND THE SLAVS BY 1000 AD

The spread of Christianity led to the division of the Slav world. The Croats (in 700 AD) and the Poles (in 999 AD) were converted to Roman Catholicism. The Serbs (in 700 AD), Bulgars (865 AD) and Russians (988 AD) were converted to Eastern (Orthodox) Catholicism. This led in particular to strong antipathy between Russians and Poles, and also between Serbs and Croats

NORSE

SWEDES

North Sea

Baltic Sea

•Novgorod

•Smolensk

RUSSIANS

SAXONS

GERMANS

Rhine

Oder

POLES

•Kiev

Volga

Don

Dniester

•Paris

FRANKS

Danube

Carpathians

MAGYARS

ALANS

Caucasus

Caspian Sea

Alps

Milan •

CROATS

Adriatic Sea

SERBS

Black Sea

Constantinople

Tiflis

Rome •

BULGARS

•Ochrid

ARMENIANS

• Tabriz

Pyrenees

GREEKS

Tarsus

Tigris

Athens

• Aleppo

• Bagdad

Kairouan •

Mediterranean Sea

Euphrates

Jerusalem •

Alexandria

Dead Sea

Nile

Red Sea

▮ The spread of Eastern, or Orthodox, Catholicism, under Constantinople's authority by 1000 AD

▨ Western, or Roman, Catholicism

▯ Areas under Muslim, or Islamic, rule

0   400
Miles

15

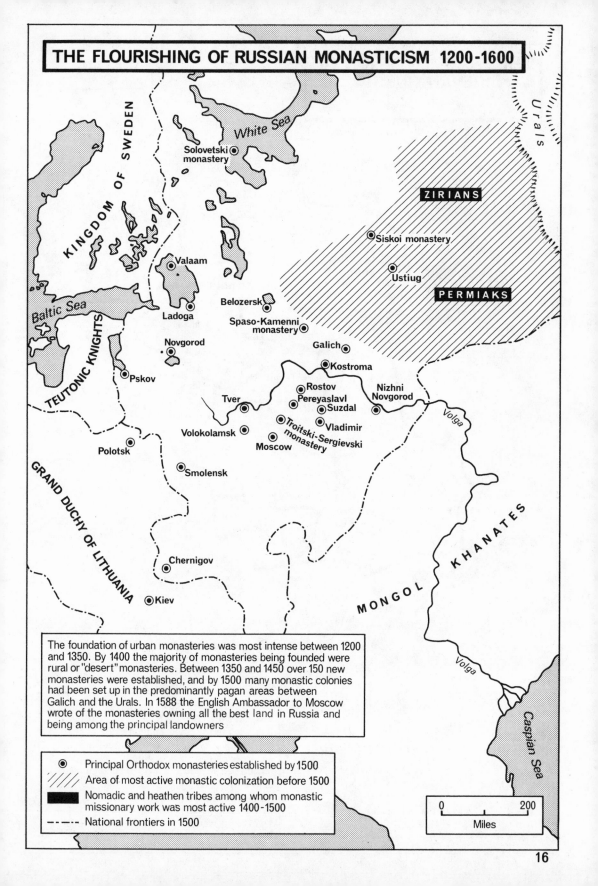

THE FLOURISHING OF RUSSIAN MONASTICISM 1200-1600

White Sea

KINGDOM OF SWEDEN

Urals

Solovetski monastery

ZIRIANS

Siskoi monastery

Ustiug

PERMIAKS

Valaam

Belozersk

Baltic Sea

Ladoga

Spaso-Kamenni monastery

Galich

Novgorod

TEUTONIC KNIGHTS

Kostroma

Pskov

Rostov

Nizhni Novgorod

Tver

Pereyaslavl

Suzdal

Volga

Volokolamsk

Vladimir

Troitski-Sergievski monastery

Polotsk

Moscow

Smolensk

GRAND DUCHY OF LITHUANIA

MONGOL KHANATES

Chernigov

Kiev

Volga

Caspian Sea

The foundation of urban monasteries was most intense between 1200 and 1350. By 1400 the majority of monasteries being founded were rural or "desert" monasteries. Between 1350 and 1450 over 150 new monasteries were established, and by 1500 many monastic colonies had been set up in the predominantly pagan areas between Galich and the Urals. In 1588 the English Ambassador to Moscow wrote of the monasteries owning all the best land in Russia and being among the principal landowners

◉ Principal Orthodox monasteries established by 1500

/// Area of most active monastic colonization before 1500

▬ Nomadic and heathen tribes among whom monastic missionary work was most active 1400-1500

–·–·– National frontiers in 1500

0   200

Miles

THE FRAGMENTATION OF KIEVAN RUSSIA 1054–1238

0   200
Miles

DEPENDENCIES OF NOVGOROD

FINNS

Ustiug

Ladoga
•Belozersk
REPUBLIC   VLADIMIR–SUZDAL
OF NOVGOROD
Reval•   •Novgorod   Kostroma•
•Yaroslavl
•Rostov   VOLGA
•Pskov   Torzhok•   BULGARS
Izborsk   Tver•   •Suzdal
Riga•   Vladimir•
Dvina   Moscow•
Murom•
LITHUANIA   Polotsk•   SMOLENSK   Riazan•
Kovno•   Vitebsk•   Viazma•   MUROM–
•Smolensk   RIAZAN
POLOTSK
•Minsk   CHERNIGOV
Vistula
TUROV   NOVGOROD–
Bialystok•   •Pinsk   SEVERSK
POLAND   •Turov   Chernigov•
VOLHYNIA   KIEV   PEREYASLAVL
Cracow•   •Kiev   •Pereyaslavl
•Zhitomir
GALICIA   Don
•Galich
Dniester   CUMANS or POLOVTSI
Carpathians
HUNGARY

Black
Sea

Constantinople•

☐ The twelve Principalities
of Russia in 1100

On the death of Yaroslav in 1054, Kievan Russia
was divided among his sons. Their constant
feuds led to the fragmentation of the once
powerful kingdom. United briefly from 1113 to 1125
by Vladimir Monomakh, the Russian lands were again
divided and in conflict during the hundred years
before the Mongol invasion of 1238. In 1199 Galicia
and Volhynia were united, and in 1254 recognised
by the Pope as an independent kingdom. In
1307 Polotsk came under Lithuanian suzerainty

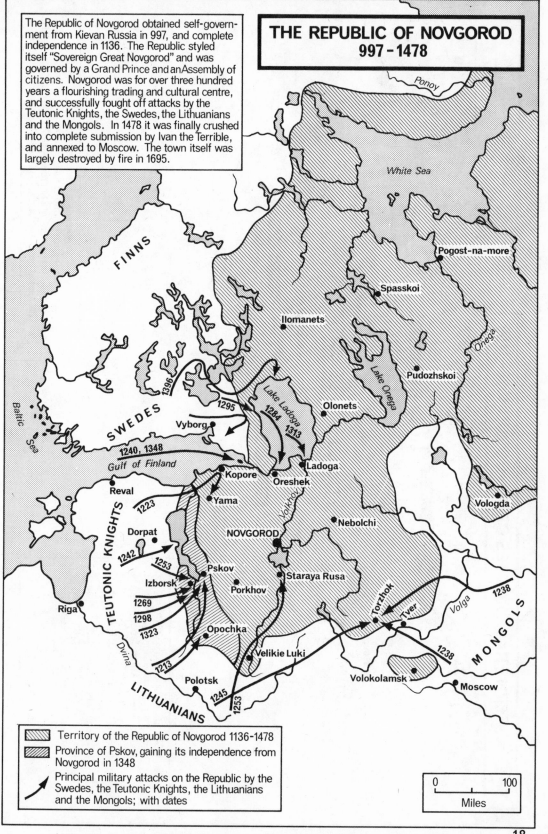

THE REPUBLIC OF NOVGOROD
997 - 1478

The Republic of Novgorod obtained self-govern-ment from Kievan Russia in 997, and complete independence in 1136. The Republic styled itself "Sovereign Great Novgorod" and was governed by a Grand Prince and an Assembly of citizens. Novgorod was for over three hundred years a flourishing trading and cultural centre, and successfully fought off attacks by the Teutonic Knights, the Swedes, the Lithuanians and the Mongols. In 1478 it was finally crushed into complete submission by Ivan the Terrible, and annexed to Moscow. The town itself was largely destroyed by fire in 1695.

Ponoy

White Sea

FINNS

Pogost-na-more

Spasskoi

Ilomanets

Pudozhskoi

Lake Onega

Onega

Olonets

Lake Ladoga

SWEDES

1396

1295

1284

1313

Vyborg

Baltic Sea

1240, 1348

Gulf of Finland

Ladoga

Kopore

Oreshek

Vologda

Reval

Yama

Volkhov

Nebolchi

1223

Dorpat

NOVGOROD

TEUTONIC KNIGHTS

1242

1253

Pskov

Staraya Rusa

Izborsk

Porkhov

Torzhok

Volga

1238

Riga

1269

1298

1323

Opochka

Tver

MONGOLS

Dvina

1213

Velikie Luki

1238

LITHUANIANS

Polotsk

1245

1253

Volokolamsk

Moscow

Territory of the Republic of Novgorod 1136-1478

Province of Pskov, gaining its independence from Novgorod in 1348

Principal military attacks on the Republic by the Swedes, the Teutonic Knights, the Lithuanians and the Mongols; with dates

0   100
Miles

18

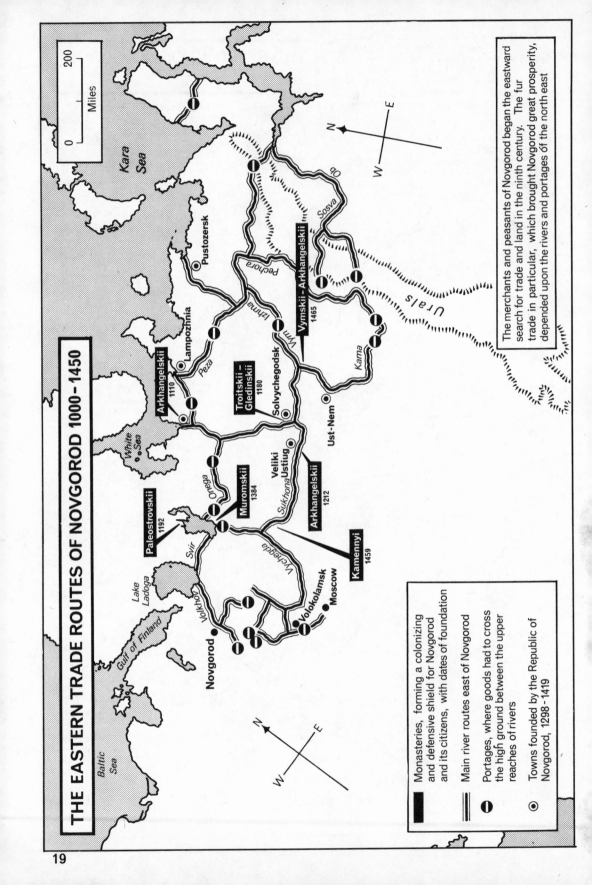

THE EASTERN TRADE ROUTES OF NOVGOROD 1000-1450

The merchants and peasants of Novgorod began the eastward search for trade and land in the ninth century. The fur trade in particular, which brought Novgorod great prosperity, depended upon the rivers and portages of the north east

Monasteries, forming a colonizing and defensive shield for Novgorod and its citizens, with dates of foundation

Main river routes east of Novgorod

Portages, where goods had to cross the high ground between the upper reaches of rivers

Towns founded by the Republic of Novgorod, 1298-1419

Kara Sea

White Sea

Baltic Sea

Lake Ladoga

Gulf of Finland

Pustozersk

Lampozhnia

Arkhangelskii 1110

Vymskii – Arkhangelskii 1465

Troitskii – Gledinskii 1180

Solvychegodsk

Ust-Nem

Veliki Ustiug

Arkhangelskii 1212

Muromskii 1384

Paleostrovskii 1192

Kamennyi 1459

Volokolamsk

Moscow

Novgorod

Ob

Sosva

Pechora

Izhma

Vym

Kama

Urals

Peza

Onega

Sukhona

Vychegda

Svir

Volkhov

Miles
0
200

19

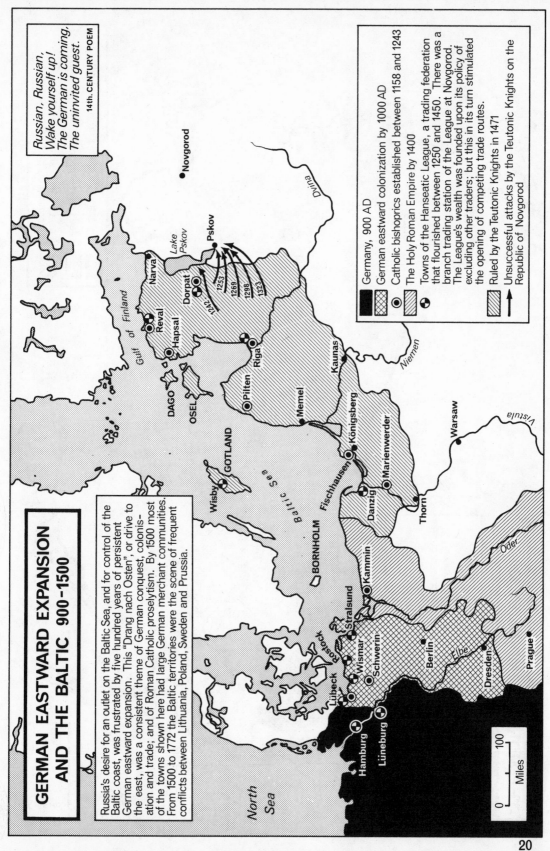

GERMAN EASTWARD EXPANSION AND THE BALTIC 900–1500

Russia's desire for an outlet on the Baltic Sea, and for control of the Baltic coast, was frustrated by five hundred years of persistent German eastward expansion. This "Drang nach Osten", or drive to the east, was a consistent theme of German conquest, colonisation and trade; and of Roman Catholic proselytism. By 1500 most of the towns shown here had large German merchant communities. From 1500 to 1772 the Baltic territories were the scene of frequent conflicts between Lithuania, Poland, Sweden and Prussia.

Russian, Russian,
Wake yourself up!
The German is coming.
The uninvited guest.

14th. CENTURY POEM

Germany, 900 AD

German eastward colonization by 1000 AD

Catholic bishoprics established between 1158 and 1243

The Holy Roman Empire by 1400

Towns of the Hanseatic League, a trading federation that flourished between 1250 and 1450. There was a branch trading station of the League at Novgorod. The League's wealth was founded upon its policy of excluding other traders; but this in its turn stimulated the opening of competing trade routes.

Ruled by the Teutonic Knights in 1471

Unsuccessful attacks by the Teutonic Knights on the Republic of Novgorod

Novgorod

Narva
Reval
Hapsal
Dorpat
Pskov
Lake Pskov
Gulf of Finland
DAGO
OSEL
Pilten
Riga
Memel
Kaunas
Niemen
Königsberg
Fischhausen
Danzig
Marienwerder
Thorn
Warsaw
Vistula
Kammin
Oder
GOTLAND
Wisby
BORNHOLM
Baltic Sea
Stralsund
Rostock
Wismar
Schwerin
Berlin
Elbe
Dresden
Prague
Lübeck
Lüneburg
Hamburg
North Sea

1242
1253
1269
1298
1323

0   100
Miles

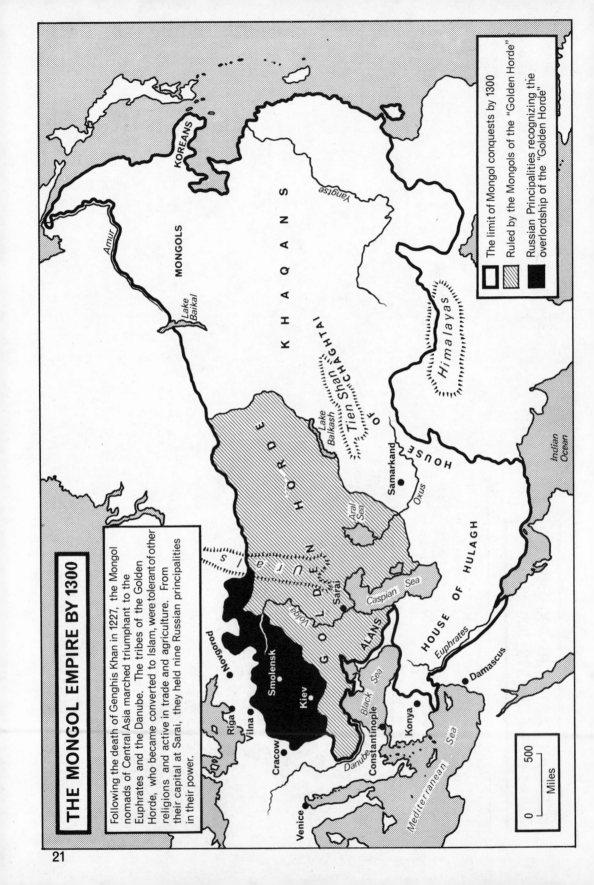

THE MONGOL EMPIRE BY 1300

Following the death of Genghis Khan in 1227, the Mongol nomads of Central Asia marched triumphant to the Euphrates and the Danube. The tribes of the Golden Horde, who became converted to Islam, were tolerant of other religions and active in trade and agriculture. From their capital at Sarai, they held nine Russian principalities in their power.

The limit of Mongol conquests by 1300

Ruled by the Mongols of the "Golden Horde"

Russian Principalities recognizing the overlordship of the "Golden Horde"

KOREANS

MONGOLS

Amur

Lake Baikal

Yangtse

KHAQANS

HOUSE OF CHAGHTAI

Tien Shan

Lake Balkash

Himalayas

Indian Ocean

Samarkand

Oxus

Aral Sea

SIBERIA

GOLDEN HORDE

Sarai

Caspian Sea

ALANS

HOUSE OF HULAGH

Euphrates

Damascus

Volga

Novgorod

Smolensk

Kiev

Riga

Vilna

Cracow

Black Sea

Konya

Danube

Constantinople

Venice

Mediterranean Sea

0   500

Miles

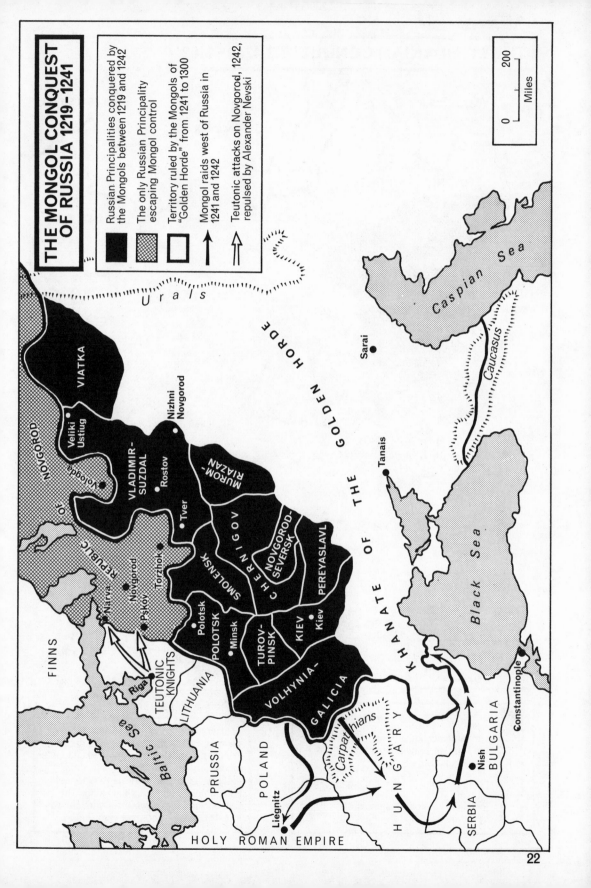

THE MONGOL CONQUEST
OF RUSSIA 1219–1241

Russian Principalities conquered by
the Mongols between 1219 and 1242

The only Russian Principality
escaping Mongol control

Territory ruled by the Mongols of
"Golden Horde" from 1241 to 1300

Mongol raids west of Russia in
1241 and 1242

Teutonic attacks on Novgorod, 1242,
repulsed by Alexander Nevski

0   200
Miles

U r a l s

Caspian Sea

Sarai

Tanais

Caucasus

VIATKA

NOVGOROD

Veliki
Ustiug

Nizhni
Novgorod

Vologda

VLADIMIR-
SUZDAL

Rostov

MUROM-
RIAZAN

Tver

REPUBLIC

Narva

Novgorod

Torzhok

Pskov

SMOLENSK

CHERNIGOV

NOVGOROD-
SEVERSK

PEREYASLAVL

FINNS

Polotsk

Minsk

POLOTSK

TUROV-
PINSK

KIEV

Kiev

Riga

TEUTONIC
KNIGHTS

LITHUANIA

VOLHYNIA-
GALICIA

Carpathians

KHANATE OF THE GOLDEN HORDE

Black Sea

Constantinople

Baltic Sea

PRUSSIA

POLAND

H U N G A R Y

Nish

BULGARIA

SERBIA

Liegnitz

HOLY ROMAN EMPIRE

22

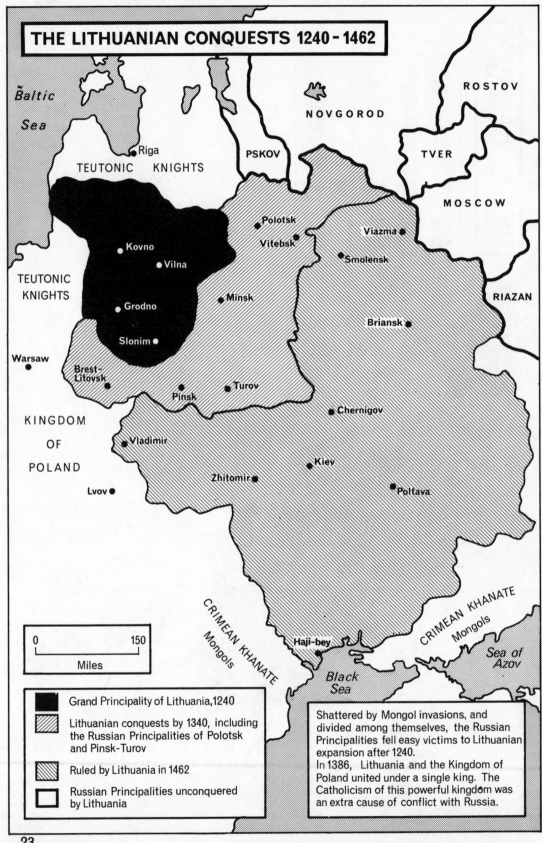

THE LITHUANIAN CONQUESTS 1240-1462

Baltic Sea

ROSTOV

NOVGOROD

TVER

Riga

TEUTONIC KNIGHTS

PSKOV

MOSCOW

Polotsk

Viazma

Vitebsk

Kovno

Smolensk

Vilna

RIAZAN

TEUTONIC KNIGHTS

Minsk

Grodno

Briansk

Slonim

Warsaw

Brest-Litovsk

Turov

Pinsk

Chernigov

KINGDOM OF POLAND

Vladimir

Kiev

Zhitomir

Poltava

Lvov

CRIMEAN KHANATE Mongols

CRIMEAN KHANATE Mongols

Sea of Azov

Haji-bey

Black Sea

0   150

Miles

Grand Principality of Lithuania,1240

Lithuanian conquests by 1340, including the Russian Principalities of Polotsk and Pinsk-Turov

Ruled by Lithuania in 1462

Russian Principalities unconquered by Lithuania

Shattered by Mongol invasions, and divided among themselves, the Russian Principalities fell easy victims to Lithuanian expansion after 1240.
In 1386, Lithuania and the Kingdom of Poland united under a single king. The Catholicism of this powerful kingdom was an extra cause of conflict with Russia.

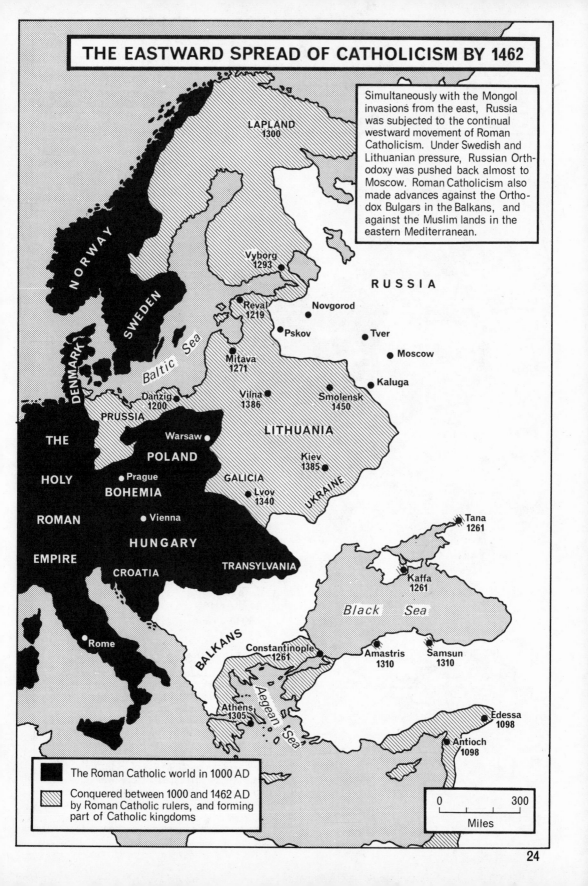

THE EASTWARD SPREAD OF CATHOLICISM BY 1462

Simultaneously with the Mongol invasions from the east, Russia was subjected to the continual westward movement of Roman Catholicism. Under Swedish and Lithuanian pressure, Russian Orthodoxy was pushed back almost to Moscow. Roman Catholicism also made advances against the Orthodox Bulgars in the Balkans, and against the Muslim lands in the eastern Mediterranean.

LAPLAND
1300

NORWAY

SWEDEN

DENMARK

Baltic Sea

Vyborg
1293

RUSSIA

Reval
1219

Novgorod

Pskov

Tver

Mitava
1271

Moscow

PRUSSIA

Danzig
1200

Kaluga

Vilna
1386

Smolensk
1450

THE

Warsaw

LITHUANIA

HOLY

POLAND

Prague

BOHEMIA

GALICIA

Kiev
1385

UKRAINE

ROMAN

Vienna

Lvov
1340

EMPIRE

HUNGARY

Tana
1261

CROATIA

TRANSYLVANIA

Kaffa
1261

Black Sea

BALKANS

Rome

Constantinople
1261

Amastris
1310

Samsun
1310

Athens
1305

Aegean Sea

Edessa
1098

Antioch
1098

	The Roman Catholic world in 1000 AD
	Conquered between 1000 and 1462 AD by Roman Catholic rulers, and forming part of Catholic kingdoms

0   300
Miles

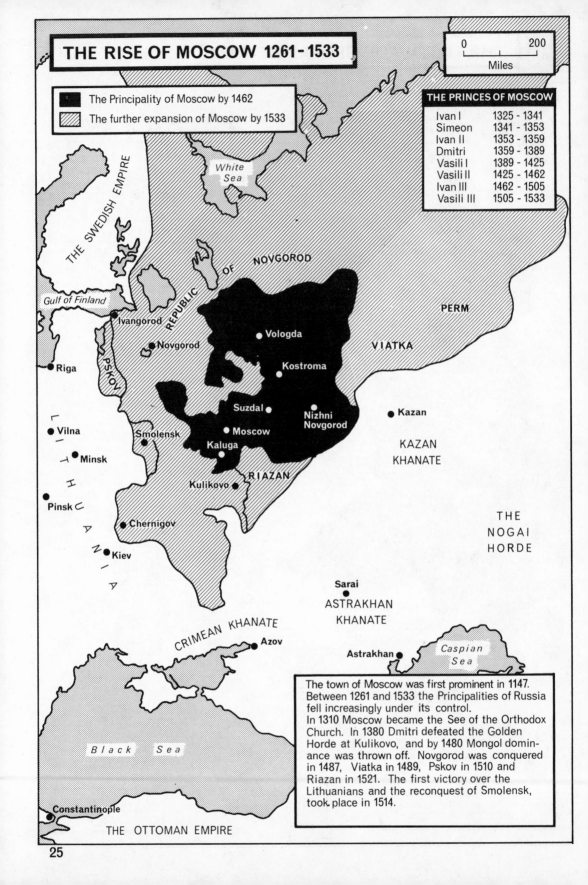

THE RISE OF MOSCOW 1261-1533

0　　　　200
Miles

■ The Principality of Moscow by 1462

▨ The further expansion of Moscow by 1533

THE PRINCES OF MOSCOW

Ivan I	1325 - 1341
Simeon	1341 - 1353
Ivan II	1353 - 1359
Dmitri	1359 - 1389
Vasili I	1389 - 1425
Vasili II	1425 - 1462
Ivan III	1462 - 1505
Vasili III	1505 - 1533

THE SWEDISH EMPIRE

White Sea

REPUBLIC OF NOVGOROD

PERM

Gulf of Finland

Ivangorod

Novgorod

VIATKA

PSKOV

Riga

Vologda

Kostroma

Suzdal

Nizhni Novgorod

Kazan

KAZAN KHANATE

L I T H U A N I A

Vilna

Minsk

Smolensk

Moscow

Kaluga

RIAZAN

Kulikovo

Chernigov

Pinsk

Kiev

THE NOGAI HORDE

Sarai

ASTRAKHAN KHANATE

CRIMEAN KHANATE

Azov

Astrakhan

Caspian Sea

Black Sea

The town of Moscow was first prominent in 1147.
Between 1261 and 1533 the Principalities of Russia
fell increasingly under its control.
In 1310 Moscow became the See of the Orthodox
Church. In 1380 Dmitri defeated the Golden
Horde at Kulikovo, and by 1480 Mongol domin-
ance was thrown off. Novgorod was conquered
in 1487, Viatka in 1489, Pskov in 1510 and
Riazan in 1521. The first victory over the
Lithuanians and the reconquest of Smolensk,
took place in 1514.

Constantinople

THE OTTOMAN EMPIRE

25

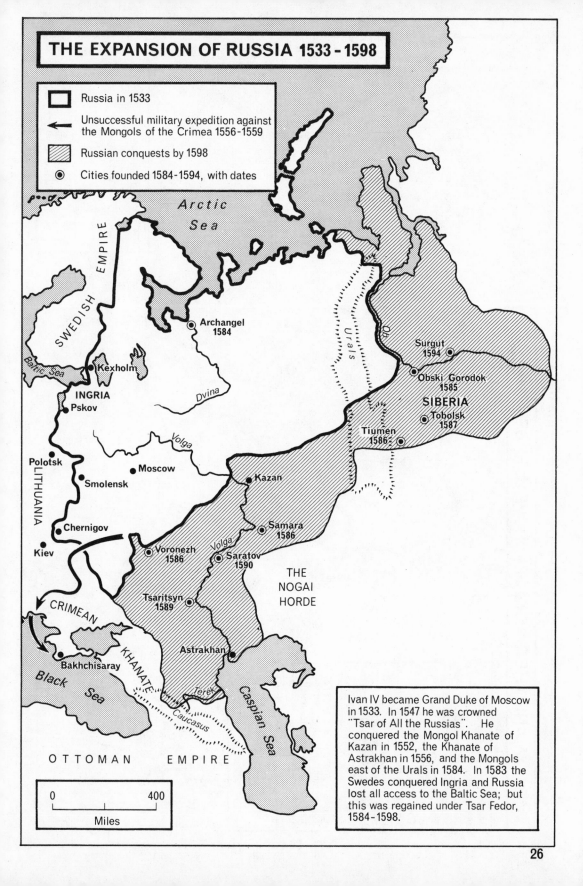

THE EXPANSION OF RUSSIA 1533 - 1598

☐ Russia in 1533

← Unsuccessful military expedition against the Mongols of the Crimea 1556-1559

▨ Russian conquests by 1598

◉ Cities founded 1584-1594, with dates

Arctic Sea

SWEDISH EMPIRE

Baltic Sea

Kexholm

INGRIA

Pskov

Polotsk

LITHUANIA

Smolensk

Moscow

Chernigov

Kiev

Volga

Archangel 1584

Dvina

Urals

Ob

Surgut 1594

Obski Gorodok 1585

SIBERIA

Tobolsk 1587

Tiumen 1586

Kazan

Samara 1586

Voronezh 1586

Saratov 1590

Volga

THE NOGAI HORDE

Tsaritsyn 1589

CRIMEAN

Bakhchisaray

Black Sea

KHANATE

Astrakhan

Terek

Caucasus

Caspian Sea

OTTOMAN EMPIRE

Ivan IV became Grand Duke of Moscow in 1533. In 1547 he was crowned "Tsar of All the Russias". He conquered the Mongol Khanate of Kazan in 1552, the Khanate of Astrakhan in 1556, and the Mongols east of the Urals in 1584. In 1583 the Swedes conquered Ingria and Russia lost all access to the Baltic Sea; but this was regained under Tsar Fedor, 1584-1598.

0 — 400

Miles

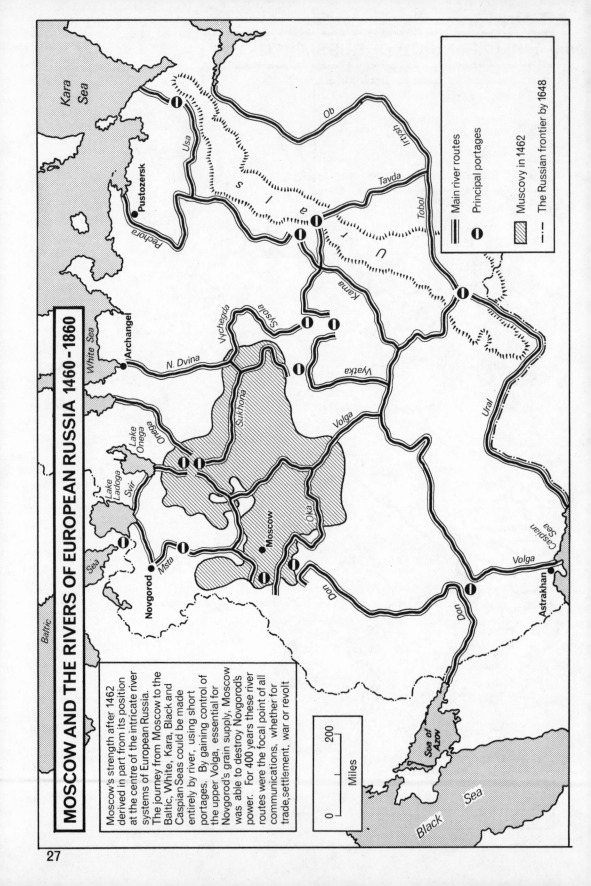

MOSCOW AND THE RIVERS OF EUROPEAN RUSSIA 1460-1860

Moscow's strength after 1462
derived in part from its position
at the centre of the intricate river
systems of European Russia.
The journey from Moscow to the
Baltic, White, Kara, Black and
Caspian Seas could be made
entirely by river, using short
portages. By gaining control of
the upper Volga, essential for
Novgorod's grain supply, Moscow
was able to destroy Novgorod's
power. For 400 years these river
routes were the focal point of all
communications, whether for
trade, settlement, war or revolt.

Legend:
- ═══ Main river routes
- Ⓘ Principal portages
- ▨ Muscovy in 1462
- ─·─· The Russian frontier by 1648

Seas and lakes: Kara Sea, Baltic Sea, White Sea, Lake Onega, Lake Ladoga, Caspian Sea, Sea of Azov, Black Sea

Rivers: Usa, Ob, Irtish, Tavda, Tobol, Pechora, Kama, Vychegda, Sysola, Vyatka, Ural, N. Dvina, Sukhona, Onega, Volga, Oka, Msta, Svir, Don

Places: Pustozersk, Archangel, Novgorod, Moscow, Astrakhan

Regions: Siberia, Urals

Scale: 0 — 200 Miles

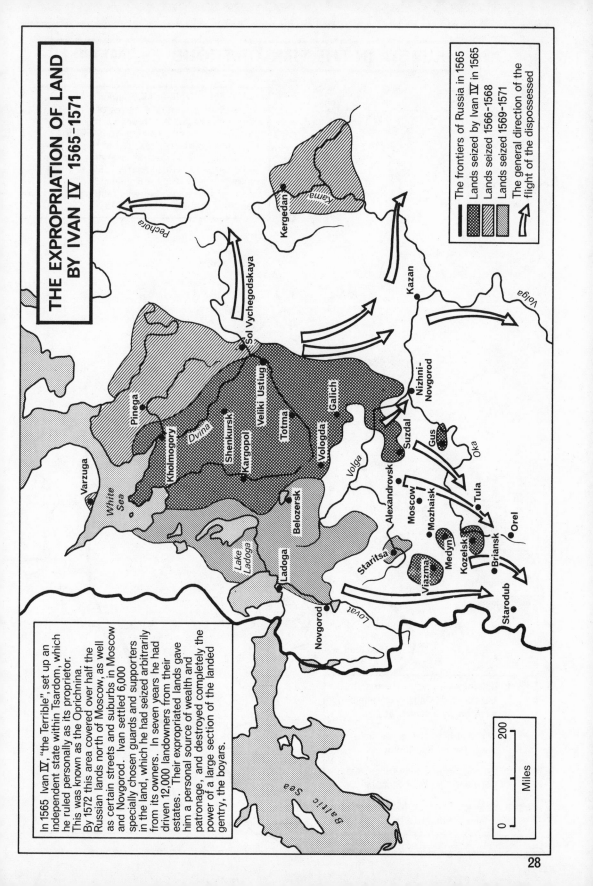

THE EXPROPRIATION OF LAND
BY IVAN IV 1565–1571

In 1565 Ivan IV, "the Terrible", set up an independent state within Tsardom, which he ruled personally as its proprietor. This was known as the Oprichnina. By 1572 this area covered over half the Russian lands north of Moscow, as well as certain streets and suburbs in Moscow and Novgorod. Ivan settled 6,000 specially chosen guards and supporters in the land, which he had seized arbitrarily from its owners. In seven years he had driven 12,000 landowners from their estates. Their expropriated lands gave him a personal source of wealth and patronage, and destroyed completely the power of a large section of the landed gentry, the boyars.

The frontiers of Russia in 1565
Lands seized by Ivan IV in 1565
Lands seized 1566–1568
Lands seized 1569–1571
The general direction of the flight of the dispossessed

Pechora

Kergedan

Kama

Sol Vychegodskaya

Kazan

Volga

Nizhni-Novgorod

Pinega

Dvina

Kholmogory

Shenkursk

Kargopol

Veliki Ustiug

Totma

Galich

Vologda

Suzdal

Gus

Oka

Varzuga

White Sea

Belozersk

Lake Ladoga

Ladoga

Alexandrovsk

Moscow

Mozhaisk

Tula

Medyn

Kozelsk

Briansk

Orel

Staritsa

Viazma

Starodub

Novgorod

Lovat

Volga

Baltic Sea

0   200
Miles

28

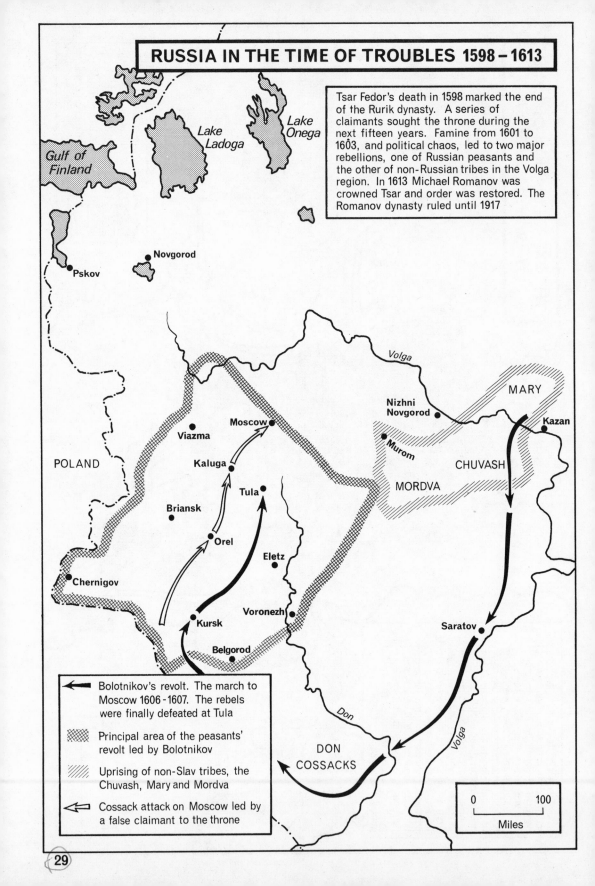

RUSSIA IN THE TIME OF TROUBLES 1598 – 1613

Tsar Fedor's death in 1598 marked the end of the Rurik dynasty. A series of claimants sought the throne during the next fifteen years. Famine from 1601 to 1603, and political chaos, led to two major rebellions, one of Russian peasants and the other of non-Russian tribes in the Volga region. In 1613 Michael Romanov was crowned Tsar and order was restored. The Romanov dynasty ruled until 1917

Gulf of Finland

Lake Ladoga

Lake Onega

Novgorod

Pskov

Volga

MARY

Nizhni Novgorod

Kazan

Moscow

Viazma

Murom

CHUVASH

Kaluga

POLAND

MORDVA

Tula

Briansk

Orel

Eletz

Chernigov

Kursk

Voronezh

Saratov

Belgorod

Don

DON COSSACKS

Volga

Bolotnikov's revolt. The march to Moscow 1606 - 1607. The rebels were finally defeated at Tula

Principal area of the peasants' revolt led by Bolotnikov

Uprising of non-Slav tribes, the Chuvash, Mary and Mordva

Cossack attack on Moscow led by a false claimant to the throne

0   100
Miles

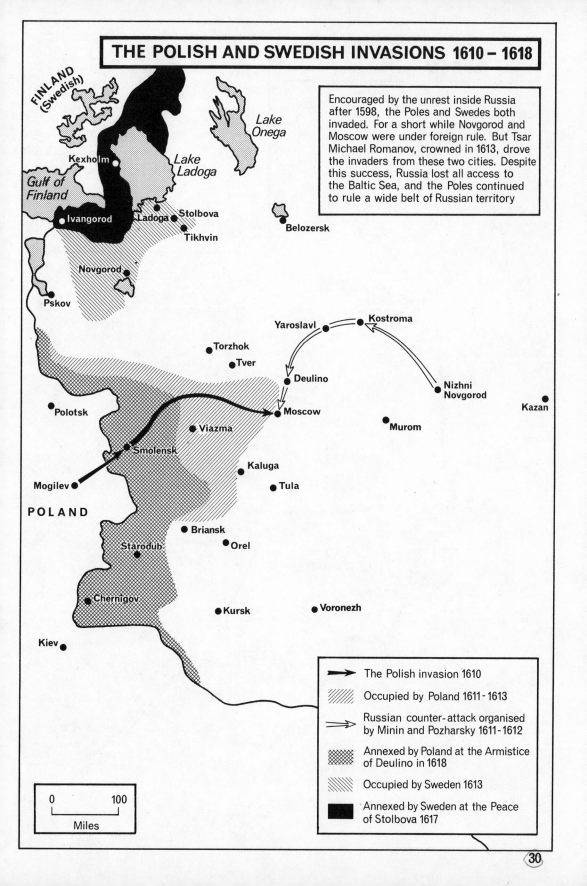

THE POLISH AND SWEDISH INVASIONS 1610 – 1618

Encouraged by the unrest inside Russia after 1598, the Poles and Swedes both invaded. For a short while Novgorod and Moscow were under foreign rule. But Tsar Michael Romanov, crowned in 1613, drove the invaders from these two cities. Despite this success, Russia lost all access to the Baltic Sea, and the Poles continued to rule a wide belt of Russian territory

FINLAND (Swedish)

Lake Onega

Kexholm

Lake Ladoga

Gulf of Finland

Ivangorod

Ladoga

Stolbova

Tikhvin

Belozersk

Novgorod

Pskov

Yaroslavl

Kostroma

Torzhok

Tver

Deulino

Nizhni Novgorod

Kazan

Polotsk

Moscow

Viazma

Murom

Smolensk

Kaluga

Mogilev

Tula

POLAND

Briansk

Starodub

Orel

Chernigov

Kursk

Voronezh

Kiev

0   100

Miles

The Polish invasion 1610

Occupied by Poland 1611-1613

Russian counter-attack organised by Minin and Pozharsky 1611-1612

Annexed by Poland at the Armistice of Deulino in 1618

Occupied by Sweden 1613

Annexed by Sweden at the Peace of Stolbova 1617

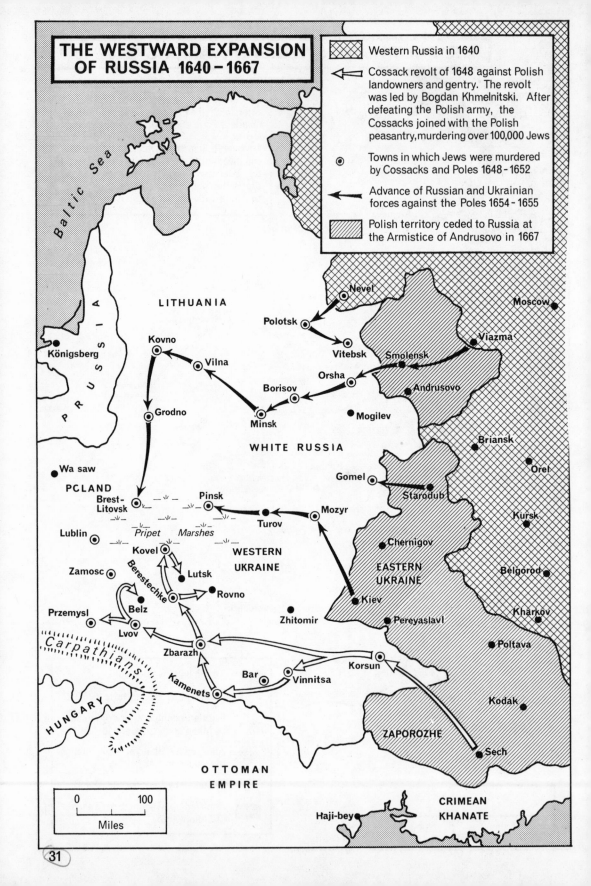

THE WESTWARD EXPANSION OF RUSSIA 1640–1667

Western Russia in 1640

Cossack revolt of 1648 against Polish landowners and gentry. The revolt was led by Bogdan Khmelnitski. After defeating the Polish army, the Cossacks joined with the Polish peasantry, murdering over 100,000 Jews

Towns in which Jews were murdered by Cossacks and Poles 1648–1652

Advance of Russian and Ukrainian forces against the Poles 1654–1655

Polish territory ceded to Russia at the Armistice of Andrusovo in 1667

Baltic Sea

LITHUANIA

Moscow

Nevel

Polotsk

Viazma

Königsberg

Kovno

Vitebsk

Smolensk

Vilna

Orsha

Andrusovo

P R U S S I A

Borisov

Grodno

Mogilev

Minsk

WHITE RUSSIA

Briansk

Orel

Wa saw

Gomel

Starodub

Kursk

PCLAND

Brest-Litovsk

Pinsk

Mozyr

Turov

Belgorod

Lublin

Pripet   Marshes

Kovel

WESTERN UKRAINE

Chernigov

EASTERN UKRAINE

Zamosc

Lutsk

Kharkov

Berestechke

Rovno

Kiev

Przemysl

Belz

Zhitomir

Lvov

Pereyaslavl

Poltava

Zbarazh

Carpathians

Kamenets

Bar

Vinnitsa

Korsun

Kodak

HUNGARY

ZAPOROZHE

Sech

OTTOMAN EMPIRE

0   100

Miles

Haji-bey

CRIMEAN KHANATE

31

SOCIAL UNREST 1648 and 1670

In 1648 uprisings took place in many of the principal Russian towns. As a result, a new code of laws was drawn up, protecting the rights of traders and town-dwellers. In 1670 a Don Cossack, Stenka Razin, led a widespread revolt of Cossacks, peasants, small traders, minor officials and the dispossessed of the Volga, Don and Donets river valleys. The revolt was crushed in 1671 and Razin broken on the wheel in Moscow.

Kargopol

Solvychegodsk

Veliki Ustiug

Cherdin

Olonets

Solikamsk

Totma

Gdov

Novgorod

Pskov

Romanov

Ostrov

Volga

Vladimir

Ruza

Yadrin

Moscow

Simbirsk

Koslov

Penza

Samara

Tambov

Donets

Kursk

Saratov

Voronezh

Don

Tsaritsyn

DON
COSSACKS

Gurev

Sea of
Azov

Astrakhan

Caspian
Sea

Black   Sea

Terski
Gorodok

◉   Urban uprisings of 1648–1650

█   The peasants' revolt led by
    Stenka Razin 1670–1671

──   The Russian frontier in 1670

0   500

Miles

32

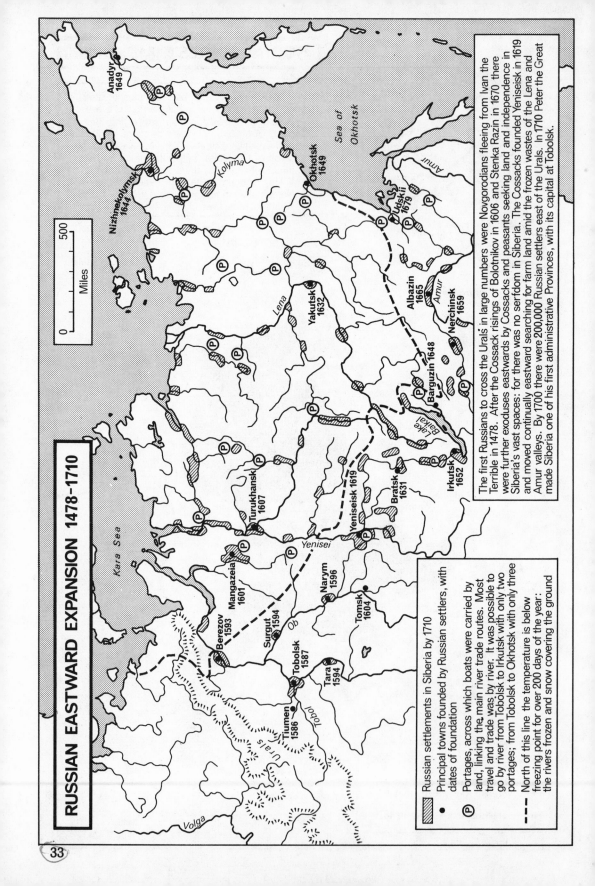

RUSSIAN EASTWARD EXPANSION 1478–1710

The first Russians to cross the Urals in large numbers were Novgorodians fleeing from Ivan the Terrible in 1478. After the Cossack risings of Bolotnikov in 1606 and Stenka Razin in 1670 there were further exoduses eastwards by Cossacks and peasants seeking land and independence in Siberia's vast spaces: for there was no serfdom in Siberia. The Cossacks founded Yeniseisk in 1619 and moved continually eastward searching for farm land amid the frozen wastes of the Lena and Amur valleys. By 1700 there were 200,000 Russian settlers east of the Urals. In 1710 Peter the Great made Siberia one of his first administrative Provinces, with its capital at Tobolsk.

Russian settlements in Siberia by 1710

Principal towns founded by Russian settlers, with dates of foundation

(P) Portages, across which boats were carried by land, linking the main river trade routes. Most travel and trade was by river. It was possible to go by river from Tobolsk to Irkutsk with only two portages; from Tobolsk to Okhotsk with only three portages.

North of this line the temperature is below freezing point for over 200 days of the year: the rivers frozen and snow covering the ground

500
Miles
0

Anadyr 1649
Nizhnekolymsk 1644
Kolyma
Okhotsk 1649
Sea of Okhotsk
Amur
Udskii 1679
Albazin 1665
Nerchinsk 1659
Amur
Barguzin 1648
Lake Baikal
Irkutsk 1652
Bratsk 1631
Yakutsk 1632
Lena
Turukhansk 1607
Yeniseisk 1619
Yenisei
Mangazeia 1601
Berezov 1593
Surgut 1594
Narym 1596
Ob
Tomsk 1604
Tobolsk 1587
Tara 1594
Tiumen 1586
Tobol
Urals
Siberia
Volga
Kara Sea

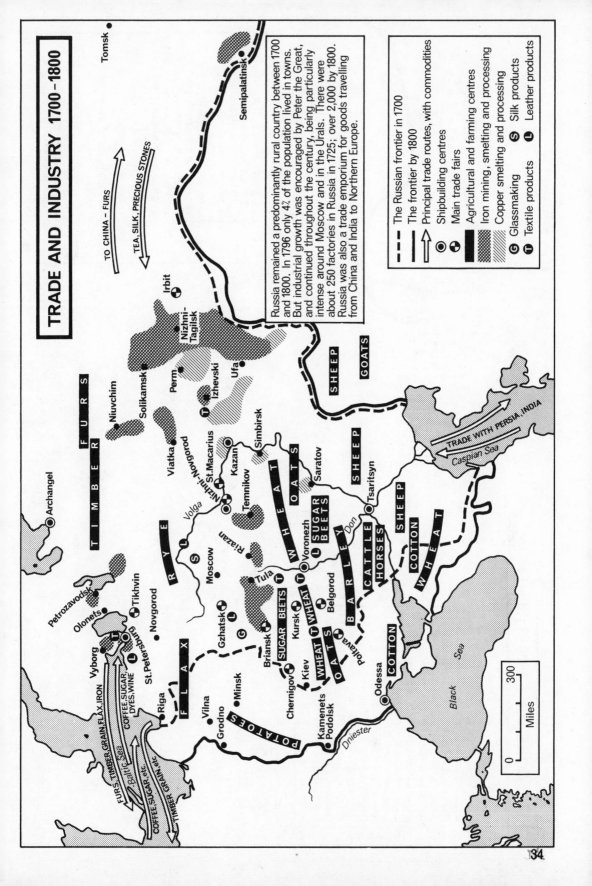

TRADE AND INDUSTRY 1700–1800

Russia remained a predominantly rural country between 1700 and 1800. In 1796 only 4% of the population lived in towns. But industrial growth was encouraged by Peter the Great, and continued throughout the century, being particularly intense around Moscow and in the Urals. There were about 250 factories in Russia in 1725; over 2,000 by 1800. Russia was also a trade emporium for goods travelling from China and India to Northern Europe.

- - - The Russian frontier in 1700
——— The frontier by 1800
⇧ Principal trade routes, with commodities
◉ Shipbuilding centres
◕ Main trade fairs
▬ Agricultural and farming centres
▨ Iron mining, smelting and processing
▥ Copper smelting and processing
Ⓖ Glassmaking   Ⓢ Silk products
Ⓣ Textile products   Ⓛ Leather products

Tomsk

Semipalatinsk

TO CHINA – FURS

TEA, SILK, PRECIOUS STONES

Irbit

Nizhni-Tagilsk

Niuvchim

Solikamsk

Perm

Izhevski

Ufa

SHEEP

GOATS

Viatka

St. Macarius

Simbirsk

SHEEP

Archangel

TIMBER

FURS

Kazan

Temnikov

Saratov

WHEAT

OATS

SUGAR BEETS

Voronezh

Tsaritsyn

SHEEP

Volga

Nizhni-Novgorod

RYE

FLAX

Moscow

Riazan

Tula

Don

BARLEY

CATTLE

HORSES

SHEEP

COTTON

WHEAT

TRADE WITH PERSIA, INDIA

Caspian Sea

Petrozavodsk

Olonets

Tikhvin

Novgorod

Gzhatsk

Briansk

Kursk

WHEAT

Belgorod

SUGAR BEETS

WHEAT

OATS

Poltava

Vyborg

St. Petersburg

FURS, TIMBER, GRAIN, FLAX, IRON

COFFEE, SUGAR, DYES, WINE

COFFEE, SUGAR, etc.

Baltic Sea

Riga

Vilna

Minsk

Grodno

Chernigov

Kiev

Kamenets Podolsk

POTATOES

Dniester

Odessa

COTTON

Black Sea

COFFEE, GRAIN, etc.

TIMBER, GRAIN

0   300   Miles

34

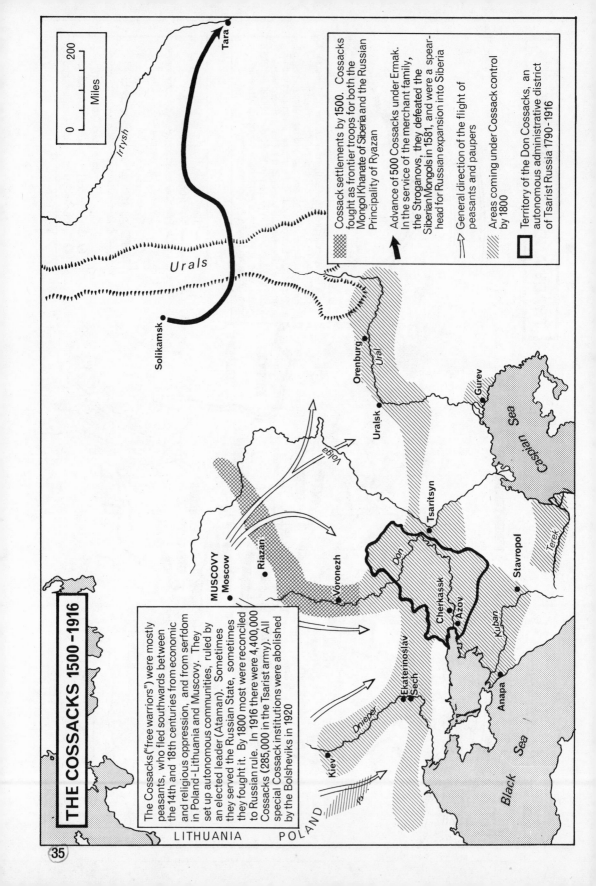

THE COSSACKS 1500 – 1916

The Cossacks ("free warriors") were mostly peasants, who fled southwards between the 14th and 18th centuries from economic and religious oppression, and from serfdom in Poland-Lithuania and Muscovy. They set up autonomous communities, ruled by an elected leader (Ataman). Sometimes they served the Russian State, sometimes they fought it. By 1800 most were reconciled to Russian rule. In 1916 there were 4,400,000 Cossacks (285,000 in the Tsarist army). All special Cossack institutions were abolished by the Bolsheviks in 1920

Cossack settlements by 1500. Cossacks fought as frontier troops for both the Mongol Khanate of Siberia and the Russian Principality of Ryazan

Advance of 500 Cossacks under Ermak. In the service of the merchant family, the Stroganovs, they defeated the Siberian Mongols in 1581, and were a spearhead for Russian expansion into Siberia

General direction of the flight of peasants and paupers

Areas coming under Cossack control by 1800

Territory of the Don Cossacks, an autonomous administrative district of Tsarist Russia 1790 - 1916

200

Miles

0

Irtysh

Urals

Tara

Solikamsk

Orenburg

Ural

Uralsk

Gurev

Caspian Sea

Tsaritsyn

Stavropol

Don

Cherkassk

Azov

Kuban

Terek

Volga

MUSCOVY

Moscow

Riazan

Voronezh

Ekaterinoslav

Sech

Dnieper

Kiev

Anapa

Black Sea

LITHUANIA

POLAND

35

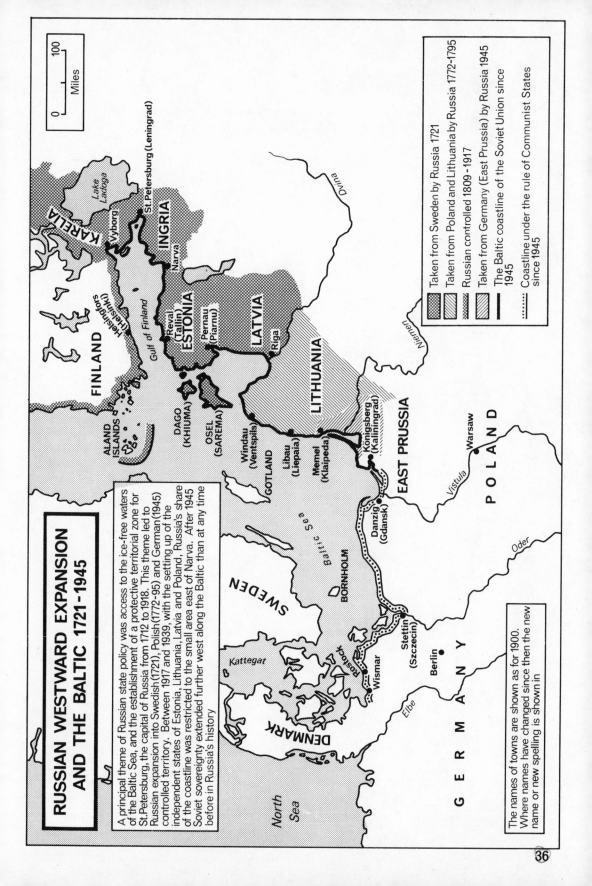

RUSSIAN WESTWARD EXPANSION AND THE BALTIC 1721-1945

A principal theme of Russian state policy was access to the ice-free waters of the Baltic Sea, and the establishment of a protective territorial zone for St.Petersburg, the capital of Russia from 1712 to 1918. This theme led to Russian expansion into Swedish (1721), Polish (1772-95) and German (1945) controlled territory. Between 1917 and 1939, with the setting up of the independent states of Estonia, Lithuania, Latvia and Poland, Russia's share of the coastline was restricted to the small area east of Narva. After 1945 Soviet sovereignty extended further west along the Baltic than at any time before in Russia's history

The names of towns are shown as for 1900. Where names have changed since then the new name or new spelling is shown in

Legend
- Taken from Sweden by Russia 1721
- Taken from Poland and Lithuania by Russia 1772-1795
- Russian controlled 1809 - 1917
- Taken from Germany (East Prussia) by Russia 1945
- The Baltic coastline of the Soviet Union since 1945
- Coastline under the rule of Communist States since 1945

Scale: 0 — 100 Miles

Lake Ladoga, KARELIA, Vyborg, St.Petersburg (Leningrad), INGRIA, Narva, FINLAND, Helsingfors (Helsinki), Gulf of Finland, Reval (Tallinn), ESTONIA, Pernau (Piarnu), LATVIA, Riga, Dvina, ALAND ISLANDS, DAGO (KHIUMA), OSEL (SAREMA), LITHUANIA, Niemen, Windau (Ventspils), GOTLAND, Libau (Liepaia), Memel (Klaipeda), Königsberg (Kaliningrad), EAST PRUSSIA, Warsaw, POLAND, Vistula, Baltic Sea, BORNHOLM, Danzig (Gdansk), Oder, SWEDEN, Stettin (Szczecin), Berlin, Rostock, Wismar, Kattegat, GERMANY, Elbe, North Sea, DENMARK

36

Section Two

IMPERIAL RUSSIA

WAR AND REVOLT UNDER PETER THE GREAT 1695 - 1723

Peter the Great's reign saw a series of widespread revolts ruthlessly crushed, the successful conquest of Swedish land, and Russian access to the ice-free waters of the Baltic Sea. But Peter was unable to drive the Turk from the Crimea, or to reach the Black Sea.

1695	Unsuccessful attack on the Turks at Azov
1696	Azov captured from the Turks. Taganrog founded as a new naval base
1700	Russians defeated by the Swedes at Narva
1709	Swedes defeated by the Russians at Poltava
1710	First Russian attacks against the Swedes, leading to Baltic annexations from Sweden in 1721
1711	Unsuccessful attack against the Turks at Jassy and Braila. Azov and Taganrog returned to Turkey
1722	Successful attack against Persia largely to forestall a Turkish advance to the Persian shore of the Caspian Sea

The privileged Moscow garrison, or Streltsy, who had helped Peter's half-sister Sophia seize power in 1682, had been exiled by him to Astrakhan in 1698. They opposed his increasingly heavy taxation and in 1705 set up a Cossack-style Government and elected an Ataman. Peter refused all pleas for mercy; the revolt was crushed and its leaders were executed with great cruelty, 1706-1708.

The Bashkirs, a Muslim nomad people subject to Russia since 1557, resented Russian colonization and sought Crimean and Turkish help to assert their independence. In 1708 they attacked Russian colonists and destroyed over 300 villages from the Ural river to the Volga, killing or capturing 13,000 settlers. The revolt was not finally crushed until 1711.

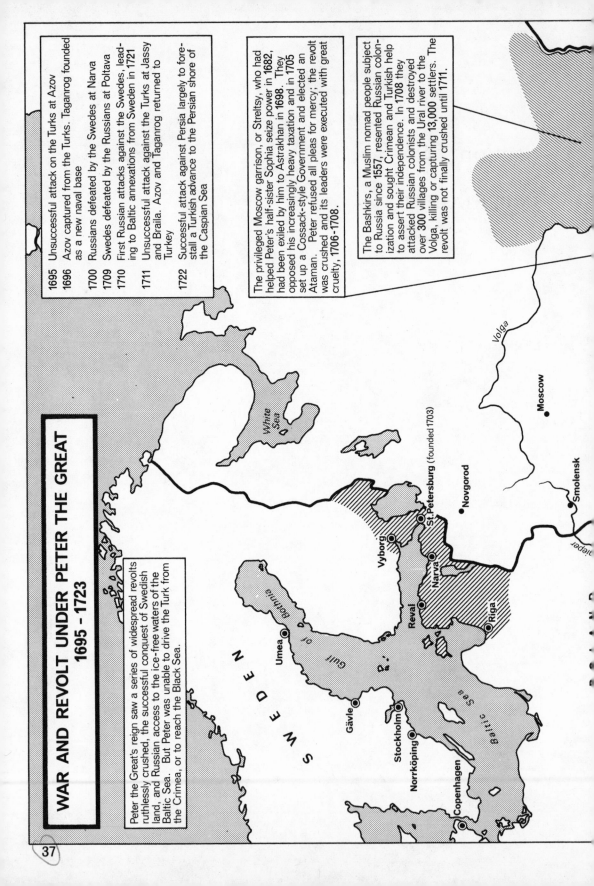

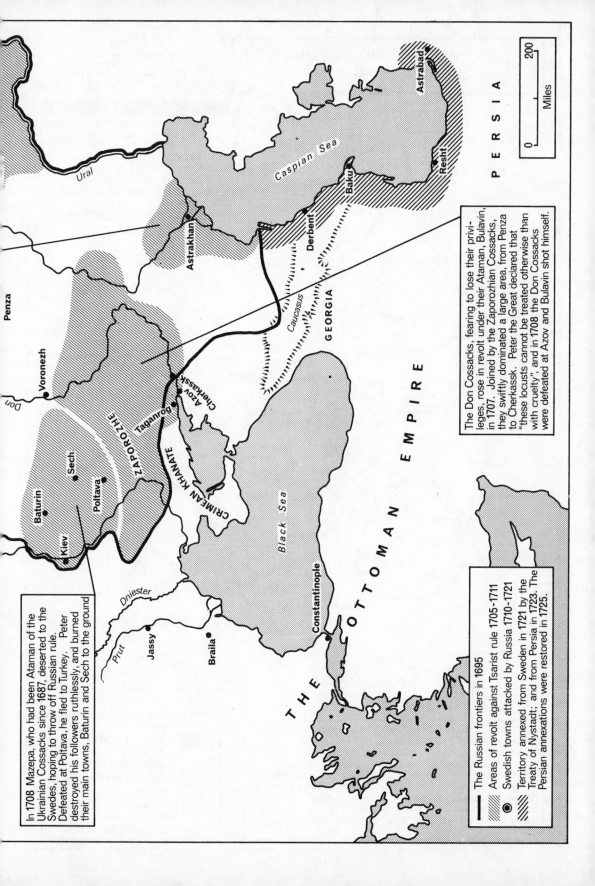

In 1708 Mazepa, who had been Ataman of the Ukrainian Cossacks since 1687, deserted to the Swedes, hoping to throw off Russian rule. Defeated at Poltava, he fled to Turkey. Peter destroyed his followers ruthlessly, and burned their main towns, Baturin and Sech to the ground

The Don Cossacks, fearing to lose their privileges, rose in revolt under their Ataman, Bulavin, in 1707. Joined by the Zaporozhian Cossacks, they swiftly dominated a large area, from Penza to Cherkassk. Peter the Great declared that "these locusts cannot be treated otherwise than with cruelty", and in 1708 the Don Cossacks were defeated at Azov and Bulavin shot himself.

The Russian frontiers in 1695

Areas of revolt against Tsarist rule 1705-1711

Swedish towns attacked by Russia 1710-1721

Territory annexed from Sweden in 1721 by the Treaty of Nystadt; and from Persia in 1723. The Persian annexations were restored in 1725.

PERSIA

THE OTTOMAN EMPIRE

Black Sea

Caspian Sea

CRIMEAN KHANATE

ZAPOROZHE

GEORGIA

Caucasus

Constantinople

Braila

Jassy

Kiev

Baturin

Poltava

Sech

Voronezh

Penza

Ural

Don

Dniester

Prut

Taganrog

Cherkassk

Azov

Derbent

Baku

Astrakhan

Astrabad

Resht

0   200
Miles

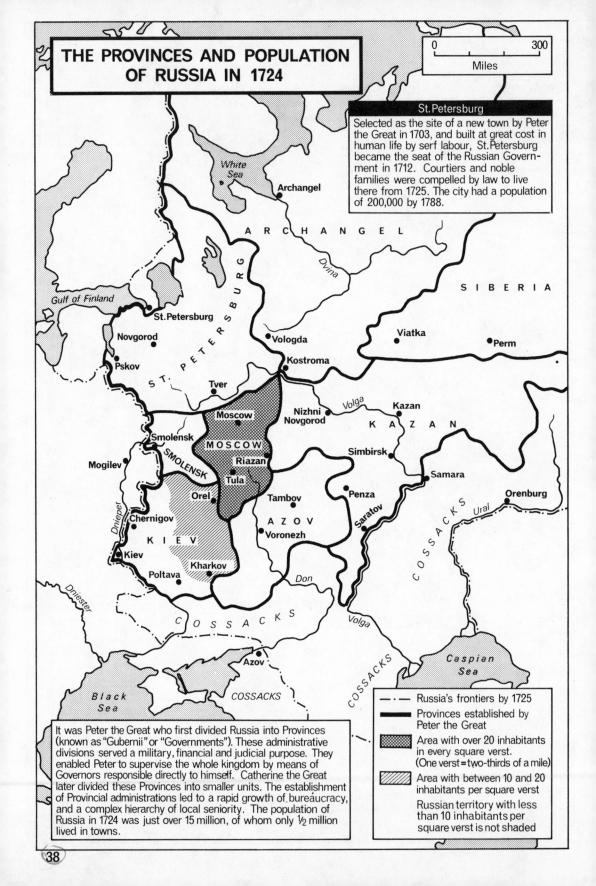

THE PROVINCES AND POPULATION OF RUSSIA IN 1724

0   300
Miles

St. Petersburg

Selected as the site of a new town by Peter the Great in 1703, and built at great cost in human life by serf labour, St. Petersburg became the seat of the Russian Government in 1712. Courtiers and noble families were compelled by law to live there from 1725. The city had a population of 200,000 by 1788.

White Sea

Archangel

A R C H A N G E L

Dvina

S I B E R I A

Gulf of Finland

St. Petersburg

Novgorod

Pskov

S T . P E T E R S B U R G

Vologda

Viatka

Perm

Kostroma

Tver

Volga

Kazan

Moscow

Nizhni Novgorod

K A Z A N

Smolensk

M O S C O W

SMOLENSK

Riazan

Simbirsk

Mogilev

Tula

Samara

Orel

Tambov

Penza

Orenburg

Chernigov

A Z O V

Saratov

Ural

C O S S A C K S

K I E V

Voronezh

Kiev

Kharkov

Poltava

Don

Volga

Dnieper

Dniester

C O S S A C K S

Azov

COSSACKS

COSSACKS

Caspian Sea

Black Sea

It was Peter the Great who first divided Russia into Provinces (known as "Gubernii" or "Governments"). These administrative divisions served a military, financial and judicial purpose. They enabled Peter to supervise the whole kingdom by means of Governors responsible directly to himself. Catherine the Great later divided these Provinces into smaller units. The establishment of Provincial administrations led to a rapid growth of bureaucracy, and a complex hierarchy of local seniority. The population of Russia in 1724 was just over 15 million, of whom only ½ million lived in towns.

—·— Russia's frontiers by 1725

▬▬ Provinces established by Peter the Great

▨ Area with over 20 inhabitants in every square verst. (One verst=two-thirds of a mile)

▧ Area with between 10 and 20 inhabitants per square verst

Russian territory with less than 10 inhabitants per square verst is not shaded

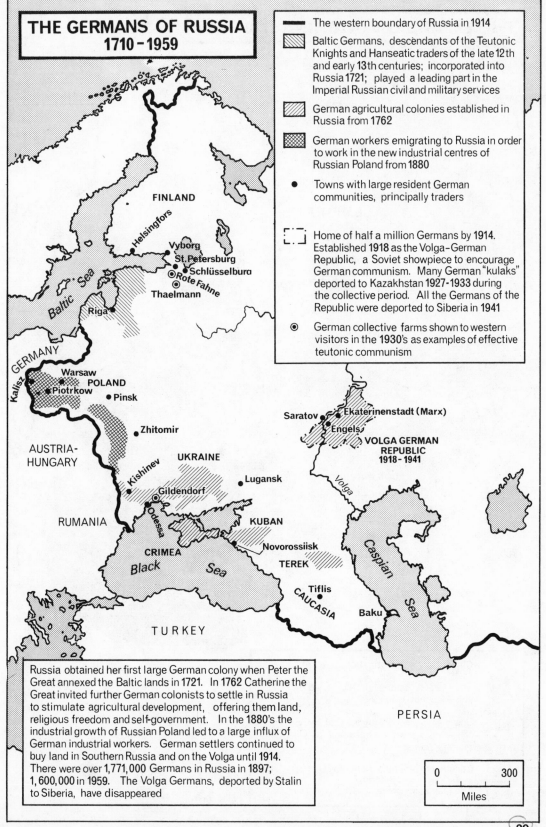

THE GERMANS OF RUSSIA
1710 - 1959

The western boundary of Russia in 1914

Baltic Germans, descendants of the Teutonic Knights and Hanseatic traders of the late 12th and early 13th centuries; incorporated into Russia 1721; played a leading part in the Imperial Russian civil and military services

German agricultural colonies established in Russia from 1762

German workers emigrating to Russia in order to work in the new industrial centres of Russian Poland from 1880

● Towns with large resident German communities, principally traders

Home of half a million Germans by 1914. Established 1918 as the Volga-German Republic, a Soviet showpiece to encourage German communism. Many German "kulaks" deported to Kazakhstan 1927-1933 during the collective period. All the Germans of the Republic were deported to Siberia in 1941

◉ German collective farms shown to western visitors in the 1930's as examples of effective teutonic communism

FINLAND

Helsingfors

Vyborg
St.Petersburg
Schlüsselburg
◉ Rote Fahne
Thaelmann

Baltic Sea

Riga

GERMANY

Kalisz
Warsaw
Piotrkow ● POLAND
● Pinsk

Saratov ● ● Ekaterinenstadt (Marx)
Engels
VOLGA GERMAN
REPUBLIC
1918 - 1941

Zhitomir

AUSTRIA-
HUNGARY

UKRAINE

Kishinev
Gildendorf ◉
Odessa

● Lugansk

RUMANIA

KUBAN

Novorossiisk

CRIMEA
Black   Sea

TEREK

Tiflis
CAUCASIA

Baku

Volga

Caspian
Sea

TURKEY

PERSIA

Russia obtained her first large German colony when Peter the Great annexed the Baltic lands in 1721. In 1762 Catherine the Great invited further German colonists to settle in Russia to stimulate agricultural development, offering them land, religious freedom and self-government. In the 1880's the industrial growth of Russian Poland led to a large influx of German industrial workers. German settlers continued to buy land in Southern Russia and on the Volga until 1914. There were over 1,771,000 Germans in Russia in 1897; 1,600,000 in 1959. The Volga Germans, deported by Stalin to Siberia, have disappeared

0   300

Miles

THE EXPANSION OF CHINA 1720–1760

THE

RUSSIAN

EMPIRE

Okhotsk⦿

Yakutsk⦿

Tobolsk⦿

Yeniseisk⦿

Tomsk⦿   Krasnoyarsk⦿

Omsk⦿   Nerchinsk⦿   Albazin

Irkutsk⦿   Lake
Baikal   Harbin

Semipalatinsk⦿   Ustkamenogorsk⦿   Maimachin

M O N G O L S

Lake
Balkhash   Hami   Peking

Kulja   Urumchi

DOMINIONS OF THE   Sian   Nanking

Yarkand   ZUNGAR KALMUKS

Khotan   C H I N A

Chengtu

T I B E T   Canton

Lhasa   Yunnan

H i m a l a y a s

⦿	Cities founded by the Russians before 1720
■	The Chinese Empire in 1720, ruled by the Manchu Dynasty
▨	Under Chinese control by 1720, providing the Manchus with a reservoir of military power
▨	Conquered by China between 1724 and 1764
▨	Conquered by China in 1780

0   500

Miles

40

RUSSIAN EXPANSION UNDER CATHERINE THE GREAT 1762–1796

The Provinces of Russia in 1750

Territory annexed by Russia 1762-1796, giving Russia an outlet on the Black Sea, and a common frontier with Prussia and Austria

White Sea

Archangel

ARCHANGEL

FINLAND

Helsingfors

ST. PETERSBURG

ESTONIA

LIVONIA

Novgorod

NOVGOROD

Vologda

Viatka

Perm

KAZAN

Pskov

Baltic Sea

KURLAND

Tver

MOSCOW

Moscow

Kazan

Ufa

UFA

PRUSSIA

Niemen

Vilna

LITHUANIA

Minsk

SMOLENSK

NIZHNI NOVGOROD

Stavropol

Samara

WHITE RUSSIA

Warsaw

Pinsk

Orel

BELGOROD

AUSTRIA

PODLESIA

KIEV

VORONEZH

Lutsk

Kiev

Dnieper

Belgorod

ASTRAKHAN

Dniester

PODOLIA

ZAPOROZHE

Jassy

Odessa

Taganrog

Astrakhan

Kutchuk Kainardji

CRIMEA

KUBAN

Sebastopol

KABARDA

Tarki

Caspian Sea

Black Sea

THE OTTOMAN EMPIRE

Constantinople

Kars

0   200

Miles

PERSIA

41

THE DESTRUCTION OF POLISH INDEPENDENCE 1768-1795

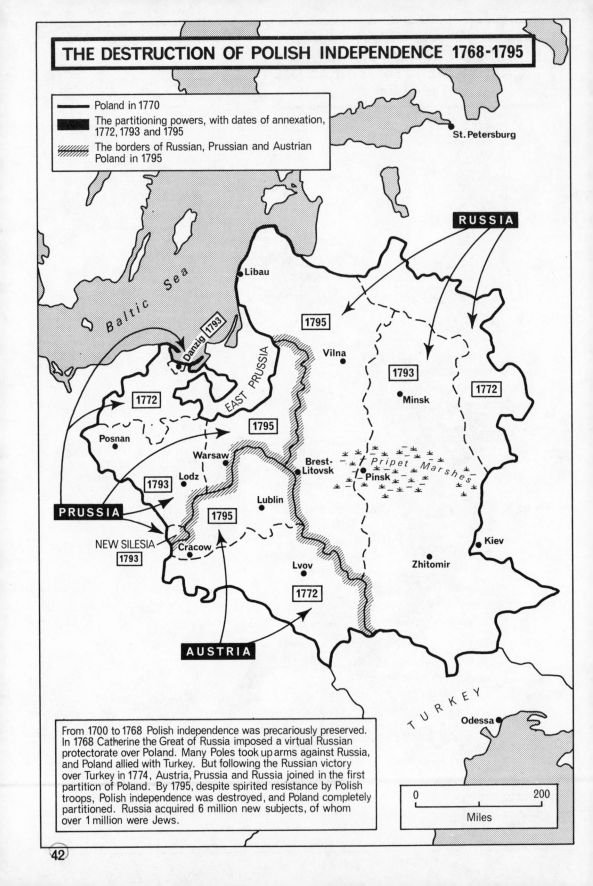

Poland in 1770

The partitioning powers, with dates of annexation, 1772, 1793 and 1795

The borders of Russian, Prussian and Austrian Poland in 1795

St. Petersburg

Baltic Sea

Libau

RUSSIA

1795

1793

1772

Vilna

Minsk

Danzig 1793

EAST PRUSSIA

1772

1795

Posnan

Warsaw

Brest-Litovsk

Pripet Marshes

Pinsk

1793

Lodz

PRUSSIA

Lublin

1795

Kiev

NEW SILESIA

Cracow

Zhitomir

1793

Lvov

1772

AUSTRIA

T U R K E Y

Odessa

From 1700 to 1768 Polish independence was precariously preserved. In 1768 Catherine the Great of Russia imposed a virtual Russian protectorate over Poland. Many Poles took up arms against Russia, and Poland allied with Turkey. But following the Russian victory over Turkey in 1774, Austria, Prussia and Russia joined in the first partition of Poland. By 1795, despite spirited resistance by Polish troops, Polish independence was destroyed, and Poland completely partitioned. Russia acquired 6 million new subjects, of whom over 1 million were Jews.

0   200

Miles

42

THE RUSSIAN ANNEXATIONS OF POLAND 1772-1795

0   150
Miles

Baltic Sea

LATVIA

Pskov

Windau

Riga

Libau

Mitau

Palanga

Dvinsk

Nevel

Memel

Dvina

Polotsk

LITHUANIA

Königsberg

Kovno

1795

Vitebsk

Smolensk

Vilna

1793

1772

EAST
PRUSSIA

Troki

Borisov

Orsha

Suvalki

Lida

Mogilev

Mstislav

Grodno

Minsk

Novogrudok

WHITE

Vilkoviski

Mir

RUSSIA

Bialystok

Baranovichi

Bobruisk

Slutsk

Warsaw

Gomel

Brest-Litovsk

Pinsk

Pripet   Marshes

Turov

Dnieper

Starodub

Pripet

Mozyr

Lublin

Kovel

Olevsk

Chernigov

VOLHYNIA

WESTERN

Lutsk

UKRAINE

Rovno

Zhitomir

Kiev

Dubno

UKRAINE

Lvov

Staro-

Berdychev

Pereyaslavl

Przemysl

Konstantinov

Boguslav

AUSTRIAN-ANNEXED
POLAND

Tarnopol

Vinnitsa

Dnieper

PODOLIA

Stanislavov

Kamenets-
Podolsk

Bug

BESSARABIA

Dniester

Balta

AUSTRIA

RUSSIAN-
ANNEXED

TURKEY

TURKEY

1791
Odessa

Kherson

Dnieper

1774

Black
Sea

The western part of Russia in 1770

Partition lines

Principal Polish military resistance
to the Russians

The western frontier of Russia 1795

PRUSSIAN-ANNEXED POLAND

GALICIA

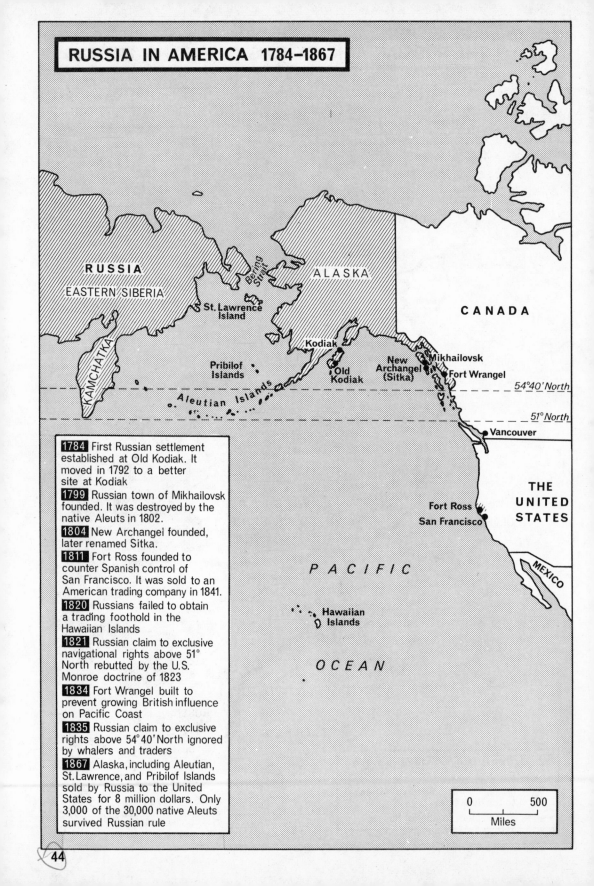

RUSSIA IN AMERICA 1784–1867

RUSSIA

EASTERN SIBERIA

Bering Strait

KAMCHATKA

St. Lawrence Island

Pribilof Islands

Aleutian Islands

ALASKA

Kodiak

Old Kodiak

New Archangel (Sitka)

Mikhailovsk

Fort Wrangel

CANADA

54°40' North

51° North

Vancouver

Fort Ross

San Francisco

THE UNITED STATES

MEXICO

PACIFIC

OCEAN

Hawaiian Islands

1784 First Russian settlement established at Old Kodiak. It moved in 1792 to a better site at Kodiak

1799 Russian town of Mikhailovsk founded. It was destroyed by the native Aleuts in 1802.

1804 New Archangel founded, later renamed Sitka.

1811 Fort Ross founded to counter Spanish control of San Francisco. It was sold to an American trading company in 1841.

1820 Russians failed to obtain a trading foothold in the Hawaiian Islands

1821 Russian claim to exclusive navigational rights above 51° North rebutted by the U.S. Monroe doctrine of 1823

1834 Fort Wrangel built to prevent growing British influence on Pacific Coast

1835 Russian claim to exclusive rights above 54°40' North ignored by whalers and traders

1867 Alaska, including Aleutian, St. Lawrence, and Pribilof Islands sold by Russia to the United States for 8 million dollars. Only 3,000 of the 30,000 native Aleuts survived Russian rule

0   500

Miles

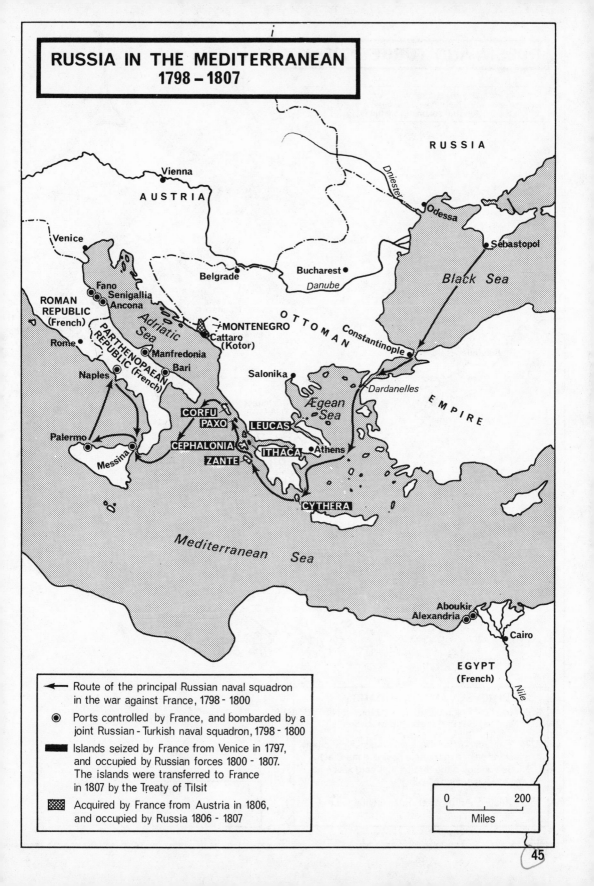

RUSSIA IN THE MEDITERRANEAN
1798 – 1807

RUSSIA

Vienna

AUSTRIA

Odessa

Venice

Dniester

Sébastopol

Belgrade

Bucharest

Black Sea

Danube

Fano
Senigallia
Ancona

ROMAN
REPUBLIC
(French)

Adriatic Sea

MONTENEGRO

OTTOMAN

Cattaro
(Kotor)

Constantinople

Rome

PARTHENOPAEAN
REPUBLIC
(French)

Manfredonia
Bari

Salonika

EMPIRE

Naples

Dardanelles

Ægean
Sea

CORFU
PAXO

LEUCAS

Athens

Palermo

CEPHALONIA

ITHACA

ZANTE

Messina

CYTHERA

Mediterranean   Sea

Aboukir
Alexandria

Cairo

EGYPT
(French)

Nile

→ Route of the principal Russian naval squadron
   in the war against France, 1798 - 1800

◉ Ports controlled by France, and bombarded by a
   joint Russian - Turkish naval squadron, 1798 - 1800

▬ Islands seized by France from Venice in 1797,
   and occupied by Russian forces 1800 - 1807.
   The islands were transferred to France
   in 1807 by the Treaty of Tilsit

▨ Acquired by France from Austria in 1806,
   and occupied by Russia 1806 - 1807

0   200
      Miles

45

RUSSIA AND TURKEY 1721-1829

The Turks are falling like skittles, but, thank God, our men stand fast, though headless
RUSSIAN SOLDIERS' SAYING

Kiev

Dnieper

Khotin
1788

Dniester

Uman
1738

Bug

Prut

BESSARABIA

Kishinev
1739

Jassy
1806

Riabaya
Mogila
1770

Bendery
1770

Ochakov
1788

1790

Perekop

177

173

1789 Fokshani
1770, 1806

Kilia
1791

Belgrade

Braila
1806

Ismail
1791, 1806

1788

C

Negotin
1810

Craiova
1807, 1828

Bucharest
1770, 1806,
1828

Bakhchisarai
1736

Vidin
1811, 1828

Danube

Rushchuk
1771
1811

Silistria
1810,
1774, 1828

1828
Kustenje
1809

Nikopol
1829

Kutchuk
Kainardji

Mangalia
1810, 1828

Shumla
1810

1774
1829

Varna
1810

Turnovo
1810

1791

TURKEY IN EUROPE

Black

Adrianople
1829

Midia
1829

Bosohorus

Enos
1829

Corlu
1829

Constantinople

The Straits

Dardanelles

Aegean Sea

TURKEY I

THE BLACK SEA AND THE STRAITS

1739 Treaty of Belgrade: Russian ships not allowed into the Sea of Azov or the Black Sea

1774 Treaty of Kutchuk Kainardji: Russian merchant ships gained the right to navigate the Black Sea and pass the Straits; but cargoes could be requisitioned at will

1829 Treaty of Adrianople: Russia obtained the right of unhindered passage of unarmed ships

0   100

Miles

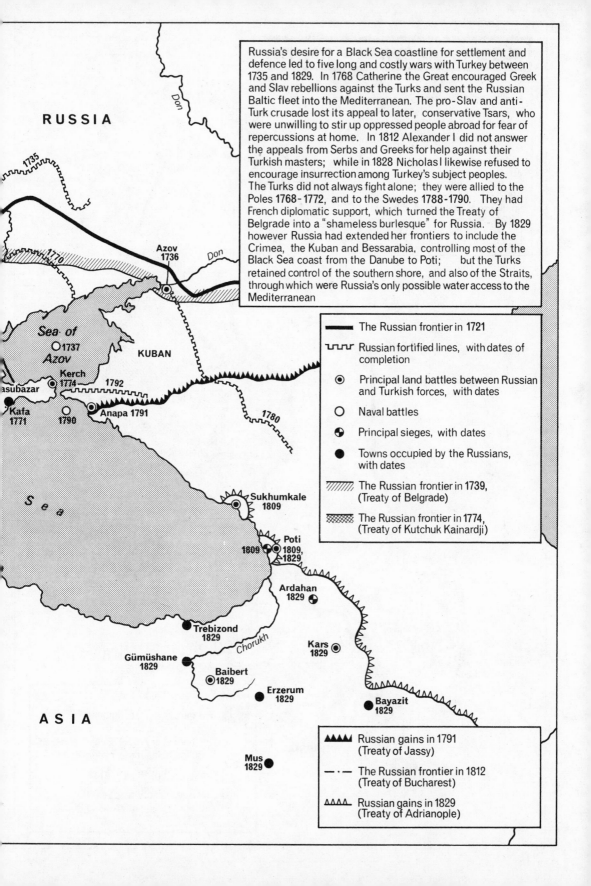

RUSSIA

Russia's desire for a Black Sea coastline for settlement and defence led to five long and costly wars with Turkey between 1735 and 1829. In 1768 Catherine the Great encouraged Greek and Slav rebellions against the Turks and sent the Russian Baltic fleet into the Mediterranean. The pro-Slav and anti-Turk crusade lost its appeal to later, conservative Tsars, who were unwilling to stir up oppressed people abroad for fear of repercussions at home. In 1812 Alexander I did not answer the appeals from Serbs and Greeks for help against their Turkish masters; while in 1828 Nicholas I likewise refused to encourage insurrection among Turkey's subject peoples. The Turks did not always fight alone; they were allied to the Poles 1768-1772, and to the Swedes 1788-1790. They had French diplomatic support, which turned the Treaty of Belgrade into a "shameless burlesque" for Russia. By 1829 however Russia had extended her frontiers to include the Crimea, the Kuban and Bessarabia, controlling most of the Black Sea coast from the Danube to Poti; but the Turks retained control of the southern shore, and also of the Straits, through which were Russia's only possible water access to the Mediterranean

Don

Azov 1736

Don

Sea of Azov 1737

KUBAN

Kerch 1774   1792

...subazar

Kafa 1771   1790   Anapa 1791

1780

S e a

Sukhumkale 1809

Poti 1809   1809, 1829

Ardahan 1829

Trebizond 1829   Chorukh

Kars 1829

Gümüshane 1829

Baibert 1829

Erzerum 1829

Bayazit 1829

ASIA

Mus 1829

The Russian frontier in 1721

Russian fortified lines, with dates of completion

⊙ Principal land battles between Russian and Turkish forces, with dates

○ Naval battles

⊕ Principal sieges, with dates

● Towns occupied by the Russians, with dates

The Russian frontier in 1739, (Treaty of Belgrade)

The Russian frontier in 1774, (Treaty of Kutchuk Kainardji)

Russian gains in 1791 (Treaty of Jassy)

— · — The Russian frontier in 1812 (Treaty of Bucharest)

Russian gains in 1829 (Treaty of Adrianople)

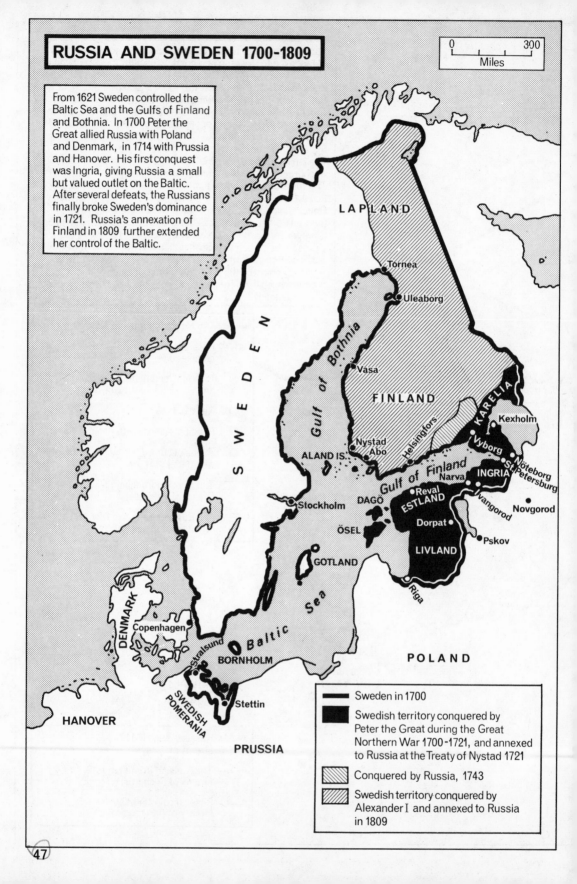

RUSSIA AND SWEDEN 1700-1809

From 1621 Sweden controlled the Baltic Sea and the Gulfs of Finland and Bothnia. In 1700 Peter the Great allied Russia with Poland and Denmark, in 1714 with Prussia and Hanover. His first conquest was Ingria, giving Russia a small but valued outlet on the Baltic. After several defeats, the Russians finally broke Sweden's dominance in 1721. Russia's annexation of Finland in 1809 further extended her control of the Baltic.

LAPLAND

Tornea

Uleaborg

Gulf of Bothnia

S W E D E N

Vasa

F I N L A N D

KARELIA

Kexholm

Helsingfors

Vyborg

Nystad
Abo

ALAND IS.

Noteborg
St Petersburg

INGRIA

Narva

Novgorod

Stockholm

DAGO

Reval

Ivangorod

ESTLAND

Dorpat

OSEL

Pskov

LIVLAND

GOTLAND

Riga

DENMARK

Copenhagen

Baltic Sea

POLAND

Stralsund

BORNHOLM

SWEDISH
POMERANIA

Stettin

HANOVER

PRUSSIA

Sweden in 1700

Swedish territory conquered by Peter the Great during the Great Northern War 1700-1721, and annexed to Russia at the Treaty of Nystad 1721

Conquered by Russia, 1743

Swedish territory conquered by Alexander I and annexed to Russia in 1809

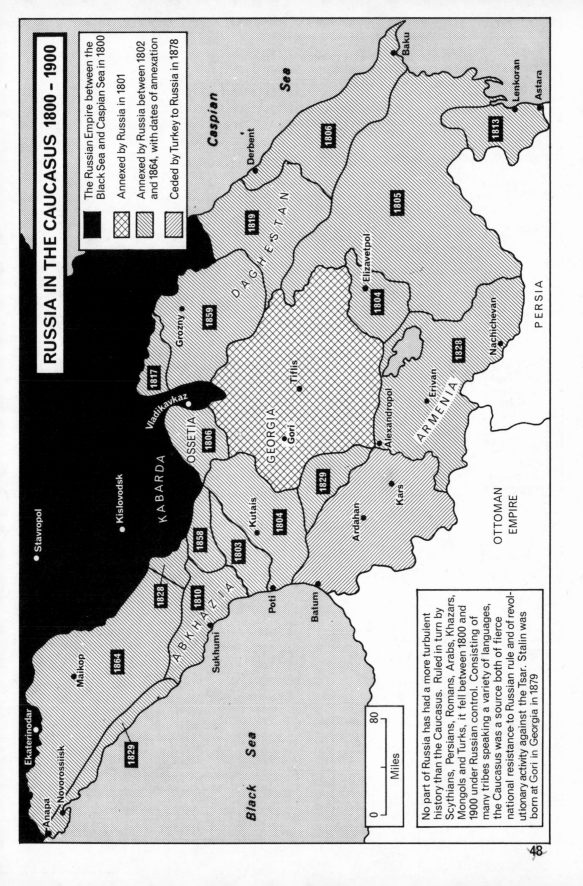

RUSSIA IN THE CAUCASUS 1800 – 1900

The Russian Empire between the Black Sea and Caspian Sea in 1800

Annexed by Russia in 1801

Annexed by Russia between 1802 and 1864, with dates of annexation

Ceded by Turkey to Russia in 1878

Caspian Sea

Black Sea

Baku
Lenkoran
Astara
1813
Derbent
1806
1805
Elizavetpol
1804
Nachichevan
1828
DAGHESTAN
1819
1859
Grozny
ARMENIA
Erivan
Alexandropol
GEORGIA
Tiflis
Gori
1817
Vladikavkaz
OSSETIA
1806
Kars
1829
Ardahan
KABARDA
Kislovodsk
Kutais
1804
1858
1803
Stavropol
ABKHAZIA
1810
1828
Poti
Batum
Sukhumi
Maikop
1864
Ekaterinodar
1829
Novorossiisk
Anapa

PERSIA

OTTOMAN EMPIRE

0   80
Miles

No part of Russia has had a more turbulent history than the Caucasus. Ruled in turn by Scythians, Persians, Romans, Arabs, Khazars, Mongols and Turks, it fell between 1800 and 1900 under Russian control. Consisting of many tribes speaking a variety of languages, the Caucasus was a source both of fierce national resistance to Russian rule and of revol-utionary activity against the Tsar. Stalin was born at Gori in Georgia in 1879

48

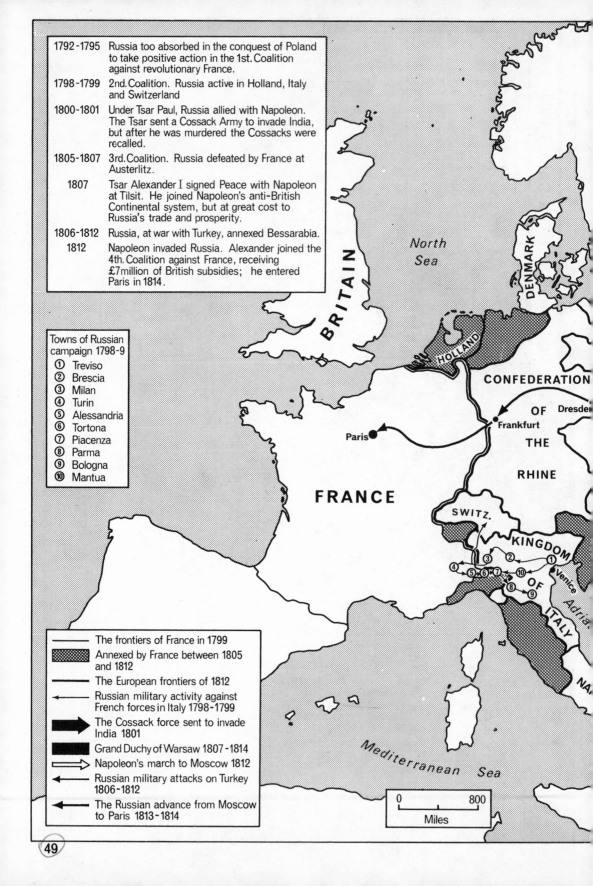

1792-1795	Russia too absorbed in the conquest of Poland to take positive action in the 1st. Coalition against revolutionary France.
1798-1799	2nd. Coalition. Russia active in Holland, Italy and Switzerland
1800-1801	Under Tsar Paul, Russia allied with Napoleon. The Tsar sent a Cossack Army to invade India, but after he was murdered the Cossacks were recalled.
1805-1807	3rd. Coalition. Russia defeated by France at Austerlitz.
1807	Tsar Alexander I signed Peace with Napoleon at Tilsit. He joined Napoleon's anti-British Continental system, but at great cost to Russia's trade and prosperity.
1806-1812	Russia, at war with Turkey, annexed Bessarabia.
1812	Napoleon invaded Russia. Alexander joined the 4th. Coalition against France, receiving £7 million of British subsidies; he entered Paris in 1814.

Towns of Russian campaign 1798-9

① Treviso
② Brescia
③ Milan
④ Turin
⑤ Alessandria
⑥ Tortona
⑦ Piacenza
⑧ Parma
⑨ Bologna
⑩ Mantua

North Sea

BRITAIN

DENMARK

HOLLAND

CONFEDERATION
OF   Dresden
Frankfurt
THE
RHINE

FRANCE

Paris

SWITZ.

KINGDOM

Venice

OF

ITALY   Adria.

NA

Mediterranean Sea

——— The frontiers of France in 1799

▦ Annexed by France between 1805 and 1812

——— The European frontiers of 1812

←— Russian military activity against French forces in Italy 1798-1799

➤ The Cossack force sent to invade India 1801

▬ Grand Duchy of Warsaw 1807-1814

⇦ Napoleon's march to Moscow 1812

←— Russian military attacks on Turkey 1806-1812

←— The Russian advance from Moscow to Paris 1813-1814

0   800
Miles

RUSSIA AND EUROPE 1789-1815

R U S S I A

Tver

Moscow

Borodino

Viazma

Riazan

Smolensk

Tula

Riga

Tilsit

Borisov

RUSSIA

Kalisz

GRAND DUCHY OF WARSAW

Baltic Sea

Napoleon championed Polish independence, and many Polish emigres joined him after 1795. In 1807 he established a Grand Duchy of Warsaw, entirely out of Prussian and Austrian Poland. The Russians planned to crush this new state, but to forestall them Napoleon marched to Moscow in 1812. 85.000 Poles served in his army. After his defeat most of the Grand Duchy was transferred to Russia, giving Russia a further 3 million Polish and 300,000 Jewish citizens.

Austerlitz

Vienna

A U S T R I A

Jassy

BESS-ARABIA

Ismail

RUMANIANS

Bucharest

Iasika

CROATS

S E R B S

Tirnovo

Shumla

Varna

Black Sea

B U L G A R S

TURKEY IN EUROPE

GREEKS

TURKEY IN ASIA

Balkan peoples under Turkish rule, whom Alexander planned to enlist in an anti-French crusade in return for helping them obtain independence from Turkey. The plan failed.

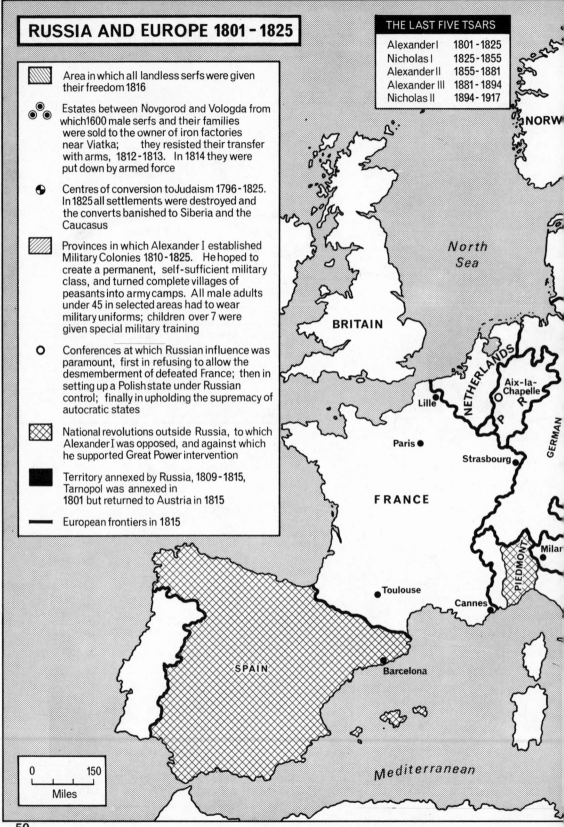

RUSSIA AND EUROPE 1801-1825

Area in which all landless serfs were given their freedom 1816

Estates between Novgorod and Vologda from which 1600 male serfs and their families were sold to the owner of iron factories near Viatka; they resisted their transfer with arms, 1812-1813. In 1814 they were put down by armed force

Centres of conversion to Judaism 1796-1825. In 1825 all settlements were destroyed and the converts banished to Siberia and the Caucasus

Provinces in which Alexander I established Military Colonies 1810-1825. He hoped to create a permanent, self-sufficient military class, and turned complete villages of peasants into army camps. All male adults under 45 in selected areas had to wear military uniforms; children over 7 were given special military training

Conferences at which Russian influence was paramount, first in refusing to allow the desmemberment of defeated France; then in setting up a Polish state under Russian control; finally in upholding the supremacy of autocratic states

National revolutions outside Russia, to which Alexander I was opposed, and against which he supported Great Power intervention

Territory annexed by Russia, 1809-1815, Tarnopol was annexed in 1801 but returned to Austria in 1815

European frontiers in 1815

NORW

North Sea

BRITAIN

NETHERLANDS

Aix-la-Chapelle

Lille

EUROPE

Paris

Strasbourg

GERMAN

FRANCE

PIEDMONT

Milan

Toulouse

Cannes

SPAIN

Barcelona

Mediterranean

0   150
Miles

FINLAND

ALAND
ISLANDS

SWEDEN

St.
Petersburg

Novgorod

Viatka ●

Vologda

Moscow ●

Tula ◓

Saratov ◓

R U S S I A

Mogilev

Baltic Sea

S S I A

Bobrov ◓

Pavlovsk ◓

POLAND

Carlsbad ○

Prague ●

Troppau ○

Lemberg ●

Tarnopol ●

BESSARABIA

Ekaterinoslav ●

Nikolaev ●

Vienna ○

AUSTRIA-
HUNGARY

Laibach ○

Bucharest ●

Black Sea

T
U
R
K
E
Y

Belgrade ●

Cattaro ●

Constantinople ●

Rome ●

NAPLES

Naples ●

GREECE

Athens ●

Sea

Like Catherine the Great on her accession,
Alexander I was looked to on his accession
(in 1801) as a potential source of liberal-
ization. In the war against Napoleon he acted
as the enemy of tyrants and friend of the
oppressed. But by 1820 he had become a
pillar of autocracy both in Russia and
abroad. Under Alexander, Russia's western
frontier reached its furthest western extent,
and from 1820 to 1917 it was unchanged

RUSSIA UNDER NICHOLAS I 1825-1855

Nicholas I, known as the Gendarme of Europe, was equally the gendarme of Russia. In 1827 he set up a special Corps of Gendarmes, as the main instrument of the political police. The country was divided into Gendarme Districts, each commanded by a General. .There were an estimated total of at least 4,000 Gendarmes in 1837, when the Districts were reorganised; and at least 8,000 by 1855. A squadron was set up to patrol the Moscow-St. Petersburg railway in 1846

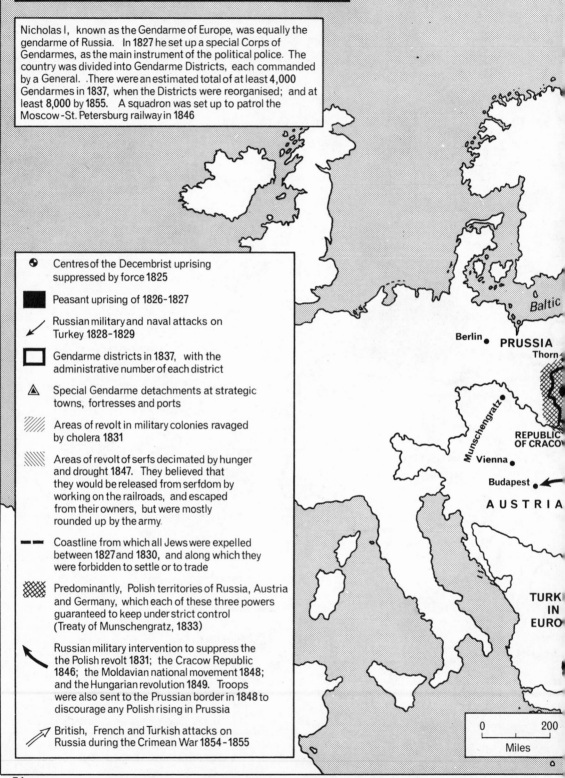

- ✪ Centres of the Decembrist uprising suppressed by force 1825

- ■ Peasant uprising of 1826-1827

- ↙ Russian military and naval attacks on Turkey 1828-1829

- ▢ Gendarme districts in 1837, with the administrative number of each district

- ▲ Special Gendarme detachments at strategic towns, fortresses and ports

- ▨ Areas of revolt in military colonies ravaged by cholera 1831

- ▨ Areas of revolt of serfs decimated by hunger and drought 1847. They believed that they would be released from serfdom by working on the railroads, and escaped from their owners, but were mostly rounded up by the army.

- – – Coastline from which all Jews were expelled between 1827 and 1830, and along which they were forbidden to settle or to trade

- ▨ Predominantly, Polish territories of Russia, Austria and Germany, which each of these three powers guaranteed to keep under strict control (Treaty of Munschengratz, 1833)

- ↖ Russian military intervention to suppress the the Polish revolt 1831; the Cracow Republic 1846; the Moldavian national movement 1848; and the Hungarian revolution 1849. Troops were also sent to the Prussian border in 1848 to discourage any Polish rising in Prussia

- ↗ British, French and Turkish attacks on Russia during the Crimean War 1854-1855

Baltic

Berlin • PRUSSIA
Thorn •

Munschengratz •

REPUBLIC OF CRACOW

Vienna •

Budapest •

AUSTRIA

TURKEY
IN
EUROPE

0   200
Miles

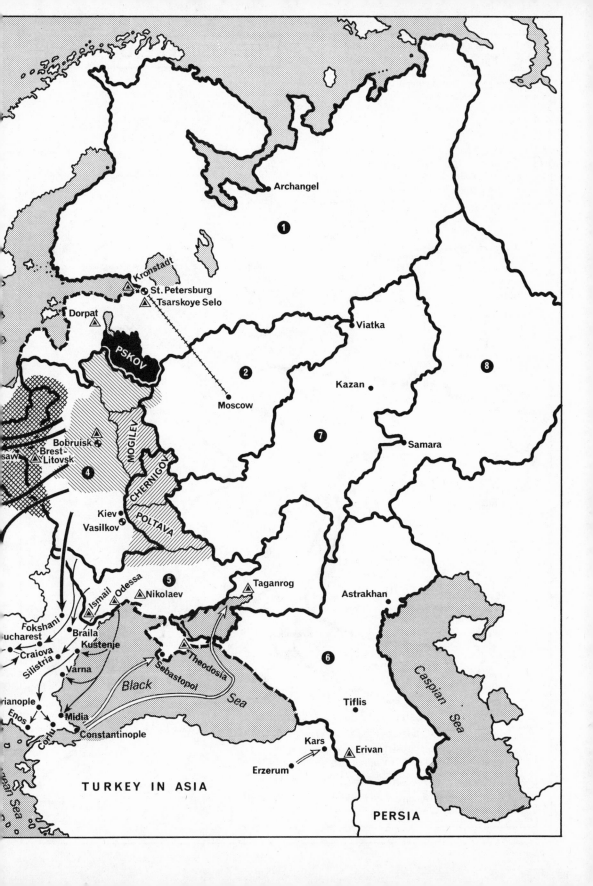

THE POLISH REVOLT IN 1831

After Napoleon's defeat in 1814, Russia set up its new Polish territory as a separate kingdom, CONGRESS POLAND, ruled directly by the Tsar. After 1814, Alexander I adopted a liberal, pro-Polish policy. But in 1825 his successor, Nicholas I, began to restrict Polish liberties. In 1830 the Poles rose in open war against Russian rule. They hoped for help from France, but it never came. The revolt was crushed by superior Russian force.

Palanga

Memel

Königsberg

Danzig

P R U S S I A

Masurian Lakes

0   50
Miles

Vilna

Suvalki

Grodno

Posen

Bialystok

R U S S I A

Warsaw

Kalisz

Lodz

Piotrkow

Pripet Marshes

Brest-Litovsk

Pinsk

Breslau

SILESIA

Czenstochowa

Krasnik

Kovel

REPUBLIC OF CRACOW

Cracow

Tarnow

GALICIA

Przemysl

Lvov

AUSTRIA

Tarnopol

Congress Poland, ruled by the Russian Tsar 1815-1914

Principal areas of Polish partisan activity in 1831 against the local Russian authorities

Battles between Russian and Polish troops in 1831

Polish troop movements. All these ended in exile across the Prussian, Austrian and Cracovian borders

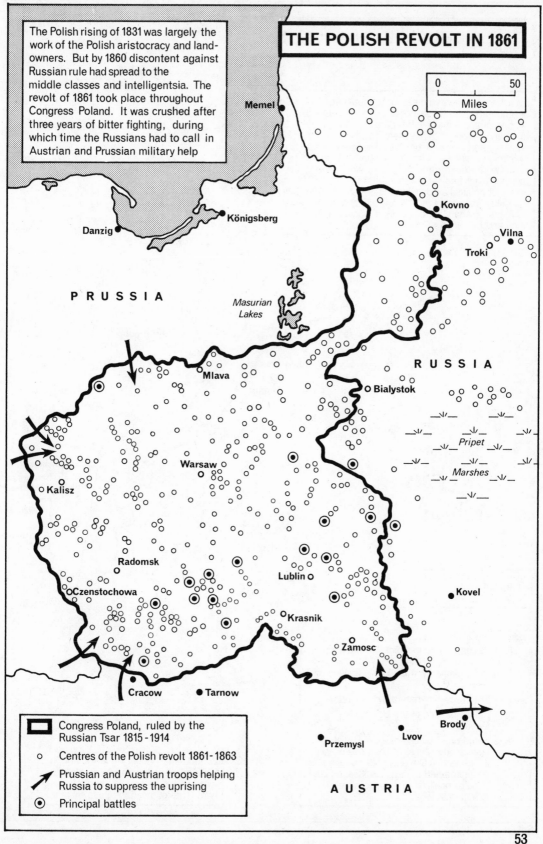

THE POLISH REVOLT IN 1861

The Polish rising of 1831 was largely the work of the Polish aristocracy and land-owners. But by 1860 discontent against Russian rule had spread to the middle classes and intelligentsia. The revolt of 1861 took place throughout Congress Poland. It was crushed after three years of bitter fighting, during which time the Russians had to call in Austrian and Prussian military help

0   50
Miles

Memel

Königsberg

Danzig

PRUSSIA

Kovno

Vilna

Troki

Masurian
Lakes

Mlava

Bialystok

RUSSIA

Pripet

Marshes

Warsaw

Kalisz

Radomsk

Lublin

Czenstochowa

Krasnik

Kovel

Zamosc

Cracow   Tarnow

Brody

Przemysl   Lvov

AUSTRIA

Congress Poland, ruled by the
Russian Tsar 1815 - 1914

○   Centres of the Polish revolt 1861-1863

Prussian and Austrian troops helping
Russia to suppress the uprising

⊙   Principal battles

53

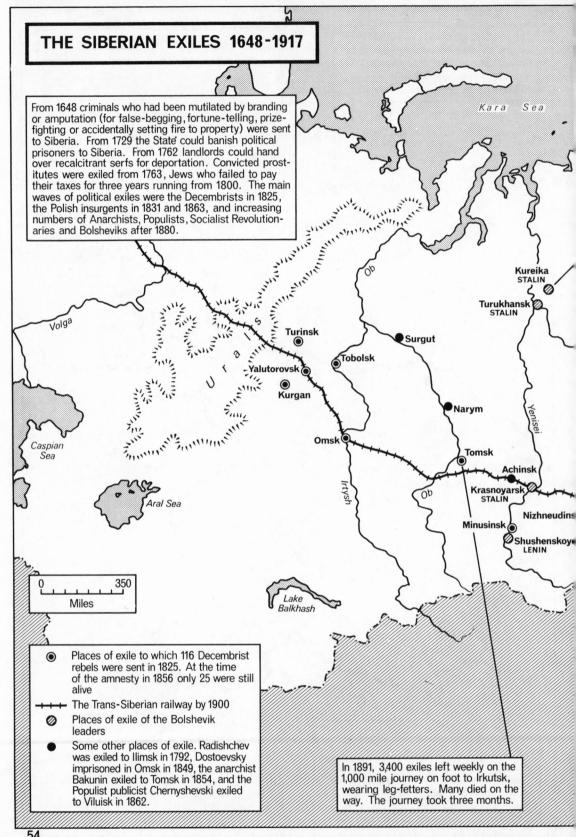

THE SIBERIAN EXILES 1648-1917

From 1648 criminals who had been mutilated by branding or amputation (for false-begging, fortune-telling, prize-fighting or accidentally setting fire to property) were sent to Siberia. From 1729 the State could banish political prisoners to Siberia. From 1762 landlords could hand over recalcitrant serfs for deportation. Convicted prostitutes were exiled from 1763, Jews who failed to pay their taxes for three years running from 1800. The main waves of political exiles were the Decembrists in 1825, the Polish insurgents in 1831 and 1863, and increasing numbers of Anarchists, Populists, Socialist Revolutionaries and Bolsheviks after 1880.

Kara Sea

Volga

Ob

Kureika
STALIN

Turukhansk
STALIN

Turinsk

Surgut

Tobolsk

Yenisei

Yalutorovsk

Kurgan

Narym

U r a l s

Omsk

Caspian Sea

Tomsk

Achinsk

Krasnoyarsk
STALIN

Irtysh

Ob

Nizhneudins

Aral Sea

Minusinsk

Shushenskoye
LENIN

```
0          350
|_|_|_|_|_|
   Miles
```

Lake Balkhash

Places of exile to which 116 Decembrist rebels were sent in 1825. At the time of the amnesty in 1856 only 25 were still alive

┼┼┼ The Trans-Siberian railway by 1900

Places of exile of the Bolshevik leaders

Some other places of exile. Radishchev was exiled to Ilimsk in 1792, Dostoevsky imprisoned in Omsk in 1849, the anarchist Bakunin exiled to Tomsk in 1854, and the Populist publicist Chernyshevski exiled to Viluisk in 1862.

In 1891, 3,400 exiles left weekly on the 1,000 mile journey on foot to Irkutsk, wearing leg-fetters. Many died on the way. The journey took three months.

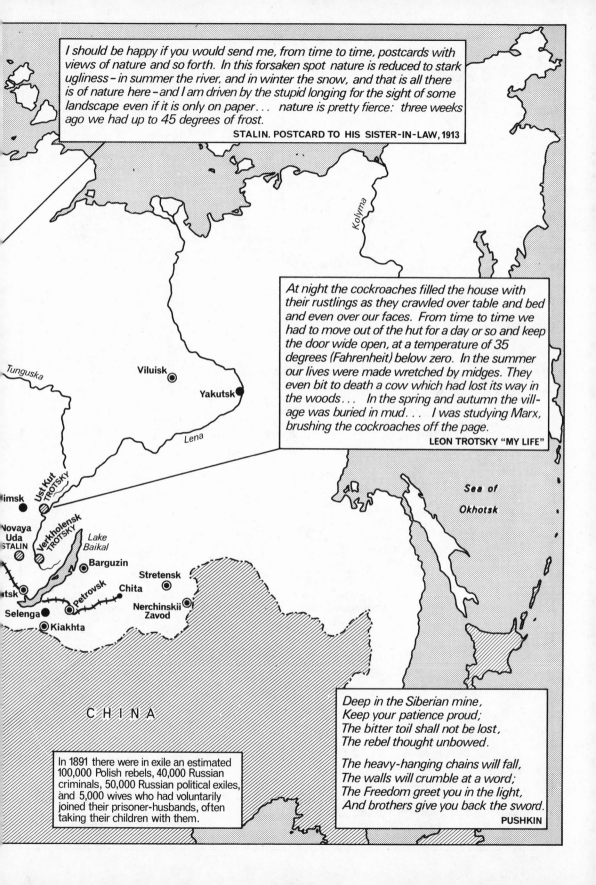

I should be happy if you would send me, from time to time, postcards with views of nature and so forth. In this forsaken spot nature is reduced to stark ugliness – in summer the river, and in winter the snow, and that is all there is of nature here – and I am driven by the stupid longing for the sight of some landscape even if it is only on paper... nature is pretty fierce: three weeks ago we had up to 45 degrees of frost.

STALIN. POSTCARD TO HIS SISTER-IN-LAW, 1913

At night the cockroaches filled the house with their rustlings as they crawled over table and bed and even over our faces. From time to time we had to move out of the hut for a day or so and keep the door wide open, at a temperature of 35 degrees (Fahrenheit) below zero. In the summer our lives were made wretched by midges. They even bit to death a cow which had lost its way in the woods... In the spring and autumn the village was buried in mud... I was studying Marx, brushing the cockroaches off the page.

LEON TROTSKY "MY LIFE"

Kolyma

Tunguska

Viluisk

Yakutsk

Lena

Ust Kut TROTSKY

imsk

Novaya Uda STALIN

Verkholensk TROTSKY

Lake Baikal

Barguzin

Stretensk

Petrovsk

Chita

tsk

Nerchinskii Zavod

Selenga

Kiakhta

Sea of Okhotsk

C H I N A

In 1891 there were in exile an estimated 100,000 Polish rebels, 40,000 Russian criminals, 50,000 Russian political exiles, and 5,000 wives who had voluntarily joined their prisoner-husbands, often taking their children with them.

Deep in the Siberian mine,
Keep your patience proud;
The bitter toil shall not be lost,
The rebel thought unbowed.

The heavy-hanging chains will fall,
The walls will crumble at a word;
The Freedom greet you in the light,
And brothers give you back the sword.

PUSHKIN

THE ANARCHISTS 1840-1906

"What is property? Property is theft" wrote the French philosopher Proudhon, the father of anarchism, in 1840. He urged the destruction of officialdom, bureaucracy money and state organisation in order to make all men equal and free. But he shunned violent revolt, fearing that revolution might bring new tyranny. The Russian, Bakunin, bent anarchism to violence. *"The passion to destroy is at the same time a passion to create,"* he wrote in 1842. Bakunin believed that the Russian peasant would be the instrument of anarchic revolt, and encouraged terrorist acts. The murder of Tsar Alexander II at St. Petersburg in 1881 encouraged further assassinations, aimed at provoking revolution. The Russian anarchist, Prince Kropotkin, said after the execution of one of the 5 assassins: *"By her death she was dealing an even more terrible blow, from which the autocracy will never recover."*

Baltic Sea

St. Petersburg

Viatka

Riga

LITHUANIA

Kovno

Vilna

Minsk

Grodno

Bialystok

Warsaw

POLAND

Moscow

Nizhni Novgorod

Volga

Tula

Orel

Samara

Nezhin

Kiev

Kharkov

UKRAINE

Ekaterinoslav

Kishinev

Odessa

Sebastopol

Yalta

Black Sea

Volga

Caspian Sea

Batum

Tiflis

CAUCASIA

Baku

⊙ Anarchist groups meeting from the 1840's to 1880's

● Revolutionary anarchist groups in existence from 1903 and "revolting" in 1905 - 1906

The "Forest Brethren" carrying out terrorist activity in 1905 - 1906

0   300
Miles

RUSSIAN INDUSTRY BY 1860

0   200
Miles

Archangel

Urals

Kama

Vyborg

Schlüsselburg

Viatka

Reval

St.Petersburg — 540,000

+ **Perm**

GOLD

COAL

Narva

LEATHER

COPPER

WOOL

Dorpat

COAL

Yaroslavl

LEATHER

Pskov

Tver

Vladimir

LINEN

Volga

Kazan

Ufa

COPPER

Libau

Mitau

Riga

Dvinsk

77,000

LEATHER

Yegorevsk

Moscow

460,000

Nizhni Novgorod

63,000

WOOL

LEATHER

Kovno

Riazan

LINEN

Vilna

69,000

Kaluga

Tula

LINEN

Grodno

LEATHER

Saratov

Bialystok

Orel

84,000

Warsaw

LINEN

WOOL

Lodz

LINEN

LINEN

Voronezh

Dnieper

Chernigov

Kiev

LINEN

68,000

Kharkov

Donets

Volga

Poltava

COAL

Kishinev

94,000

64,000

Nikolaev

Don

Caspian Sea

Odessa

120,000

TOBACCO

Caucasus

POPULATION
1811: 41,000,000
1863: 74,000,000

Black Sea

Baku

OIL

── The Russian frontier 1815 - 1914

● Principal cities, with their estimated population in 1860

╫╫╫ Railways built by 1860

┼┼┼ Railways under construction in 1860

⊙ Factory development before 1860

◉ Towns with large factory growth from 1860

▬ Industries expanding rapidly from 1860

▓ Centres of the iron and steel production

▨ Sugar factories

PRINCIPAL IMPORTS: Cotton, machine tools, alcohol, dyes, fruit and nuts, wool, tea, olive and vegetable oil, silk, sugar, zinc, steel, iron, copper, horses, cattle, poultry, salt. Over 80% of all imports and exports went through the ports of St. Petersburg and Odessa

PRINCIPAL EXPORTS: Wheat, rye, cereals, flour, flax, hemp, wool, animal fat, lard, seeds, wood, wood products, paper

56

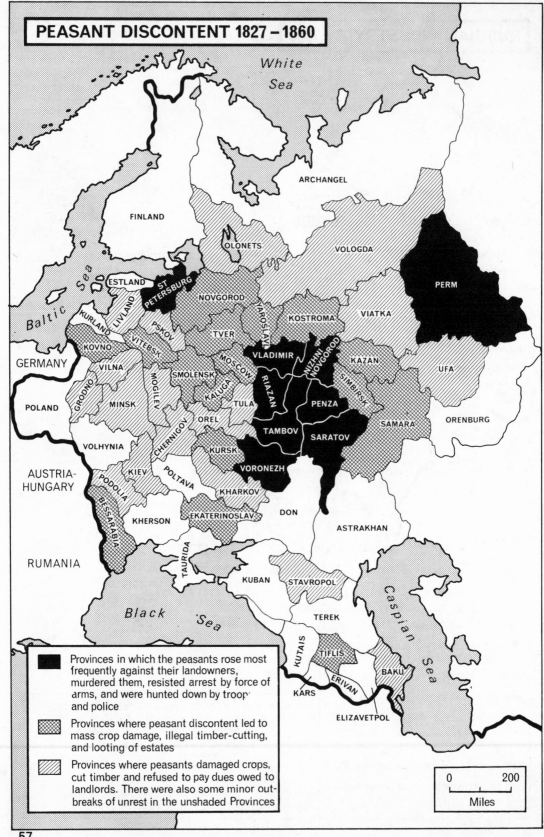

PEASANT DISCONTENT 1827–1860

White Sea

ARCHANGEL

FINLAND

OLONETS

VOLOGDA

Baltic Sea

ESTLAND

ST PETERSBURG

NOVGOROD

PERM

KURLAND

LIVLAND

PSKOV

YAROSLAVL

KOSTROMA

VIATKA

KOVNO

VITEBSK

TVER

VLADIMIR

NIZHNI NOVGOROD

KAZAN

UFA

GERMANY

VILNA

GRODNO

MOGILEV

SMOLENSK

MOSCOW

KALUGA

RIAZAN

SIMBIRSK

POLAND

MINSK

TULA

PENZA

ORENBURG

OREL

SAMARA

CHERNIGOV

KURSK

TAMBOV

SARATOV

VOLHYNIA

KIEV

POLTAVA

VORONEZH

AUSTRIA-HUNGARY

PODOLIA

BESSARABIA

KHARKOV

EKATERINOSLAV

DON

ASTRAKHAN

RUMANIA

KHERSON

TAURIDA

KUBAN

STAVROPOL

Black Sea

Caspian Sea

TEREK

KUTAIS

TIFLIS

BAKU

ERIVAN

KARS

ELIZAVETPOL

Provinces in which the peasants rose most frequently against their landowners, murdered them, resisted arrest by force of arms, and were hunted down by troops and police

Provinces where peasant discontent led to mass crop damage, illegal timber-cutting, and looting of estates

Provinces where peasants damaged crops, cut timber and refused to pay dues owed to landlords. There were also some minor outbreaks of unrest in the unshaded Provinces

0   200
Miles

57

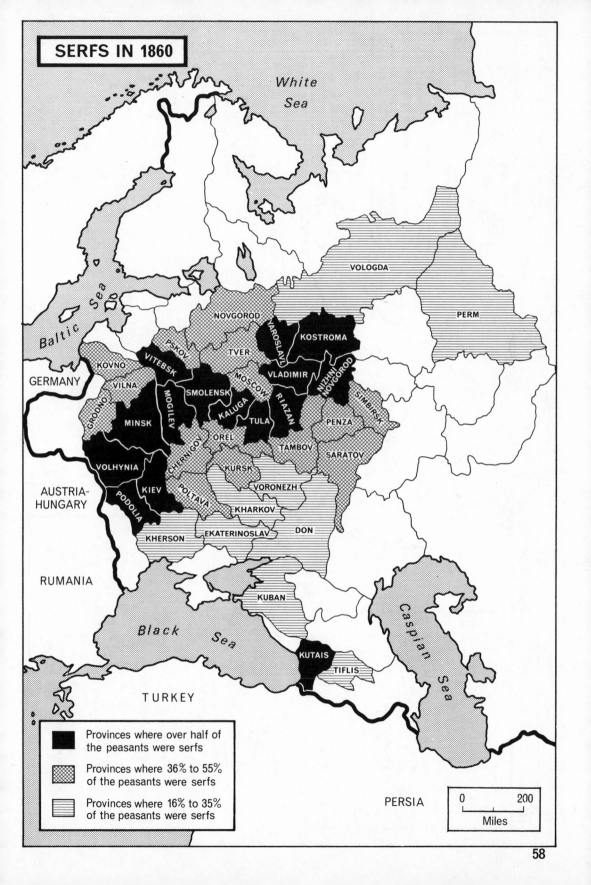

SERFS IN 1860

White
Sea

Baltic Sea

GERMANY

VOLOGDA

PERM

NOVGOROD

PSKOV

VITEBSK

KOVNO

VILNA

GRODNO

MOGILEV

SMOLENSK

MINSK

TVER

MOSCOW

YAROSLAVL

KOSTROMA

VLADIMIR

NIZHNI NOVGOROD

KALUGA

TULA

RIAZAN

SIMBIRSK

PENZA

AUSTRIA-
HUNGARY

VOLHYNIA

KIEV

PODOLIA

CHERNIGOV

OREL

POLTAVA

KURSK

VORONEZH

TAMBOV

SARATOV

E KHARKOV

RUMANIA

KHERSON

EKATERINOSLAV

DON

KUBAN

Black   Sea

Caspian Sea

KUTAIS

TIFLIS

TURKEY

PERSIA

■ Provinces where over half of
the peasants were serfs

▨ Provinces where 36% to 55%
of the peasants were serfs

▤ Provinces where 16% to 35%
of the peasants were serfs

0   200
Miles

58

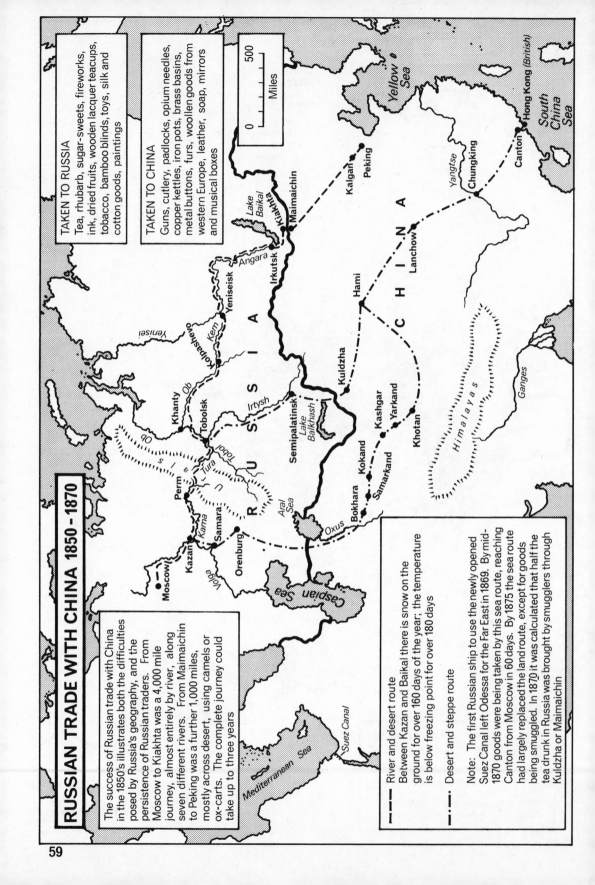

RUSSIAN TRADE WITH CHINA 1850 – 1870

The success of Russian trade with China in the 1850's illustrates both the difficulties posed by Russia's geography, and the persistence of Russian traders. From Moscow to Kiakhta was a 4,000 mile journey, almost entirely by river, along seven different rivers. From Maimaichin to Peking was a further 1,000 miles, mostly across desert, using camels or ox-carts. The complete journey could take up to three years

TAKEN TO RUSSIA
Tea, rhubarb, sugar-sweets, fireworks, ink, dried fruits, wooden lacquer teacups, tobacco, bamboo blinds, toys, silk and cotton goods, paintings

TAKEN TO CHINA
Guns, cutlery, padlocks, opium needles, copper kettles, iron pots, brass basins, metal buttons, furs, woollen goods from western Europe, leather, soap, mirrors and musical boxes

- - - River and desert route
Between Kazan and Baikal there is snow on the ground for over 160 days of the year; the temperature is below freezing point for over 180 days

-·-· Desert and steppe route

Note: The first Russian ship to use the newly opened Suez Canal left Odessa for the Far East in 1869. By mid-1870 goods were being taken by this sea route, reaching Canton from Moscow in 60 days. By 1875 the sea route had largely replaced the land route, except for goods being smuggled. In 1870 it was calculated that half the tea drunk in Russia was brought by smugglers through Kuldzha or Maimaichin

500
0
Miles

59

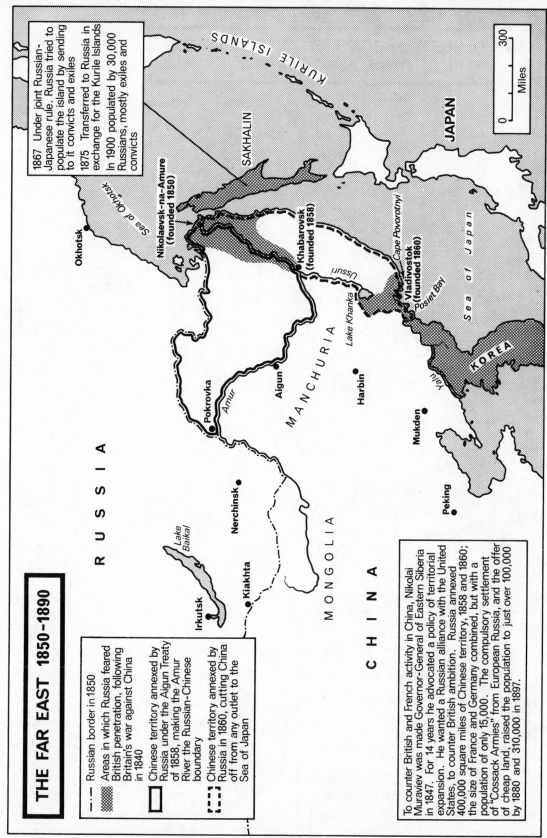

THE FAR EAST 1850–1890

Legend:

- –·– Russian border in 1850
- ░ Areas in which Russia feared British penetration, following Britain's war against China in 1840
- ▭ Chinese territory annexed by Russia under the Aigun Treaty of 1858, making the Amur River the Russian-Chinese boundary
- ⬚ Chinese territory annexed by Russia in 1860, cutting China off from any outlet to the Sea of Japan

1867 Under joint Russian-Japanese rule. Russia tried to populate the island by sending to it convicts and exiles

1875 Transferred to Russia in exchange for the Kurile Islands In 1900 populated by 30,000 Russians, mostly exiles and convicts

To counter British and French activity in China, Nikolai Muraviev was made Governor-General of Eastern Siberia in 1847. For 14 years he advocated a policy of territorial expansion. He wanted a Russian alliance with the United States, to counter British ambition. Russia annexed 400,000 square miles of Chinese territory, 1858 and 1860; the size of France and Germany combined, but with a population of only 15,000. The compulsory settlement of "Cossack Armies" from European Russia, and the offer of cheap land, raised the population to just over 100,000 by 1880 and 310,000 in 1897.

Map labels:

KURILE ISLANDS

JAPAN

SAKHALIN

Sea of Okhotsk

Okhotsk

Nikolaevsk-na-Amure (founded 1850)

Khabarovsk (founded 1858)

Cape Povorotnyi

Vladivostok (founded 1860)

Posiet Bay

Sea of Japan

Ussuri

Lake Khanka

KOREA

MANCHURIA

Yalu

Pokrovka

Aigun

Harbin

Amur

Mukden

Nerchinsk

Peking

RUSSIA

Lake Baikal

Irkutsk

Kiakhta

MONGOLIA

CHINA

0   300
Miles

60

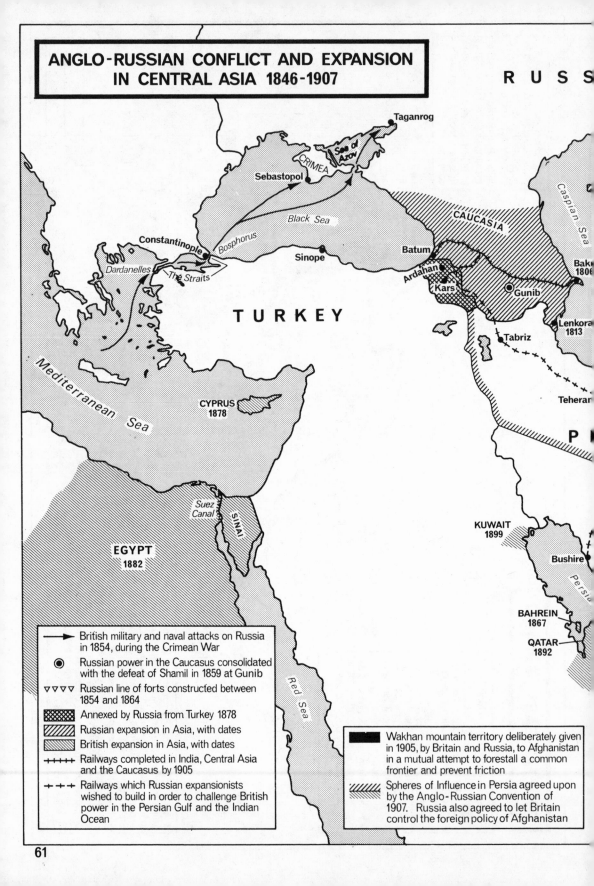

ANGLO-RUSSIAN CONFLICT AND EXPANSION IN CENTRAL ASIA 1846-1907

RUSS

Taganrog

Sea of Azov

CRIMEA

Sebastopol

Black Sea

CAUCASIA

Caspian Sea

Constantinople

Bosphorus

Batum

Bak 1806

Dardanelles

The Straits

Sinope

Ardahan

Kars

Gunib

Lenkora 1813

TURKEY

Tabriz

Teheran

Mediterranean Sea

CYPRUS 1878

P

Suez Canal

SINAI

KUWAIT 1899

Bushire

EGYPT 1882

Persi

Red Sea

BAHREIN 1867

QATAR 1892

→	British military and naval attacks on Russia in 1854, during the Crimean War
⊙	Russian power in the Caucasus consolidated with the defeat of Shamil in 1859 at Gunib
▽▽▽▽	Russian line of forts constructed between 1854 and 1864
▨	Annexed by Russia from Turkey 1878
▨	Russian expansion in Asia, with dates
▨	British expansion in Asia, with dates
+++++	Railways completed in India, Central Asia and the Caucasus by 1905
+-+-+	Railways which Russian expansionists wished to build in order to challenge British power in the Persian Gulf and the Indian Ocean

▰	Wakhan mountain territory deliberately given in 1905, by Britain and Russia, to Afghanistan in a mutual attempt to forestall a common frontier and prevent friction
▨	Spheres of Influence in Persia agreed upon by the Anglo-Russian Convention of 1907. Russia also agreed to let Britain control the foreign policy of Afghanistan

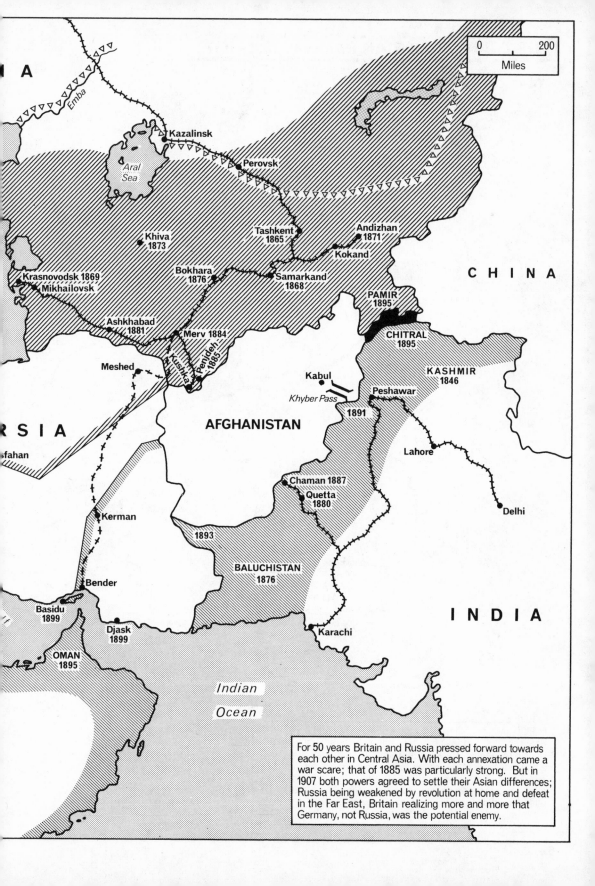

Kazalinsk

Emba

Aral
Sea

Perovsk

Khiva
1873

Tashkent
1865

Andizhan
1871

Kokand

CHINA

Krasnovodsk 1869

Mikhailovsk

Bokhara
1876

Samarkand
1868

PAMIR
1895

Ashkhabad
1881

Merv 1884

CHITRAL
1895

Meshed

Penjdeh
1885

Kushka

KASHMIR
1846

Kabul

Peshawar

RSIA

Khyber Pass

1891

AFGHANISTAN

sfahan

Lahore

Chaman 1887

Quetta
1880

Kerman

Delhi

1893

BALUCHISTAN
1876

INDIA

Bender

Basidu
1899

Djask
1899

Karachi

OMAN
1895

Indian

Ocean

For 50 years Britain and Russia pressed forward towards
each other in Central Asia. With each annexation came a
war scare; that of 1885 was particularly strong. But in
1907 both powers agreed to settle their Asian differences;
Russia being weakened by revolution at home and defeat
in the Far East, Britain realizing more and more that
Germany, not Russia, was the potential enemy.

0   200

Miles

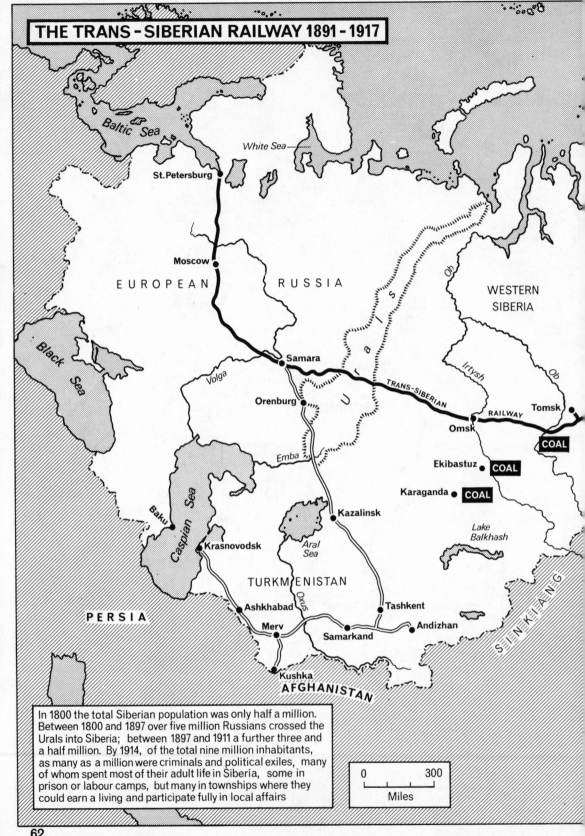

THE TRANS - SIBERIAN RAILWAY 1891 - 1917

Baltic Sea

White Sea

St.Petersburg

Moscow

EUROPEAN   RUSSIA

WESTERN
SIBERIA

Ob

Black Sea

Samara

Volga

Orenburg

Urals

Irtysh

Ob

TRANS-SIBERIAN

RAILWAY

Tomsk

Omsk

COAL

Emba

Ekibastuz   **COAL**

Karaganda   **COAL**

Baku

Caspian Sea

Kazalinsk

*Aral
Sea*

*Lake
Balkhash*

Krasnovodsk

TURKMENISTAN

Oxus

PERSIA

Ashkhabad

Tashkent

Merv

Samarkand

Andizhan

S I N K I A N G

Kushka
AFGHANISTAN

In 1800 the total Siberian population was only half a million.
Between 1800 and 1897 over five million Russians crossed the
Urals into Siberia; between 1897 and 1911 a further three and
a half million. By 1914, of the total nine million inhabitants,
as many as a million were criminals and political exiles, many
of whom spent most of their adult life in Siberia, some in
prison or labour camps, but many in townships where they
could earn a living and participate fully in local affairs

0   300

Miles

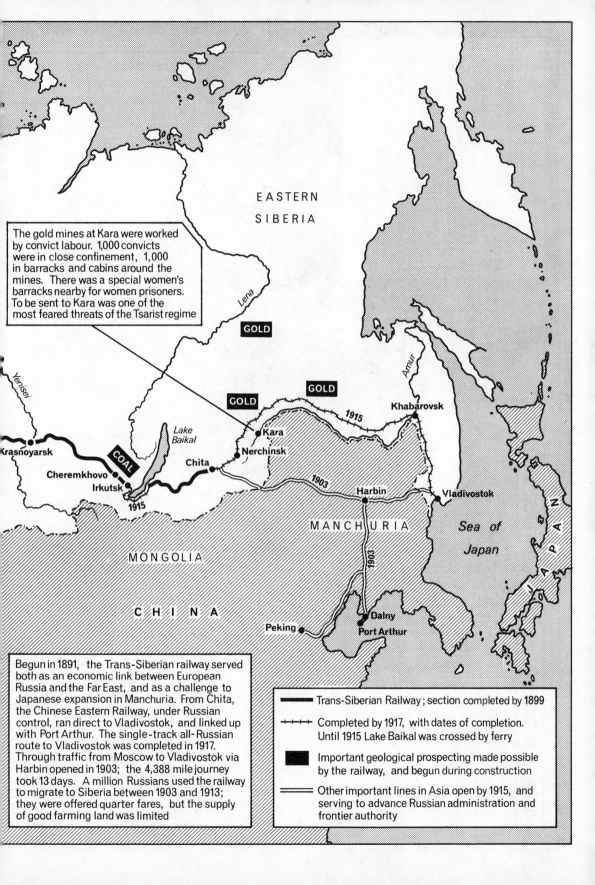

EASTERN
SIBERIA

Lena

The gold mines at Kara were worked
by convict labour. 1,000 convicts
were in close confinement, 1,000
in barracks and cabins around the
mines. There was a special women's
barracks nearby for women prisoners.
To be sent to Kara was one of the
most feared threats of the Tsarist regime

Yenisei

Amur

GOLD

GOLD

GOLD

Khabarovsk

1915

Lake
Baikal

Kara

Nerchinsk

Krasnoyarsk

COAL

Chita

1903

Harbin

Vladivostok

Cheremkhovo

Irkutsk

1915

1903

Sea of
Japan

MANCHURIA

MONGOLIA

J A P A N

C H I N A

Dalny

Peking

Port Arthur

Begun in 1891, the Trans-Siberian railway served
both as an economic link between European
Russia and the Far East, and as a challenge to
Japanese expansion in Manchuria. From Chita,
the Chinese Eastern Railway, under Russian
control, ran direct to Vladivostok, and linked up
with Port Arthur. The single-track all-Russian
route to Vladivostok was completed in 1917.
Through traffic from Moscow to Vladivostok via
Harbin opened in 1903; the 4,388 mile journey
took 13 days. A million Russians used the railway
to migrate to Siberia between 1903 and 1913;
they were offered quarter fares, but the supply
of good farming land was limited

Trans-Siberian Railway; section completed by 1899

+++++ Completed by 1917, with dates of completion.
Until 1915 Lake Baikal was crossed by ferry

Important geological prospecting made possible
by the railway, and begun during construction

Other important lines in Asia open by 1915, and
serving to advance Russian administration and
frontier authority

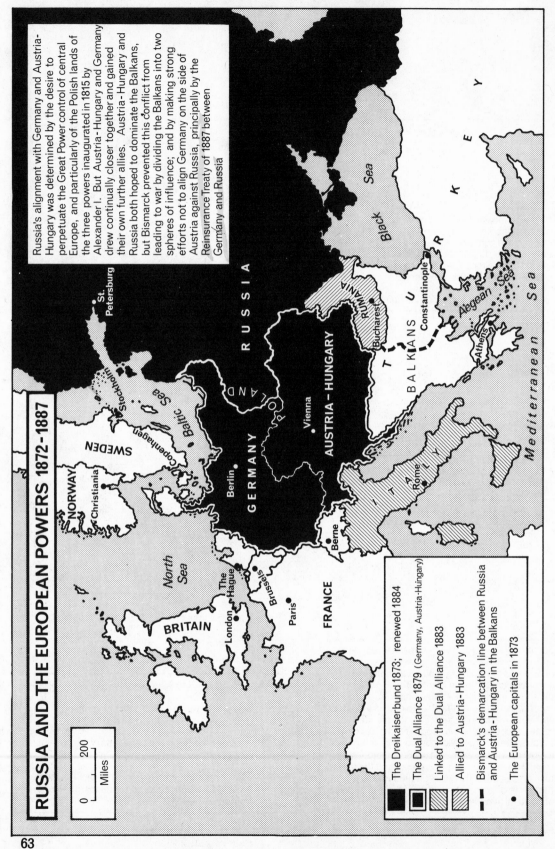

RUSSIA AND THE EUROPEAN POWERS 1872-1887

Russia's alignment with Germany and Austria-Hungary was determined by the desire to perpetuate the Great Power control of central Europe, and particularly of the Polish lands of the three powers inaugurated in 1815 by Alexander I. But Austria-Hungary and Germany drew continually closer together and gained their own further allies. Austria-Hungary and Russia both hoped to dominate the Balkans, but Bismarck prevented this conflict from leading to war by dividing the Balkans into two spheres of influence; and by making strong efforts not to align Germany on the side of Austria against Russia, principally by the Reinsurance Treaty of 1887 between Germany and Russia

The Dreikaiserbund 1873; renewed 1884

The Dual Alliance 1879 (Germany, Austria-Hungary)

Linked to the Dual Alliance 1883

Allied to Austria-Hungary 1883

Bismarck's demarcation line between Russia and Austria-Hungary in the Balkans

The European capitals in 1873

200

0   Miles

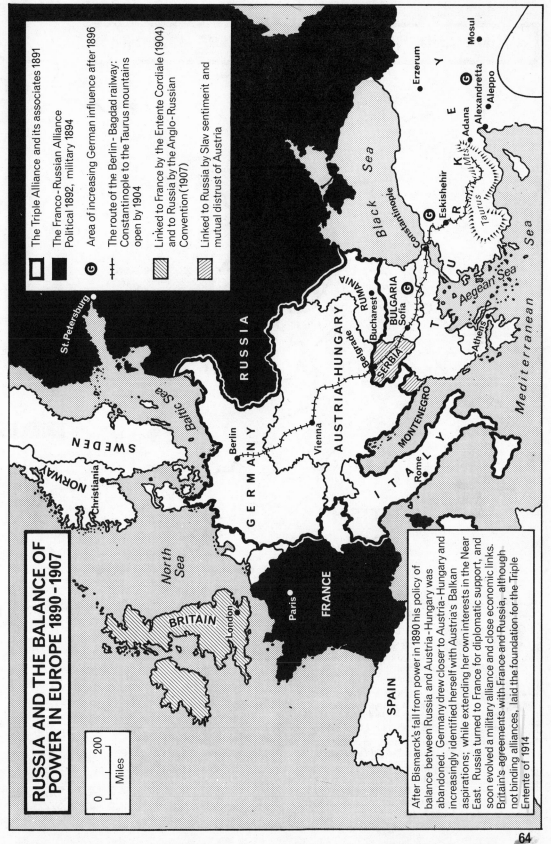

RUSSIA AND THE BALANCE OF POWER IN EUROPE 1890-1907

Legend:

The Triple Alliance and its associates 1891

The Franco-Russian Alliance Political 1892, military 1894

Area of increasing German influence after 1896

The route of the Berlin–Bagdad railway: Constantinople to the Taurus mountains open by 1904

Linked to France by the Entente Cordiale (1904) and to Russia by the Anglo-Russian Convention (1907)

Linked to Russia by Slav sentiment and mutual distrust of Austria

Scale: 0 200 Miles

After Bismarck's fall from power in 1890 his policy of balance between Russia and Austria-Hungary was abandoned. Germany drew closer to Austria-Hungary and increasingly identified herself with Austria's Balkan aspirations; while extending her own interests in the Near East. Russia turned to France for diplomatic support, and soon evolved a military alliance and close economic links. Britain's agreements with France and Russia, although not binding alliances, laid the foundation for the Triple Entente of 1914

Labels on map: St. Petersburg, SWEDEN, NORWAY, Christiania, Baltic Sea, North Sea, BRITAIN, London, Paris, FRANCE, SPAIN, GERMANY, Berlin, Vienna, AUSTRIA-HUNGARY, ITALY, Rome, RUSSIA, SERBIA, Belgrade, MONTENEGRO, RUMANIA, Bucharest, BULGARIA, Sofia, Constantinople, TURKEY, Eskishehir, Erzerum, Taurus Mts., Adana, Alexandretta, Aleppo, Mosul, Athens, Aegean Sea, Black Sea, Mediterranean Sea

CHINA AND THE EUROPEAN POWERS 1898-1904

RUSSIA

Lake Balkhash

Tashkent

Issyk Kul

Kuldzha

Hami

Kashgar

S I N K I A N G

Yarkand

Lop Nor

Khotan

AFGHANISTAN

Koko Nor

Peshawar

K A S H M I R

T I B E T

Indus

BRITAIN

Delhi

Lhasa

Guru

Ganges

B E N G A L

BRITISH
INDIA

Yunna

Calcutta

BURMA

Bay of Bengal

The Chinese frontier in 1897

Ports annexed by the European Powers in 1898

Port which the United States wished to annex in
1900, but was stopped from doing so by Japan.
In 1898 the United States had defeated Spain and
annexed the Philippines

Proposed partition of China between Russia,
Britain, France and Germany. The idea was aband-
oned, as too many interests clashed. The British in
India, for example, wanted to control the area

Russian exploration, trade and diplomatic influence
in Tibet, 1900-1904, resented by Britain

British military Mission under Younghusband,
which defeated the Tibetans at Guru in 1904 and
entered Lhasa. In 1907 Russia agreed to allow
Britain to be the dominant foreign power in Tibet

Indian
Ocean

SIAM

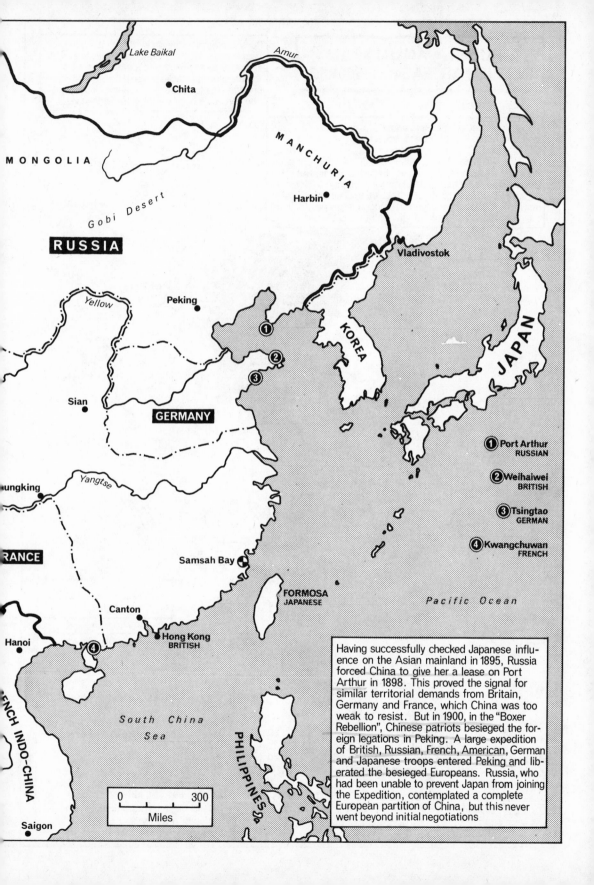

Lake Baikal

Amur

Chita

MONGOLIA

MANCHURIA

Gobi Desert

Harbin

RUSSIA

Vladivostok

Yellow

Peking

KOREA

JAPAN

Sian

GERMANY

① Port Arthur
RUSSIAN

② Weihaiwei
BRITISH

③ Tsingtao
GERMAN

④ Kwangchuwan
FRENCH

ungking

Yangtse

RANCE

Samsah Bay

FORMOSA
JAPANESE

Pacific Ocean

Hanoi

Canton

Hong Kong
BRITISH

ENCH INDO-CHINA

*South China
Sea*

PHILIPPINES

Saigon

| 0 | 300 |
Miles

Having successfully checked Japanese influence on the Asian mainland in 1895, Russia
forced China to give her a lease on Port
Arthur in 1898. This proved the signal for
similar territorial demands from Britain,
Germany and France, which China was too
weak to resist. But in 1900, in the "Boxer
Rebellion", Chinese patriots besieged the foreign legations in Peking. A large expedition
of British, Russian, French, American, German
and Japanese troops entered Peking and liberated the besieged Europeans. Russia, who
had been unable to prevent Japan from joining
the Expedition, contemplated a complete
European partition of China, but this never
went beyond initial negotiations

RUSSIA AND JAPAN IN THE FAR EAST 1860-1895

Kamchatka: part of Russia in 1650. Since 1750 used largely as a place of exile for criminals and political prisoners. Russian schoolboys were often threatened that slackers would be "sent to Kamchatka"—the furthest corner of the classroom. The peninsula has over 20 active volcanoes.

The struggle between Russia and Japan in the Far East was long and bitter. In 1860 Russia acquired an outlet on the Sea of Japan. The Japanese at once adopted a forward policy in China and Korea. When Japan defeated China in 1895 she expected to make wide territorial gains. But Russia, France, Britain and Germany combined to deprive Japan of the fruits of victory. This led to deep anti-Russian resentment throughout Japan. Throughout this period, European penetration in south China continued unabated.

RUSSIA

SIBERIA

KAMCHATKA

Sea of Okhotsk

Petropavlovsk

EASTERN

Nikolaevsk

SAKHALIN

Amur

MANCHURIA

Khabarosvk

KURILE ISLANDS

Uruppu

Harbin

Sungari

Ussuri

Etorofu

Changchun

Kirin

Mukden

Vladivostok

Yalu

Sea of Japan

Pacific

Peking

Wonsan

Ocean

Tientsin

Weihaiwei

Port Arthur

Seoul

Inchon

KOREA

JAPAN

Tsingtao

Yellow Sea

Pusan

Yellow

CHINA

0   500

Miles

Nanking

Hankow

Shanghai

Yangtse

Oshima

Okinawa

Macao (Portuguese 1557)

Kowloon (British 1861)

RYUKYU ISLANDS

Hongkong (British 1841)

FORMOSA

South China Sea

PHILIPPINES (Spanish 1521)

■ Territory annexed by Russia from China in 1858-1860

⌐ ┐ Islands annexed by Japan from China in 1874

⋯ Islands annexed by Japan in return for Russian control of Sakhalin

◉ Korean ports open, as the result of Japanese pressure, to Japanese trade 1876-1878

▨ Occupied by Japan during the war with China, 1894-95. Russia, France, Britain and Germany combined to prevent Japan keeping any of this territory

□ Only Chinese territory actually annexed by Japan after the war of 1894-1895

0   300
Miles

WAR DEAD 1904-05
Russian   120,000
Japanese   75,000

R U S S I A

Chita
Nerchinsk
Amur
Argun
Hailar
M A N C H U R I A
Tsitsihar
Harbin
Sungari
CHINA
Mukden
Yalu
Peking
Port Arthur
Seoul
Yellow Sea
KOREA
Vladivostok
Sea of Japan
Tsushima Strait
Nikolaevsk
Khabarovsk
Amur
SAKHALIN
Tokyo
J A P A N

The Trans-Siberian Railway by 1895

Under increasing Russian control
after 1895

Leased by Russia from China in
1898, together with the right to
build a railway to Harbin;
(completed by 1904)

The Chinese Eastern Railway,
controlled by Russia after its
completion in 1903

Russian economic penetration.
Russia refused to allow Japan a
sphere of influence in Korea

Japanese naval and military
attacks 1904-1905

Annexed by Japan in 1905

After successfully halting Japanese expansion
in 1895, the Russians adopted an active
expansionist policy. For 10 years they pressed
forward in Manchuria, and discussed the
partition of China with the British Government
in 1900. But Japan sought revenge for the
humiliation of 1895, and in 1902 neutralized
Britain by the Anglo-Japanese Alliance. In
February 1904, under Russian provocation,
Japan attacked Port Arthur. Russia was
defeated on land and sea, and a peace treaty
was signed in the United States in Sept.1905.
The grave demoralization created by Russia's
defeat led to a mass of revolutionary outbreaks
in Russia, and to a serious weakening of the
Tsarist mystique.

PRELUDE TO REVOLUTION 1894 - 1904

Despite the abolition of Serfdom in 1860, peasant poverty remained widespread. Despite Russia's economic expansion in the 1890's, urban hardship was widespread. Revolutionary groups competed for allegiance, offering various panaceas: anarchy, the total destruction of the autocracy, and a new world based upon the dignity of labour. There were frequent strikes and riots after 1890. The Tsarist police struggled to prevent the mounting violence. An increasing number of political activists were exiled to Siberia. Discontent continued unabated: the General Jewish Labour League (the 'Bund') was founded in 1897, the Social Democrat Labour Party in 1898, the Socialist Revolutionary Party in 1901. By 1904 every town in Russia, and almost every factory, however small, was caught in the upsurge of popular revolt, strikes and riots

The emperor of all the Russias is an autocratic and unlimited monarch. God himself commands that his supreme power be obeyed, out of conscience as well as fear

ARTICLE ONE, FUNDAMENTAL LAWS OF THE EMPIRE 1892

Ufa 1903

Volga

Ivanovo

St. Petersburg 1902, 1904

Moscow

Don

TAMBOV

RIAZAN

TULA

OREL

FINNS

BALTS

Riga

Minsk

POLES

Baltic Sea

68

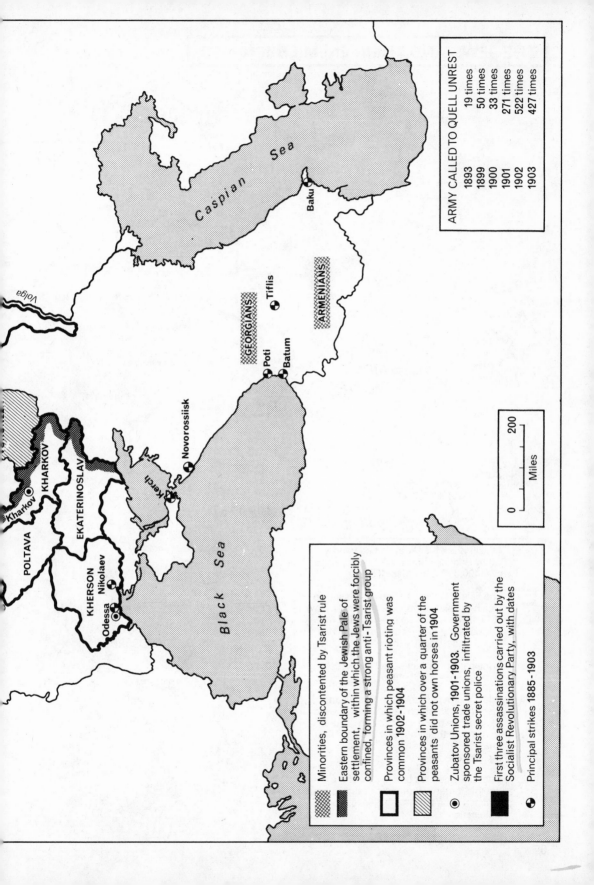

ARMY CALLED TO QUELL UNREST

1893	19 times
1899	50 times
1900	33 times
1901	271 times
1902	522 times
1903	427 times

Caspian Sea

Baku

Volga

GEORGIANS

Tiflis

ARMENIANS

Poti

Batum

Novorossiisk

Kerch

Black Sea

POLTAVA

KHARKOV

Kharkov

EKATERINOSLAV

KHERSON

Nikolaev

Odessa

0   200

Miles

Minorities, discontented by Tsarist rule

Eastern boundary of the Jewish Pale of
settlement, within which the Jews were forcibly
confined, forming a strong anti-Tsarist group

Provinces in which peasant rioting was
common 1902-1904

Provinces in which over a quarter of the
peasants did not own horses in 1904

Zubatov Unions, 1901-1903. Government
sponsored trade unions, infiltrated by
the Tsarist secret police

First three assassinations carried out by the
Socialist Revolutionary Party, with dates

Principal strikes 1885-1903

THE JEWS AND THEIR ENEMIES 1648-1917

1903
1906 St. Petersburg

Tsarskoye Selo
1905

1891. 2,000 Jews deported
many of them in chains

Baltic Sea

Dusiata

Mogilev

Minsk

Starodub

Bialystok

Gomel

Berlin
1911

Sedlits

Brest-
Litovsk

Konotop

Xanten

Lodz

Nezhin

GERMANY

Czestochowa

Kiev

Zhitomir

Pereyaslavl

Smel

Elizavetgrad

Balta

Tisza-
Eszlar

Ananaye

Nikolaevka

Kishinev

AUSTRIA - HUNGARY

Odessa

RUMANIA

BULGARIA

////// Area in which the Ukrainian peasantry, led by Bogdan Khmelnitski, massacred over 100,000 Jews 1648-1656

The Pale of Settlement inside Russia, to which Russian Jews were confined by law 1815-1917. Of Russia's 5 million Jews in 1880, only 300,000 had managed to live outside, mostly illegally

⊙ Principal mob attacks, or "pogroms", against Jews, 1871-1906

✪ Ritual murder charges, in Russia and elsewhere, in which Jews were accused of using the blood of Christian children to mix with their Passover bread. These charges led to harsh mob violence against the Jews

◮ Publishing centres before 1917 of the anti-semitic forgery, "Protocols of Zion", which claimed to be the Jewish plan for world domination

Vologda

Nizhni
Novgorod ◎

◎ Murom   ◉ Simbirsk

Moscow

891. 20,000 Jews expelled

● Saratov

◎ Tsaritsyn

aterinoslav   ◎ Rostov

elitopol
◎

◎Simferopol   ● Kutais

ack Sea

Caspian Sea

The three main anti-Jewish groups in Imperial Russia were the peasants and Cossacks
of the Ukraine, the intellectual Slavophils, and the Tsarist Government, and
aristocracy. The peasants and Cossacks saw the rich Jew as an exploiter, the poor
Jew as a rival, and the intellectual Jew as a dangerous revolutionary. The Slavophils
believed in the sacred mission of the Slav peoples, under the guidance of their Orthodox
Tsar; they wanted Russia to adopt a strong pro-Slav, and anti-Turk policy, and saw
the Jew as anti-Christ, an alien on Russian soil, and a subversive influence acting
against Russian interests. Both peasants and Slavophils were in many ways supported
by the Government, whose laws discriminated against the Jews, and whose Pale
of Settlement confined them

200

Miles

—— National boundaries
    of 1914

1882 500,000 Jews living in rural areas
of the Pale were forced to leave their homes
and live in towns or townlets (shtetls) in the
Pale. 250,000 Jews living along the western
frontier zone were also moved into the
Pale. A further 700,000 Jews living east of
the Pale were driven into the Pale by 1891

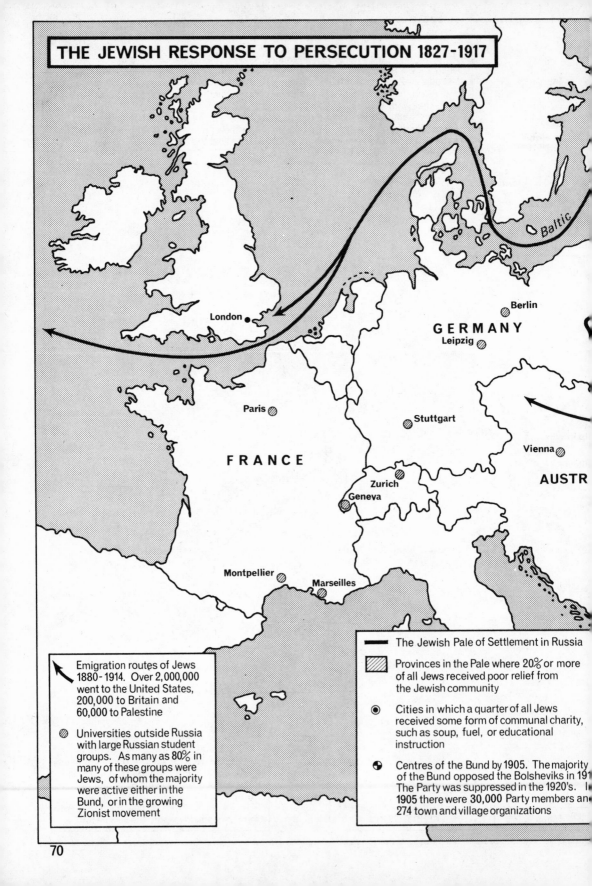

THE JEWISH RESPONSE TO PERSECUTION 1827-1917

Baltic

Berlin

GERMANY

Leipzig

London

Paris

Stuttgart

FRANCE

Zurich

Geneva

Vienna

AUSTR

Montpellier

Marseilles

Emigration routes of Jews 1880-1914. Over 2,000,000 went to the United States, 200,000 to Britain and 60,000 to Palestine

Universities outside Russia with large Russian student groups. As many as 80% in many of these groups were Jews, of whom the majority were active either in the Bund, or in the growing Zionist movement

The Jewish Pale of Settlement in Russia

Provinces in the Pale where 20% or more of all Jews received poor relief from the Jewish community

Cities in which a quarter of all Jews received some form of communal charity, such as soup, fuel, or educational instruction

Centres of the Bund by 1905. The majority of the Bund opposed the Bolsheviks in 191 The Party was suppressed in the 1920's. I 1905 there were **30,000** Party members an 274 town and village organizations

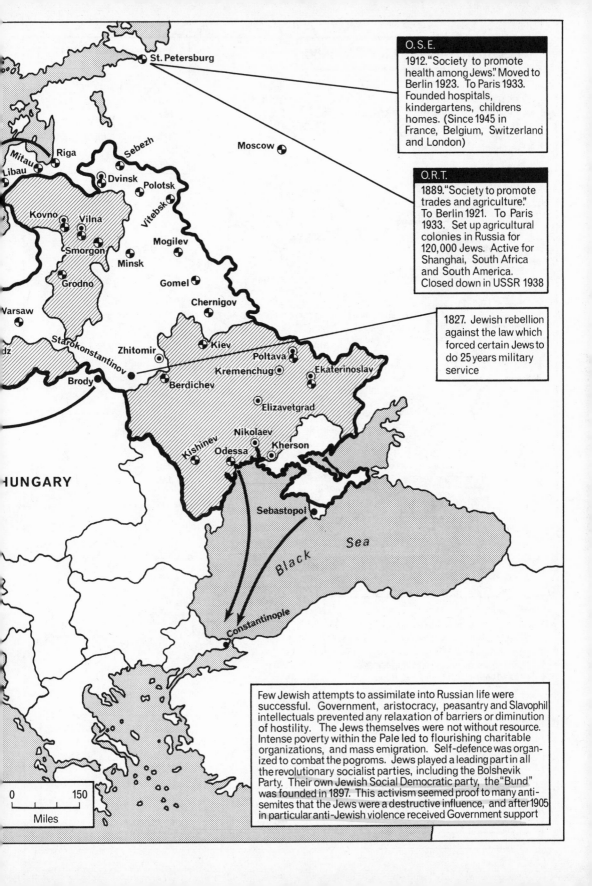

St. Petersburg

Moscow

Sebezh

Riga

Mitau
Libau

Dvinsk
Polotsk

Vitebsk

Kovno
Vilna

Smorgon

Mogilev

Grodno

Minsk

Gomel

Chernigov

Warsaw

Starokonstantinov

dz

Zhitomir

Kiev

Poltava

Brody

Berdichev

Kremenchug

Ekaterinoslav

Elizavetgrad

Kishinev

Nikolaev

Odessa

Kherson

HUNGARY

Sebastopol

Black Sea

Constantinople

O.S.E.

1912. "Society to promote health among Jews." Moved to Berlin 1923. To Paris 1933. Founded hospitals, kindergartens, childrens homes. (Since 1945 in France, Belgium, Switzerland and London)

O.R.T.

1889. "Society to promote trades and agriculture." To Berlin 1921. To Paris 1933. Set up agricultural colonies in Russia for 120,000 Jews. Active for Shanghai, South Africa and South America. Closed down in USSR 1938

1827. Jewish rebellion against the law which forced certain Jews to do 25 years military service

Few Jewish attempts to assimilate into Russian life were successful. Government, aristocracy, peasantry and Slavophil intellectuals prevented any relaxation of barriers or diminution of hostility. The Jews themselves were not without resource. Intense poverty within the Pale led to flourishing charitable organizations, and mass emigration. Self-defence was organized to combat the pogroms. Jews played a leading part in all the revolutionary socialist parties, including the Bolshevik Party. Their own Jewish Social Democratic party, the "Bund" was founded in 1897. This activism seemed proof to many anti-semites that the Jews were a destructive influence, and after 1905 in particular anti-Jewish violence received Government support

0   150

Miles

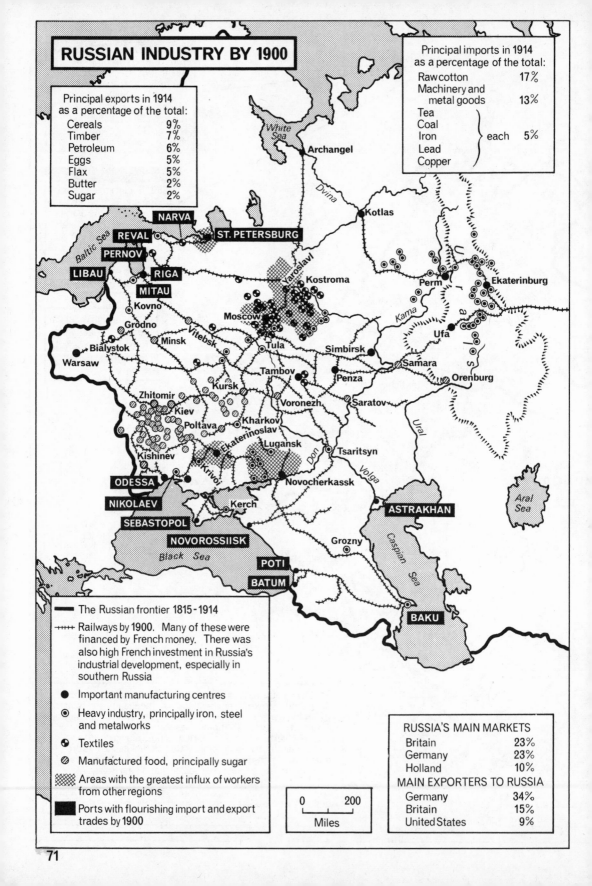

RUSSIAN INDUSTRY BY 1900

Principal imports in 1914
as a percentage of the total:

Raw cotton		17%
Machinery and metal goods		13%
Tea		
Coal		
Iron	each	5%
Lead		
Copper		

Principal exports in 1914
as a percentage of the total:

Cereals	9%
Timber	7%
Petroleum	6%
Eggs	5%
Flax	5%
Butter	2%
Sugar	2%

White Sea

Archangel

Kotlas

Dvina

NARVA

REVAL
PERNOV
ST. PETERSBURG

Baltic Sea

LIBAU
RIGA
MITAU
Kovno
Grodno
Bialystok
Warsaw
Minsk
Vitebsk

Yaroslavl
Kostroma
Moscow
Tula
Simbirsk
Samara
Tambov
Penza
Kursk
Voronezh
Saratov
Zhitomir
Kiev
Poltava
Kharkov
Ekaterinoslav
Lugansk
Kishinev
Krivoi
ODESSA
NIKOLAEV
Kerch
Novocherkassk
Tsaritsyn
Don
Volga

Perm
Ekaterinburg
Kama
Ufa
Orenburg

Ural
Urals

Aral Sea

SEBASTOPOL
NOVOROSSIISK
Black Sea
POTI
BATUM

Grozny

ASTRAKHAN

Caspian Sea

BAKU

The Russian frontier 1815-1914

+++++ Railways by 1900. Many of these were
financed by French money. There was
also high French investment in Russia's
industrial development, especially in
southern Russia

● Important manufacturing centres

⊙ Heavy industry, principally iron, steel
and metalworks

⊕ Textiles

⊘ Manufactured food, principally sugar

▨ Areas with the greatest influx of workers
from other regions

▮ Ports with flourishing import and export
trades by 1900

0   200
Miles

RUSSIA'S MAIN MARKETS
Britain	23%
Germany	23%
Holland	10%

MAIN EXPORTERS TO RUSSIA
Germany	34%
Britain	15%
United States	9%

71

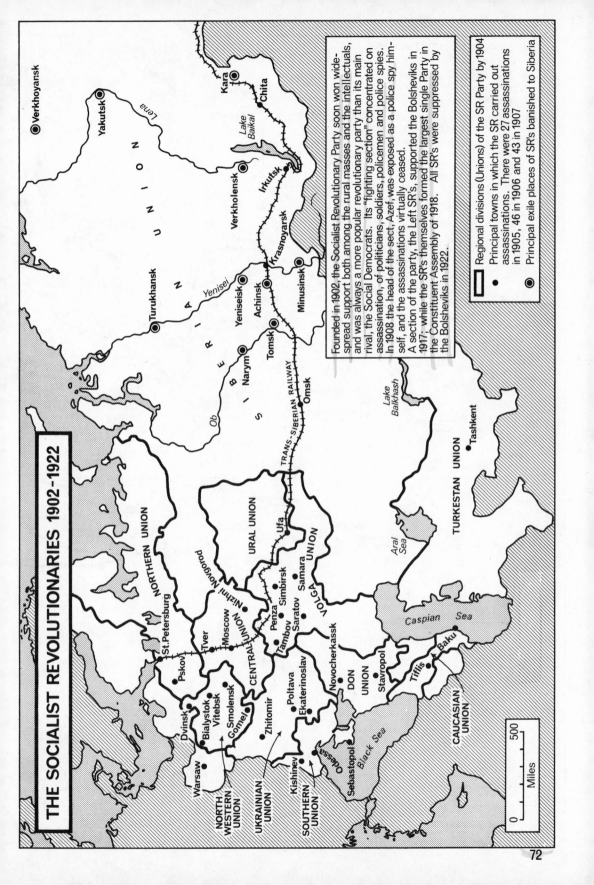

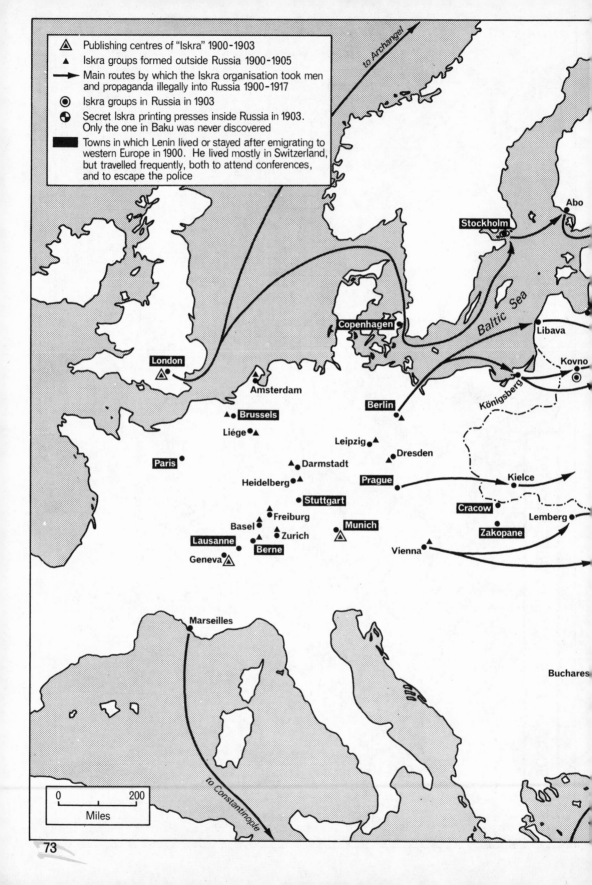

△ Publishing centres of "Iskra" 1900-1903

▲ Iskra groups formed outside Russia 1900-1905

→ Main routes by which the Iskra organisation took men and propaganda illegally into Russia 1900-1917

◉ Iskra groups in Russia in 1903

◐ Secret Iskra printing presses inside Russia in 1903. Only the one in Baku was never discovered

■ Towns in which Lenin lived or stayed after emigrating to western Europe in 1900. He lived mostly in Switzerland, but travelled frequently, both to attend conferences, and to escape the police

to Archangel

Abo

Stockholm

Baltic Sea

Copenhagen

Libava

Kovno

London

Königsberg

Amsterdam

Berlin

Brussels

Liége

Leipzig

Dresden

Paris

Darmstadt

Kielce

Heidelberg

Prague

Stuttgart

Cracow

Freiburg

Lemberg

Basel

Munich

Zakopane

Lausanne

Zurich

Berne

Vienna

Geneva

Marseilles

Buchares

0   200
Miles

to Constantinople

73

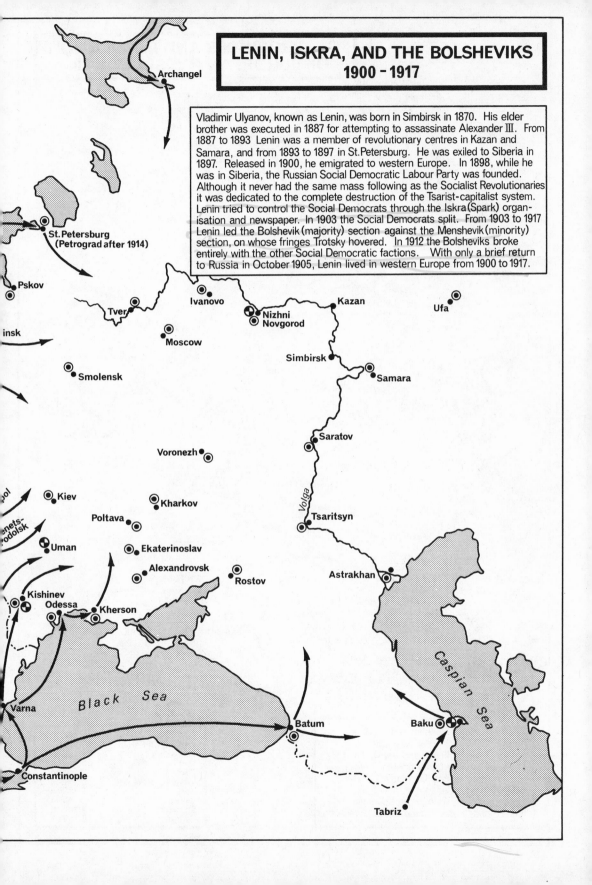

LENIN, ISKRA, AND THE BOLSHEVIKS
1900 - 1917

Vladimir Ulyanov, known as Lenin, was born in Simbirsk in 1870. His elder brother was executed in 1887 for attempting to assassinate Alexander III. From 1887 to 1893 Lenin was a member of revolutionary centres in Kazan and Samara, and from 1893 to 1897 in St.Petersburg. He was exiled to Siberia in 1897. Released in 1900, he emigrated to western Europe. In 1898, while he was in Siberia, the Russian Social Democratic Labour Party was founded. Although it never had the same mass following as the Socialist Revolutionaries it was dedicated to the complete destruction of the Tsarist-capitalist system. Lenin tried to control the Social Democrats through the Iskra (Spark) organisation and newspaper. In 1903 the Social Democrats split. From 1903 to 1917 Lenin led the Bolshevik (majority) section against the Menshevik (minority) section, on whose fringes Trotsky hovered. In 1912 the Bolsheviks broke entirely with the other Social Democratic factions. With only a brief return to Russia in October 1905, Lenin lived in western Europe from 1900 to 1917.

Archangel

St.Petersburg
(Petrograd after 1914)

Pskov

insk

Tver

Ivanovo

Nizhni
Novgorod

Kazan

Ufa

Moscow

Smolensk

Simbirsk

Samara

Saratov

Voronezh

Volga

Kiev

Kharkov

Poltava

enets-
odolsk

Uman

Ekaterinoslav

Tsaritsyn

Alexandrovsk

Rostov

Astrakhan

Kishinev
Odessa

Kherson

Varna

Black   Sea

Caspian   Sea

Batum

Baku

Constantinople

Tabriz

THE PROVINCES AND POPULATION OF EUROPEAN RUSSIA IN 1900

White Sea

NORWAY

SWEDEN

Baltic Sea

GERMANY

POLISH PROVINCES

AUSTRIA-HUNGARY

RUMANIA

TURKEY

PERSIA

ARCHANGEL

FINLAND

OLONETS

VOLOGDA

ESTLAND

ST PETERSBURG

LIVLAND

KURLAND

NOVGOROD

PERM

KOVNO

VITEBSK

PSKOV

YAROSLAVL

KOSTROMA

VIATKA

VILNA

MOGILEV

TVER

VLADIMIR

NIZHNI NOVGOROD

KAZAN

UFA

SMOLENSK

MOSCOW

GRODNO

MINSK

KALUGA

RIAZAN

SIMBIRSK

CHERNIGOV

OREL

TULA

PENZA

SAMARA

ORENBURG

VOLHYNIA

KIEV

POLTAVA

KURSK

TAMBOV

SARATOV

PODOLIA

VORONEZH

BESSARABIA

KHARKOV

DON

ASTRAKHAN

KHERSON

EKATERINOSLAV

TAURIDA

KUBAN

STAVROPOL

Black Sea

TEREK

Caspian Sea

TRANS-CAUCASIAN PROVINCES

The first official Russian census was held in 1897. The total population was just over 129 million - nearly as large as the combined populations of Britain, France, and Germany. Over 80% of all Russians were peasants. Finland was an autonomous Duchy, and, like Poland, was subdivided into Provinces

MAIN NATIONAL & ETHNIC GROUPS IN EUROPEAN RUSSIA IN 1900	
Russians	55 million
Ukrainians	22 million
Poles	8 million
White Russians	6 million
Jews	5 million
Balts	4 million
Caucasians	3 million
Germans	2 million

74

THE 1905 REVOLUTION IN THE COUNTRYSIDE

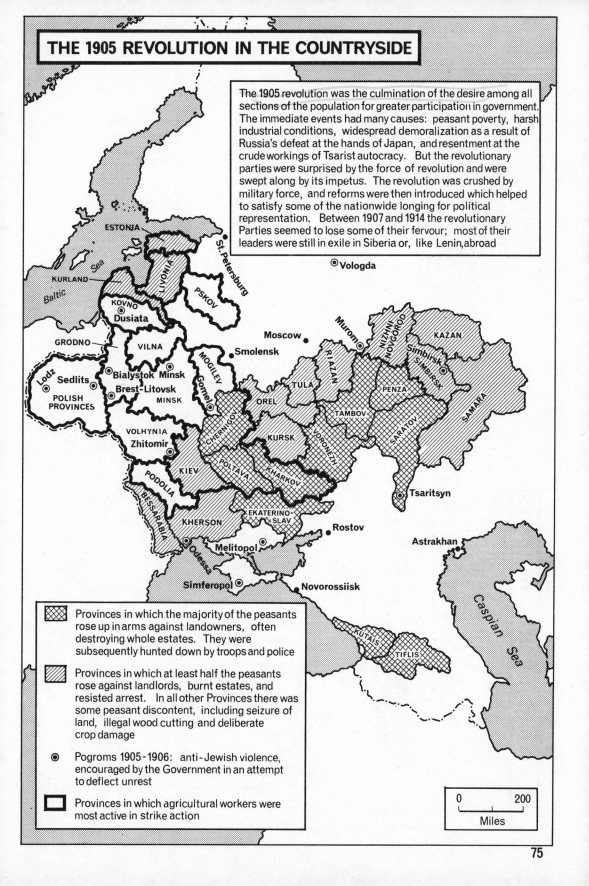

The 1905 revolution was the culmination of the desire among all sections of the population for greater participation in government. The immediate events had many causes: peasant poverty, harsh industrial conditions, widespread demoralization as a result of Russia's defeat at the hands of Japan, and resentment at the crude workings of Tsarist autocracy. But the revolutionary parties were surprised by the force of revolution and were swept along by its impetus. The revolution was crushed by military force, and reforms were then introduced which helped to satisfy some of the nationwide longing for political representation. Between 1907 and 1914 the revolutionary Parties seemed to lose some of their fervour; most of their leaders were still in exile in Siberia or, like Lenin, abroad

⊗ Vologda

Baltic Sea
Caspian Sea

ESTONIA
St. Petersburg
KURLAND
LIVONIA
PSKOV
KOVNO
Dusiata
GRODNO
VILNA
Moscow
Smolensk
Murom
NIZHNI NOVGOROD
KAZAN
RIAZAN
Simbirsk
SIMBIRSK
Lodz
Sedlits
Bialystok Minsk
MOGILEV
TULA
PENZA
SAMARA
Brest-Litovsk
MINSK
Gomel
OREL
TAMBOV
POLISH PROVINCES
VOLHYNIA
Zhitomir
CHERNIGOV
KURSK
VORONEZH
SARATOV
PODOLIA
KIEV
POLTAVA
KHARKOV
BESSARABIA
Tsaritsyn
KHERSON
EKATERINO-SLAV
Rostov
Astrakhan
Odessa
Melitopol
Simferopol
Novorossiisk
KUTAIS
TIFLIS

Provinces in which the majority of the peasants rose up in arms against landowners, often destroying whole estates. They were subsequently hunted down by troops and police

Provinces in which at least half the peasants rose against landlords, burnt estates, and resisted arrest. In all other Provinces there was some peasant discontent, including seizure of land, illegal wood cutting and deliberate crop damage

⊙ Pogroms 1905-1906: anti-Jewish violence, encouraged by the Government in an attempt to deflect unrest

Provinces in which agricultural workers were most active in strike action

0   200
Miles

75

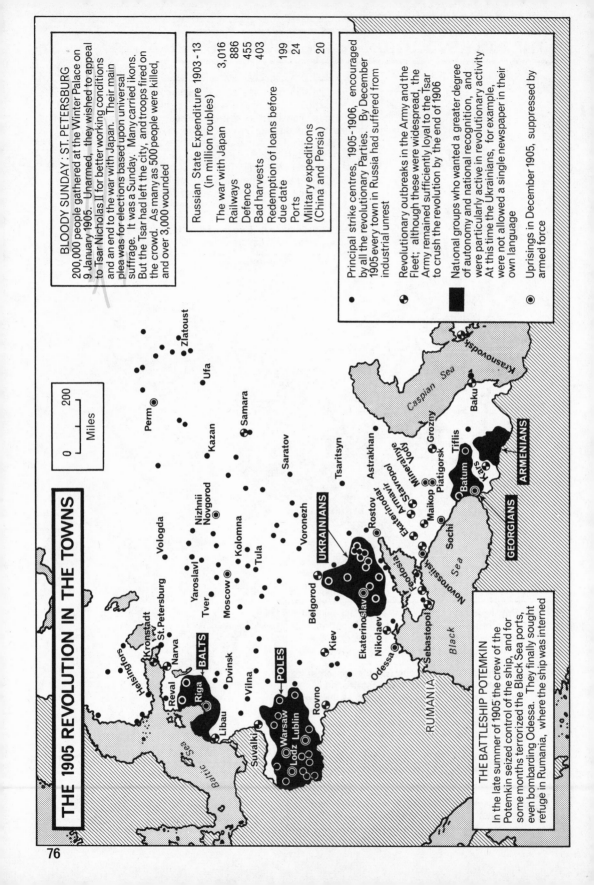

THE 1905 REVOLUTION IN THE TOWNS

BLOODY SUNDAY : ST. PETERSBURG
200,000 people gathered at the Winter Palace on 9 January 1905. Unarmed, they wished to appeal to Tsar Nicholas II for better working conditions and an end to the war with Japan. Their main plea was for elections based upon universal suffrage. It was a Sunday. Many carried ikons. But the Tsar had left the city, and troops fired on the crowd. As many as 500 people were killed, and over 3,000 wounded

Russian State Expenditure 1903 - 13 (in million roubles)	
The war with Japan	3,016
Railways	886
Defence	455
Bad harvests	403
Redemption of loans before due date	199
Ports	24
Military expeditions (China and Persia)	20

● Principal strike centres, 1905 - 1906, encouraged by all the revolutionary Parties. By December 1905 every town in Russia had suffered from industrial unrest

⊕ Revolutionary outbreaks in the Army and the Fleet; although these were widespread, the Army remained sufficiently loyal to the Tsar to crush the revolution by the end of 1906

■ National groups who wanted a greater degree of autonomy and national recognition, and were particularly active in revolutionary activity At this time the Ukrainians, for example, were not allowed a single newspaper in their own language

◉ Uprisings in December 1905, suppressed by armed force

THE BATTLESHIP POTEMKIN
In the late summer of 1905 the crew of the Potemkin seized control of the ship, and for some months terrorized the Black Sea ports, even bombarding Odessa. They finally sought refuge in Rumania, where the ship was interned

0   200   Miles

THE MOSCOW UPRISING 1905

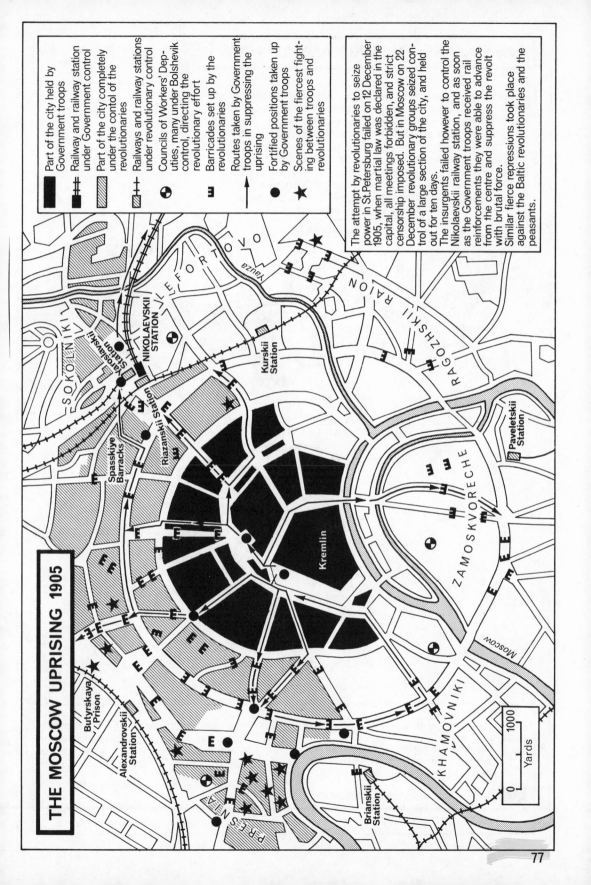

Legend:

- Part of the city held by Government troops
- Railway and railway station under Government control
- Part of the city completely under the control of the revolutionaries
- Railways and railway stations under revolutionary control
- Councils of Workers' Deputies, many under Bolshevik control, directing the revolutionary effort
- Barricades set up by the revolutionaries
- Routes taken by Government troops in suppressing the uprising
- Fortified positions taken up by Government troops
- Scenes of the fiercest fighting between troops and revolutionaries

The attempt by revolutionaries to seize power in St.Petersburg failed on 12 December 1905, when martial law was declared in the capital, all meetings forbidden, and strict censorship imposed. But in Moscow on 22 December revolutionary groups seized control of a large section of the city, and held out for ten days.

The insurgents failed however to control the Nikolaevskii railway station, and as soon as the Government troops received rail reinforcements they were able to advance from the centre and suppress the revolt with brutal force.

Similar fierce repressions took place against the Baltic revolutionaries and the peasants.

Map labels: SOKOLNIKI, LEFORTOVO, Yauza, RAGOZHSKII RAION, Yaroslavskii Station, NIKOLAEVSKII STATION, Kurskii Station, Spasskiye Barracks, Riazanskii Station, Paveletskii Station, Kremlin, ZAMOSKVORECHE, Moscow, KHAMOVNIKI, Butyrskaya Prison, Alexandrovskii Station, PRESNIA, Brianskii Station, 0 1000 Yards

RUSSIA AND THE BALKANS 1876-1885

0   100
Miles

Russia wanted to drive the Turk from Europe and dominate the Balkans.   Britain supported Russian protests against Turkish atrocities against the Bulgarians in 1875, which led Russia to attack Turkey. After defeating the Turks at Plevna in 1876 Russia tried to set up a large independent Bulgaria, but Britain and Austria-Hungary challenged Russia's aspirations, and under German mediation Russia agreed to the creation of a much smaller Bulgaria. Austria advanced her own Balkan interests by occupying the former Turkish province of Bosnia, which she formally annexed in 1908, and entering Novi Pazar.

RUSSIA

AUSTRIA-HUNGARY

RUMANIA

BOSNIA
Sarajevo

Belgrade

Bucharest

Constanza

SERBIA

Danube

Plevna

Silistria

BULGARIA

Varna

NOVI PAZAR

Nish

Tirnovo

Adriatic Sea

Sofia

Burgas

EAST RUMELIA

Black Sea

Cattaro

Skopje

Adrianople

Midia

MONTENEGRO

Constantinople

MACEDONIA

Kavalla

Rodosto

San Stephano

Dedeagatch

Chanak

TURKEY –

IN – ASIA

Aegean Sea

GREECE

Athens

– · – The boundary of Turkey-in-Europe 1876

Russian proposal for an independent "Big Bulgaria", agreed to by the Turks at the Treaty of San Stephano 1878

Bulgaria, autonomous, not independent, as allowed by Britain and Germany by the Treaty of Berlin 1878

Turkish territory added to Serbia, Rumania and Montenegro (who each gained their independence from Turkey) by the Treaty of Berlin 1878; and to Greece in 1881

Occupied by Austria-Hungary in 1878

Added to Bulgaria in 1885, when Bulgaria became fully independent of Turkey

RUSSIA, THE BALKANS, AND THE COMING OF WAR 1912–1914

0 ——————— 500
Miles

North Sea

BRITAIN

Baltic Sea

Reval
St. Petersburg

Riga
BALTIC PROVINCES

Moscow

RUSSIA

Danzig

Berlin

GERMANY

Breslau

Warsaw
POLISH PROVINCES

Pripet Marshes

Kiev

VOLHYNIA

Paris

FRANCE

Lemberg

Vienna

Budapest

AUSTRIA - HUNGARY

Adriatic Sea

BOSNIA
Sarajevo

Belgrade
SERBIA

RUMANIA

Black Sea

BULGARIA

MONTENEGRO

ALBANIA
Skopje

Constantinople

Bosphorus

GREECE

Dardanelles

TURKEY

Russia's mid-century alignment with Germany was changed during the 1880's to a new alignment with France, while at the same time Austria and Germany drew closer together. In the two Balkan Wars of 1912 and 1913 Turkey was driven almost entirely from Europe, but Russia's position did not improve; for as a result of Turkey's defeat Austrian influence increased even further. In June 1914 a Bosnian Serb murdered the Austrian heir to the throne, Archduke Franz-Ferdinand, at Sarajevo. Austria invaded Serbia on 28 July 1914. Russia then declared war on Austria. Germany supported her ally Austria and declared war on Russia. France and Britain joined Russia against Germany and Austria. Turkey attacked Russia in October 1914

Countries in which Austrian and German influence worked against Russia. Greece had a pro-German King; Turkey a pro-German Minister of War and virtual dictator; Bulgaria and Rumania had both accepted alliance with the Central Powers

Area of Russia in which Germany hoped to expand as a result of war

Russia's only two Balkan Allies, both threatened by Austria. Austria had created the state of Albania in 1912 in order to cut Serbia off from the sea.

Countries in western Europe sympathetic to Russia. France had a military alliance with Russia dating from 1894. Britain a convention dating from 1907

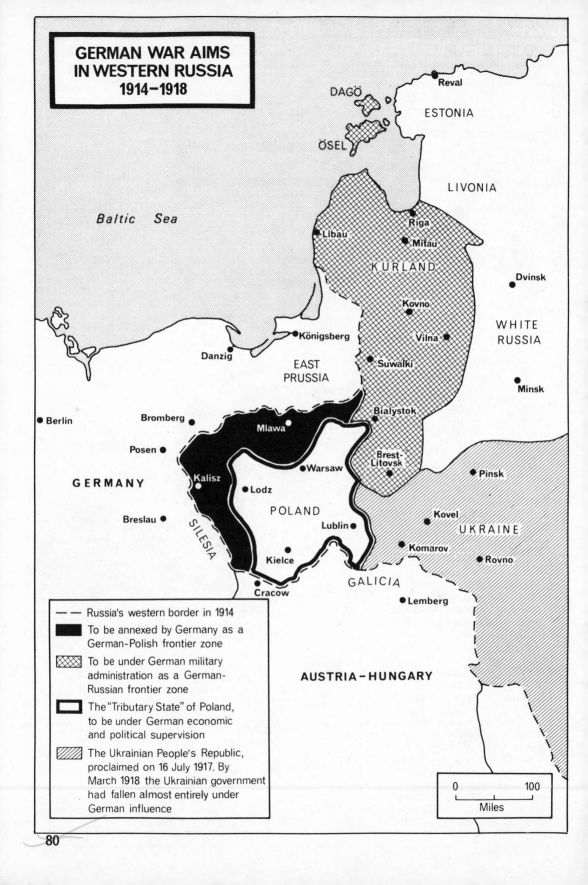

GERMAN WAR AIMS
IN WESTERN RUSSIA
1914–1918

DAGÖ

Reval

ESTONIA

ÖSEL

LIVONIA

Baltic Sea

Libau

Riga

Mitau

KURLAND

Dvinsk

Kovno

WHITE
RUSSIA

Königsberg

Vilna

Danzig

Suwalki

Minsk

EAST
PRUSSIA

Berlin

Bromberg

Mlawa

Bialystok

Posen

Warsaw

Brest-
Litovsk

Pinsk

GERMANY

Kalisz

Lodz

POLAND

Kovel

UKRAINE

Breslau

Lublin

SILESIA

Komarov

Rovno

Kielce

GALICIA

Cracow

Lemberg

AUSTRIA–HUNGARY

Russia's western border in 1914

To be annexed by Germany as a
German-Polish frontier zone

To be under German military
administration as a German-
Russian frontier zone

The "Tributary State" of Poland,
to be under German economic
and political supervision

The Ukrainian People's Republic,
proclaimed on 16 July 1917. By
March 1918 the Ukrainian government
had fallen almost entirely under
German influence

0   100

Miles

THE EASTERN FRONT 1914

Baltic Sea

GERMANY

EAST PRUSSIA

- Danzig
- Königsberg
- Gumbinnen
- Vilkoviski
- Elbing
- Suvalki
- Masurian Lakes
- Augustow
- Tannenberg
- Bialystok
- Mlawa

Vistula

RUSSIA

Bug

- Plotsk
- Warsaw
- Brest–Litovsk
- Kutno

Vistula

- Kalisz
- Lodz
- Piotrkow
- Kielce
- Lublin
- Novo Radomsk
- Krasnik
- Komarov
- Czestochowa

SILESIA

- Cracow
- Tarnow
- GALICIA
- Przemysl
- Lemberg
- Gorlice

Carpathians

AUSTRIA-HUNGARY

0   50
Miles

Russian advance into East Prussia 4-23 August. Between August 26 and September 13 they were defeated at Tannenberg and the Masurian Lakes, and driven back into Russia

Russian territory conquered by Germany September 28-December 31. At the Battle of Lodz, in November, the Germans prevented a Russian advance into Silesia

⟹ Austrian advances into Russia

← Russian counter-attacks into Austria

Conquered by Russia from Austria

— The front line on 31 December 1914

⊙ Russian victories

⊕ German victories

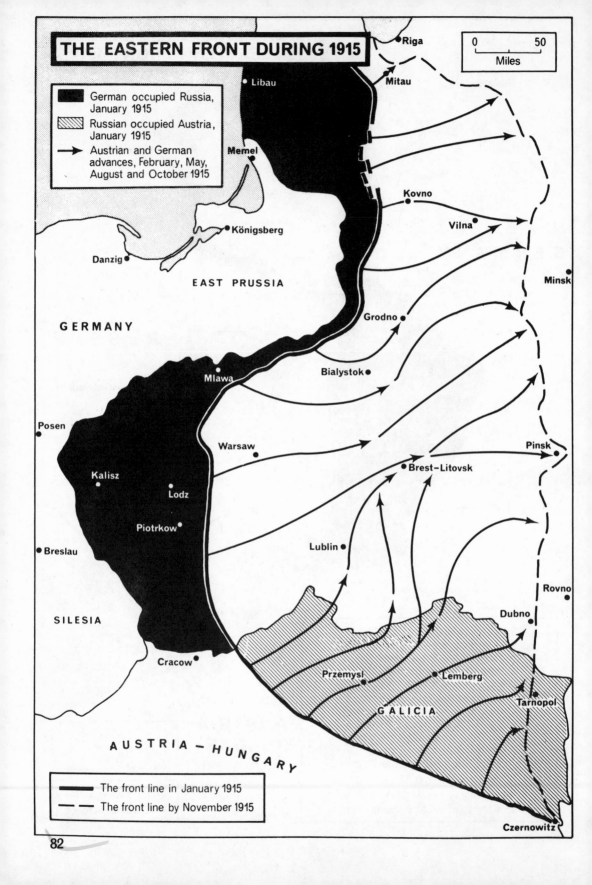

THE EASTERN FRONT DURING 1915

0   50
Miles

■ German occupied Russia,
   January 1915

▨ Russian occupied Austria,
   January 1915

→ Austrian and German
   advances, February, May,
   August and October 1915

Riga

Mitau

Libau

Memel

Königsberg

Danzig

EAST PRUSSIA

GERMANY

Kovno

Vilna

Minsk

Grodno

Mlawa

Bialystok

Posen

Warsaw

Pinsk

Kalisz

Lodz

Brest–Litovsk

Piotrkow

Lublin

Breslau

Rovno

SILESIA

Dubno

Cracow

Przemysl

Lemberg

Tarnopol

GALICIA

AUSTRIA – HUNGARY

Czernowitz

▬▬ The front line in January 1915

– – – The front line by November 1915

82

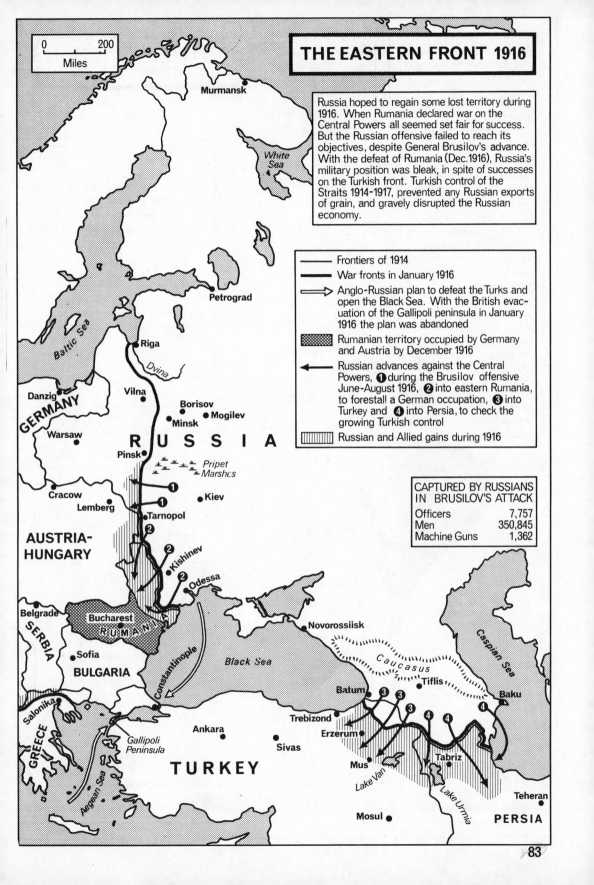

THE EASTERN FRONT 1916

Russia hoped to regain some lost territory during 1916. When Rumania declared war on the Central Powers all seemed set fair for success. But the Russian offensive failed to reach its objectives, despite General Brusilov's advance. With the defeat of Rumania (Dec.1916), Russia's military position was bleak, in spite of successes on the Turkish front. Turkish control of the Straits 1914-1917, prevented any Russian exports of grain, and gravely disrupted the Russian economy.

———	Frontiers of 1914
▬▬▬	War fronts in January 1916
⇨	Anglo-Russian plan to defeat the Turks and open the Black Sea. With the British evacuation of the Gallipoli peninsula in January 1916 the plan was abandoned
▨	Rumanian territory occupied by Germany and Austria by December 1916
←	Russian advances against the Central Powers, ❶ during the Brusilov offensive June-August 1916, ❷ into eastern Rumania, to forestall a German occupation, ❸ into Turkey and ❹ into Persia, to check the growing Turkish control
▥	Russian and Allied gains during 1916

CAPTURED BY RUSSIANS
IN BRUSILOV'S ATTACK

Officers	7,757
Men	350,845
Machine Guns	1,362

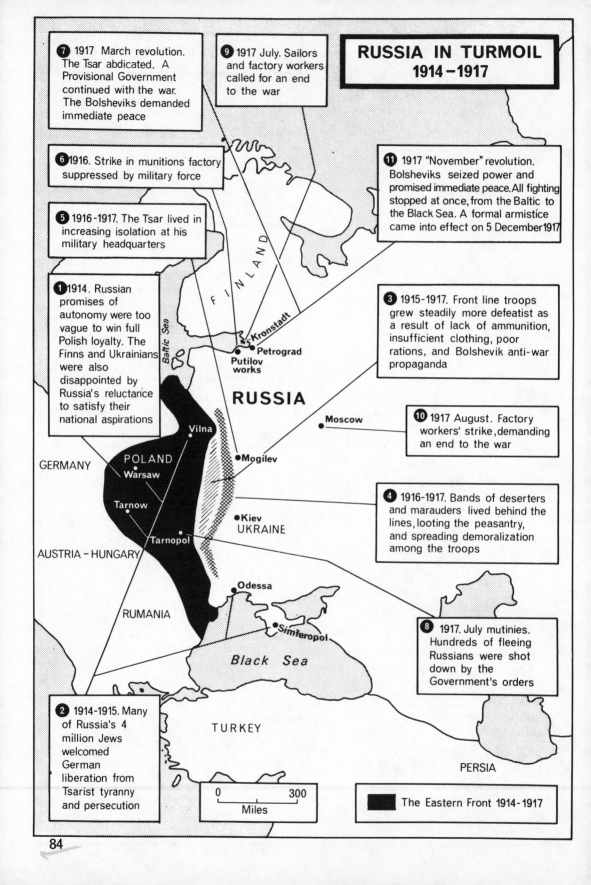

RUSSIA IN TURMOIL
1914 – 1917

7 1917 March revolution. The Tsar abdicated. A Provisional Government continued with the war. The Bolsheviks demanded immediate peace

9 1917 July. Sailors and factory workers called for an end to the war

6 1916. Strike in munitions factory suppressed by military force

11 1917 "November" revolution. Bolsheviks seized power and promised immediate peace. All fighting stopped at once, from the Baltic to the Black Sea. A formal armistice came into effect on 5 December 1917

5 1916-1917. The Tsar lived in increasing isolation at his military headquarters

1 1914. Russian promises of autonomy were too vague to win full Polish loyalty. The Finns and Ukrainians were also disappointed by Russia's reluctance to satisfy their national aspirations

3 1915-1917. Front line troops grew steadily more defeatist as a result of lack of ammunition, insufficient clothing, poor rations, and Bolshevik anti-war propaganda

10 1917 August. Factory workers' strike, demanding an end to the war

4 1916-1917. Bands of deserters and marauders lived behind the lines, looting the peasantry, and spreading demoralization among the troops

8 1917. July mutinies. Hundreds of fleeing Russians were shot down by the Government's orders

2 1914-1915. Many of Russia's 4 million Jews welcomed German liberation from Tsarist tyranny and persecution

FINLAND

Baltic Sea

Kronstadt

Petrograd

Putilov works

RUSSIA

Moscow

Mogilev

Vilna

POLAND

Warsaw

GERMANY

Tarnow

Tarnopol

AUSTRIA – HUNGARY

Kiev
UKRAINE

Odessa

RUMANIA

Simferopol

Black Sea

TURKEY

PERSIA

0   300
Miles

The Eastern Front 1914-1917

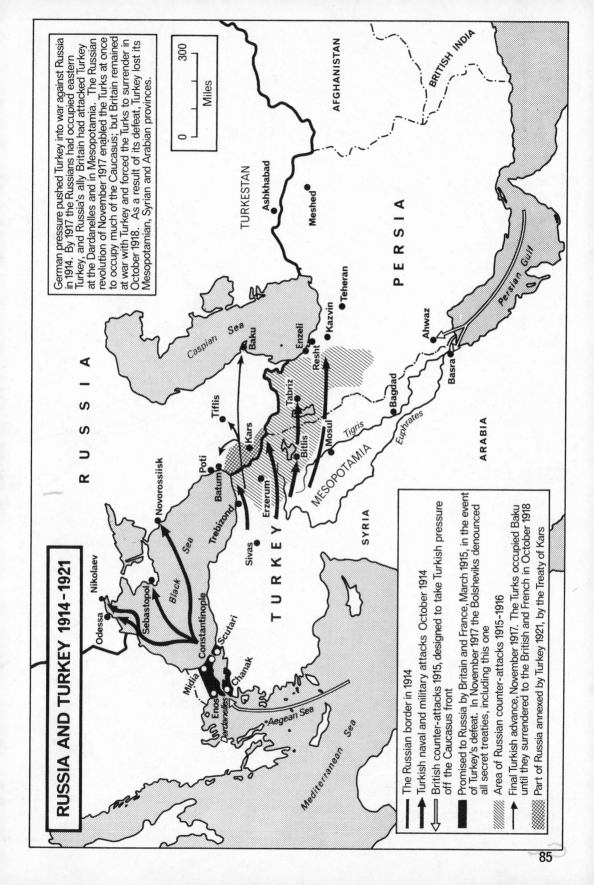

RUSSIA AND TURKEY 1914–1921

German pressure pushed Turkey into war against Russia in 1914. By 1917 the Russians had occupied eastern Turkey, and Russia's ally Britain had attacked Turkey at the Dardanelles and in Mesopotamia. The Russian revolution of November 1917 enabled the Turks at once to occupy much of the Caucasus; but Britain remained at war with Turkey and forced the Turks to surrender in October 1918. As a result of its defeat, Turkey lost its Mesopotamian, Syrian and Arabian provinces.

300

0

Miles

AFGHANISTAN

BRITISH INDIA

TURKESTAN

Ashkhabad

Meshed

P E R S I A

R U S S I A

Caspian Sea

Baku

Enzeli

Resht

Kazvin

Teheran

Ahwaz

Persian Gulf

Nikolaev

Odessa

Sebastopol

Novorossiisk

Poti

Batum

Tiflis

Kars

Tabriz

Bitlis

Mosul

Basra

Bagdad

Tigris

Euphrates

Black Sea

Trebizond

Erzerum

Sivas

MESOPOTAMIA

SYRIA

ARABIA

Constantinople

Scutari

Chanak

Midia

Enos

Dardanelles

Aegean Sea

Mediterranean Sea

T U R K E Y

The Russian border in 1914

Turkish naval and military attacks October 1914

British counter-attacks 1915, designed to take Turkish pressure off the Caucasus front

Promised to Russia by Britain and France, March 1915, in the event of Turkey's defeat. In November 1917 the Bolsheviks denounced all secret treaties, including this one

Area of Russian counter-attacks 1915–1916

Final Turkish advance, November 1917. The Turks occupied Baku until they surrendered to the British and French in October 1918

Part of Russia annexed by Turkey 1921, by the Treaty of Kars

85

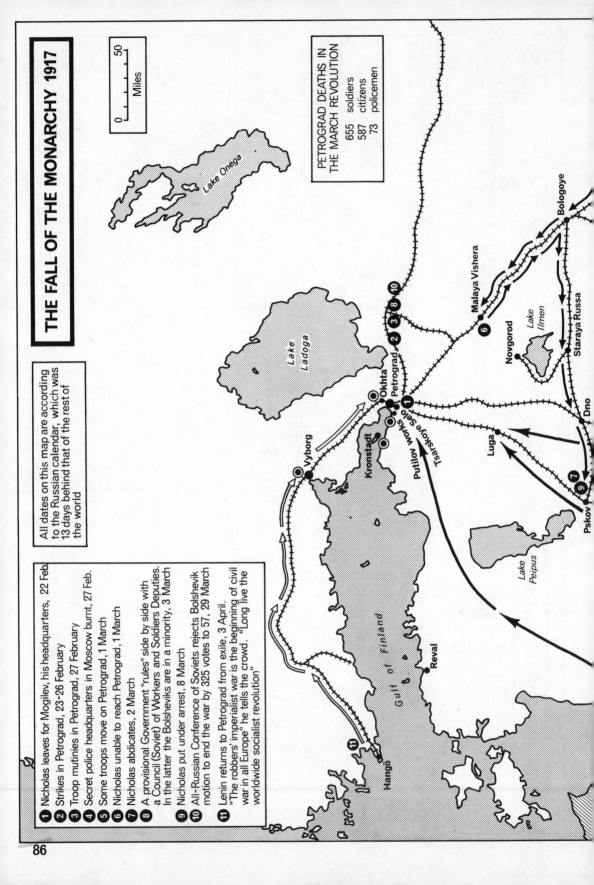

THE FALL OF THE MONARCHY 1917

All dates on this map are according to the Russian calendar, which was 13 days behind that of the rest of the world

PETROGRAD DEATHS IN
THE MARCH REVOLUTION

655 soldiers
587 citizens
73 policemen

1. Nicholas leaves for Mogilev, his headquarters, 22 Feb.
2. Strikes in Petrograd, 23-26 February
3. Troop mutinies in Petrograd, 27 February
4. Secret police headquarters in Moscow burnt, 27 Feb.
5. Some troops move on Petrograd, 1 March
6. Nicholas unable to reach Petrograd, 1 March
7. Nicholas abdicates, 2 March
8. A provisional Government "rules" side by side with a Council (Soviet) of Workers and Soldiers Deputies. In the latter the Bolsheviks are in a minority, 3 March
9. Nicholas put under arrest, 8 March
10. All-Russian Conference of Soviets rejects Bolshevik motion to end the war by 325 votes to 57, 29 March
11. Lenin returns to Petrograd from exile, 3 April. "The robbers' imperialist war is the beginning of civil war in all Europe" he tells the crowd. "Long live the worldwide socialist revolution"

Lake Onega

Miles
0   50

Lake Ladoga

Okhta

Petrograd

Vyborg

Kronstadt

Putilov works

Tsarskoye Selo

Malaya Vishera

Novgorod

Lake Ilmen

Bologoye

Staraya Russa

Dno

Luga

Pskov

Lake Peipus

Gulf of Finland

Reval

Hangö

86

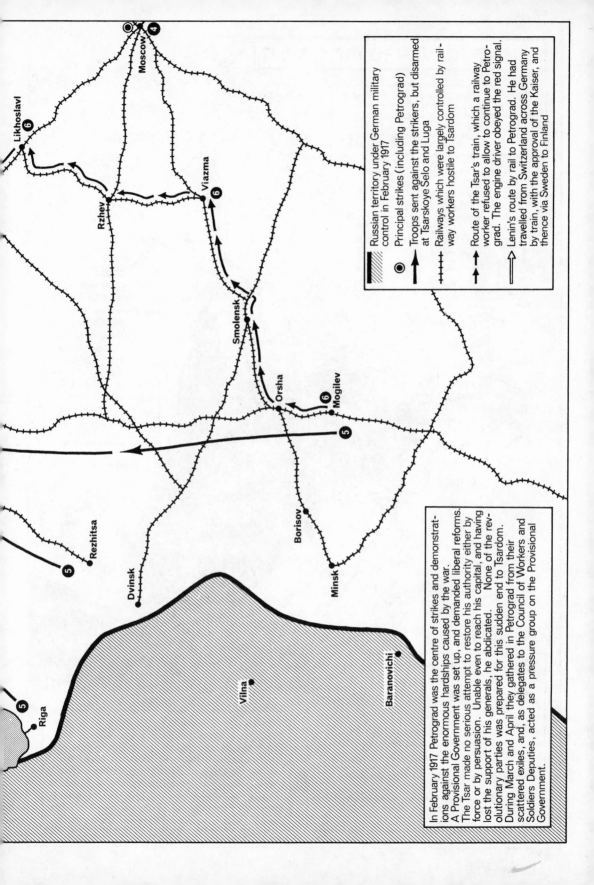

Legend:

- Russian territory under German military control in February 1917
- ◉ Principal strikes (including Petrograd)
- ↑ Troops sent against the strikers, but disarmed at Tsarskoye Selo and Luga
- ┼┼┼ Railways which were largely controlled by railway workers hostile to Tsardom
- ↑ Route of the Tsar's train, which a railway worker refused to allow to continue to Petrograd. The engine driver obeyed the red signal.
- ⇧ Lenin's route by rail to Petrograd. He had travelled from Switzerland across Germany by train, with the approval of the Kaiser, and thence via Sweden to Finland

In February 1917 Petrograd was the centre of strikes and demonstrations against the enormous hardships caused by the war. A Provisional Government was set up, and demanded liberal reforms. The Tsar made no serious attempt to restore his authority either by force or by persuasion. Unable even to reach his capital, and having lost the support of his generals, he abdicated. None of the revolutionary parties was prepared for this sudden end to Tsardom. During March and April they gathered in Petrograd from their scattered exiles, and, as delegates to the Council of Workers and Soldiers Deputies, acted as a pressure group on the Provisional Government.

Moscow · 4

Likhoslavl · 6

Rzhev

Viazma · 6

Smolensk

Orsha

Mogilev · 6

5

Borisov

Rezhitsa

5

Dvinsk

Minsk

Vilna

Baranovichi

Riga · 5

LENIN'S RETURN TO RUSSIA 1917

Our tactics: absolute distrust; no support of new Government; Kerensky particularly suspect; to arm proletariat only guarantee; no rapprochement with other parties. This last is conditio sine qua non

**LENIN TO BOLSHEVIKS IN SWEDEN
TELEGRAM FROM BERN 26 MARCH 1917**

0   250
Miles

North Cape

Murmansk

SWEDEN

Scapa Flow

BRITAIN

Liverpool

North Sea

Stockholm

Hangö   **Vyborg**

Baltic Sea   **Petrograd**

Trelleborg

On 7 August 1914 Lenin was arrested in Cracow by the Austrians as an enemy alien and spy. He was released on 23 Aug., the Austrian Government having been persuaded that he was even more an enemy of Tsardom, and could "render great services" to Austria by fomenting anti-Tsarist troubles

London

English Channel

Berlin

GERMANY

Cracow

RUSSIA

Paris

FRANCE

Berne
SWITZ.   **Innsbruck**   **Vienna**

**AUSTRIA–
HUNGARY**

Odessa

ITALY

BULGARIA

Black Sea

Aegean Sea

TURKEY

■ The Central Powers and their conquests in February 1917

—▪— Lenin's route from Austria to Switzerland, 1914

····▶ Lenin's first proposed route back to Russia, which proved impossible for fear of arrest by the British

➡ Lenin's actual route 9-16 April 1917

▨ Sea routes to Russia closed by Central Power minefields

When revolution broke out in Petrograd in February 1917, Lenin, the Bolshevik leader, was in Switzerland. Wartime was not conducive to travel, nor did his plan to go through Britain prove possible. Instead, the German Government, eager to see dissension and chaos in Russia, agreed with alacrity to his request to travel across "enemy" territory, and provided him with facilities. Thus Imperial Germany served as a hand-maiden to the Russian revolution of October 1917

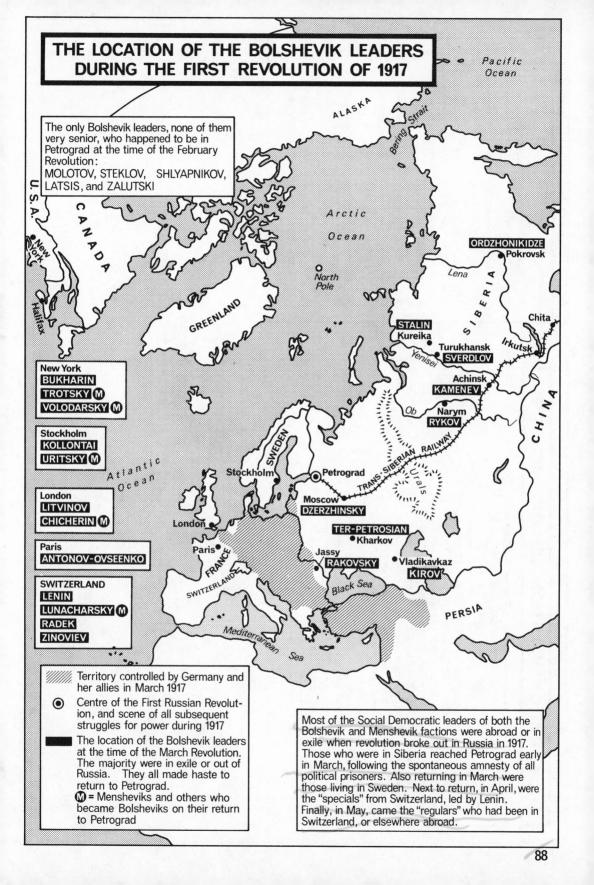

THE LOCATION OF THE BOLSHEVIK LEADERS DURING THE FIRST REVOLUTION OF 1917

The only Bolshevik leaders, none of them very senior, who happened to be in Petrograd at the time of the February Revolution:
MOLOTOV, STEKLOV, SHLYAPNIKOV, LATSIS, and ZALUTSKI

New York
BUKHARIN
TROTSKY Ⓜ
VOLODARSKY Ⓜ

Stockholm
KOLLONTAI
URITSKY Ⓜ

London
LITVINOV
CHICHERIN Ⓜ

Paris
ANTONOV-OVSEENKO

SWITZERLAND
LENIN
LUNACHARSKY Ⓜ
RADEK
ZINOVIEV

Pacific Ocean
ALASKA
Bering Strait
U.S.A.
CANADA
New York
Halifax
Arctic Ocean
North Pole
GREENLAND
Lena
SIBERIA
ORDZHONIKIDZE
Pokrovsk
Chita
STALIN
Kureika
Turukhansk
SVERDLOV
Irkutsk
Yenisei
Achinsk
KAMENEV
CHINA
Ob
Narym
RYKOV
SWEDEN
Atlantic Ocean
Stockholm
Petrograd
TRANS-SIBERIAN RAILWAY
Urals
Moscow
DZERZHINSKY
London
TER-PETROSIAN
Paris
Kharkov
FRANCE
Jassy
RAKOVSKY
Vladikavkaz
KIROV
SWITZERLAND
Black Sea
PERSIA
Mediterranean Sea

//// Territory controlled by Germany and her allies in March 1917

◉ Centre of the First Russian Revolution, and scene of all subsequent struggles for power during 1917

▬ The location of the Bolshevik leaders at the time of the March Revolution. The majority were in exile or out of Russia. They all made haste to return to Petrograd.
Ⓜ = Mensheviks and others who became Bolsheviks on their return to Petrograd

Most of the Social Democratic leaders of both the Bolshevik and Menshevik factions were abroad or in exile when revolution broke out in Russia in 1917. Those who were in Siberia reached Petrograd early in March, following the spontaneous amnesty of all political prisoners. Also returning in March were those living in Sweden. Next to return, in April, were the "specials" from Switzerland, led by Lenin. Finally, in May, came the "regulars" who had been in Switzerland, or elsewhere abroad.

THE WAR AND REVOLUTION JULY AND AUGUST 1917

In March 1917 the Provisional Government assured Britain and France that it would continue the war against the Central Powers. But the offensive launched on 1 July ended two weeks later in mutiny and failure. Mass demonstrations in Petrograd on 16 and 17 July, though leaderless, showed how hated the war had become, and the Bolsheviks soon dominated the Soviets by their cry of "Bread and Peace". The Provisional Government then published evidence of financial dealings between the Bolsheviks and German agents, forced Lenin to go into hiding in Finland, and arrested Trotsky. In August General Kornilov led an army against Petrograd, intending to crush the Soviets and stiffen the Provisional Government against concessions.
The Bolsheviks took a leading part in the defence of the city, and greatly increased their military power, having been armed by the Provisional Government. They also gained support among the masses, who feared the return of autocracy

The eastern front on 1 July 1917

Austrian territory conquered by Russia 1-16 July 1917

Russian proposals for further offensive action during the second two weeks of July

Subject peoples insisting on independence from Russian rule, and gravely hampering the war effort when their demands were rejected or disregarded

Principal areas of mutiny 17-30 July 1917

Kornilov's unsuccessful attack on the capital August 1917

Factory groups between Petrograd and the front with increasingly strong Bolshevik influence July-September 1917

Military units between Petrograd and the front with increasingly strong Bolshevik sections July-September 1917

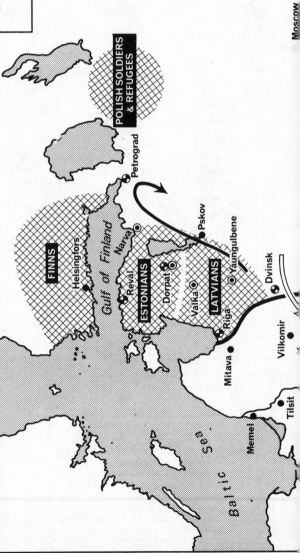

POLISH SOLDIERS & REFUGEES

Petrograd

FINNS

Helsingfors

Gulf of Finland

Reval

ESTONIANS

Narva

Pskov

Dorpat

Valka

Vaungulbene

LATVIANS

Riga

Dvinsk

Mitava

Vilkomir

Memel

Tilsit

Baltic Sea

Moscow

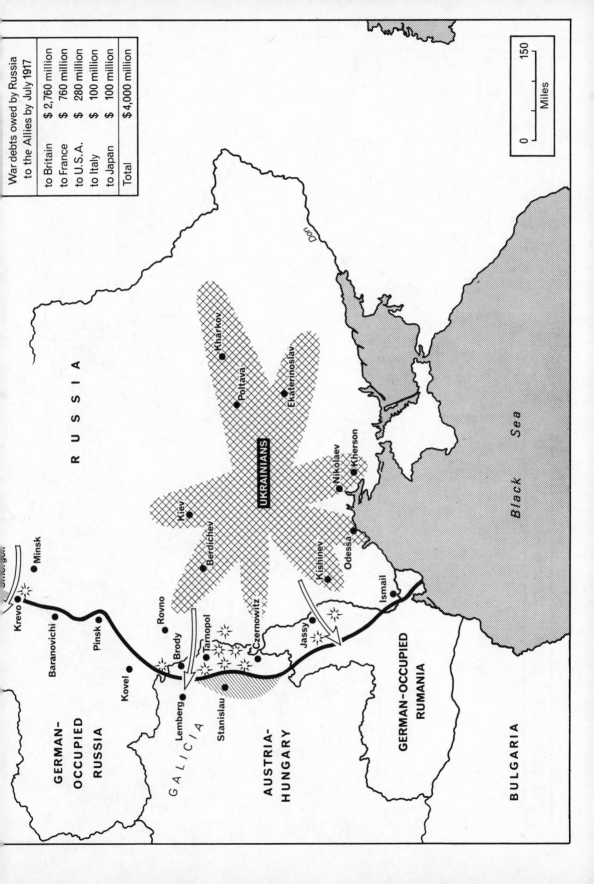

War debts owed by Russia
to the Allies by July 1917

to Britain	$	2,760 million
to France	$	760 million
to U.S.A.	$	280 million
to Italy	$	100 million
to Japan	$	100 million
Total		$4,000 million

RUSSIA

GERMAN-
OCCUPIED
RUSSIA

Minsk

Krevo
Baranovichi
Pinsk
Kovel
Rovno
Brody
Lemberg
Stanislau

GALICIA

Tarnopol
Czernowitz
Jassy

AUSTRIA-
HUNGARY

Berdichev
Kiev

Kishinev
Odessa
Nikolaev
Kherson
Ismail

UKRAINIANS

Poltava
Kharkov
Ekaterinoslav

Don

GERMAN-OCCUPIED
RUMANIA

BULGARIA

Black Sea

Miles
0   150

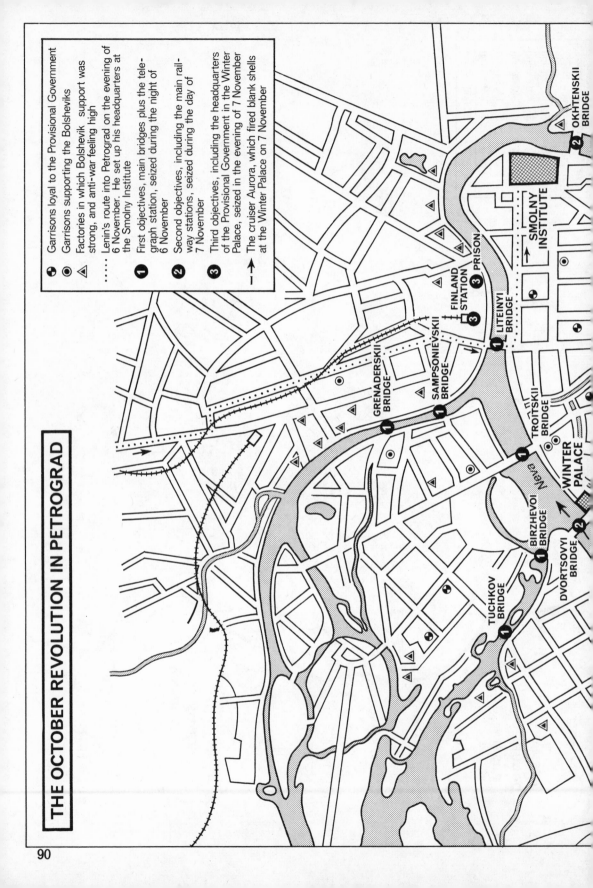

THE OCTOBER REVOLUTION IN PETROGRAD

⊕ Garrisons loyal to the Provisional Government

◉ Garrisons supporting the Bolsheviks

◁ Factories in which Bolshevik support was strong, and anti-war feeling high

⋯⋯ Lenin's route into Petrograd on the evening of 6 November. He set up his headquarters at the Smolny Institute

❶ First objectives, main bridges plus the telegraph station, seized during the night of 6 November

❷ Second objectives, including the main railway stations, seized during the day of 7 November

❸ Third objectives, including the headquarters of the Provisional Government in the Winter Palace, seized in the evening of 7 November

↑ The cruiser Aurora, which fired blank shells at the Winter Palace on 7 November

OKHTENSKII BRIDGE ❷

SMOLNY INSTITUTE

FINLAND STATION ❸

❸ PRISON

LITEINYI BRIDGE ❶

GRENADERSKII BRIDGE

SAMPSONIEVSKII BRIDGE ❶

❶

TROITSKII BRIDGE

BIRZHEVOI BRIDGE ❶

Neva

WINTER PALACE ❷

DVORTSOVYI BRIDGE ❶

TUCHKOV BRIDGE ❶

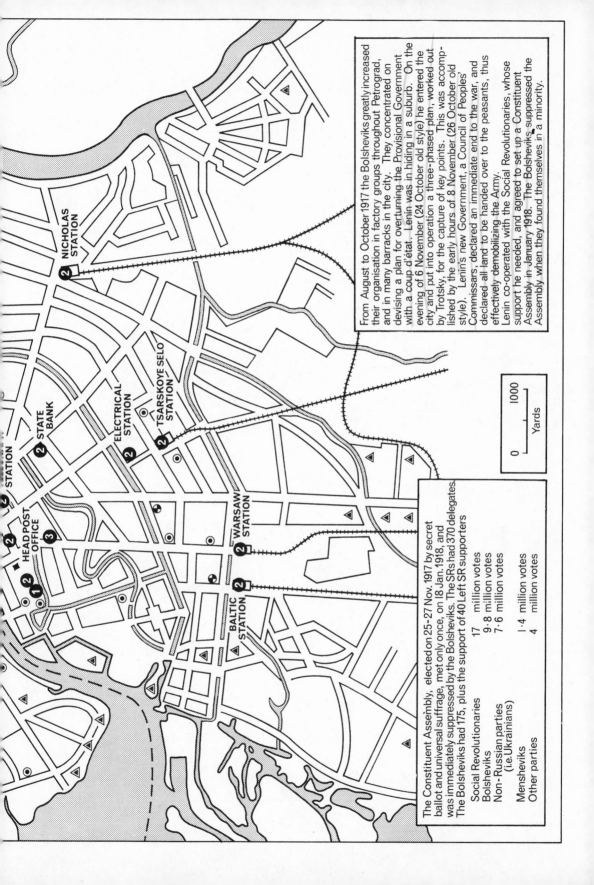

From August to October 1917 the Bolsheviks greatly increased their organisation in factory groups throughout Petrograd, and in many barracks in the city. They concentrated on devising a plan for overturning the Provisional Government with a coup d'état. Lenin was in hiding in a suburb. On the evening of 6 November (24 October old style) he entered the city and put into operation a three-phased plan, worked out by Trotsky, for the capture of key points. This was accomplished by the early hours of 8 November (26 October old style). Lenin's new Government, a Council of Peoples' Commissars, declared an immediate end to the war, and declared all land to be handed over to the peasants, thus effectively demobilizing the Army. Lenin co-operated with the Social Revolutionaries, whose support he needed, and agreed to set up a Constituent Assembly in January 1918. The Bolsheviks suppressed the Assembly when they found themselves in a minority.

The Constituent Assembly, elected on 25-27 Nov. 1917 by secret ballot and universal suffrage, met only once, on 18 Jan.1918, and was immediately suppressed by the Bolsheviks. The SRs had 370 delegates. The Bolsheviks had 175, plus the support of 40 Left SR supporters

Social Revolutionaries	17	million votes
Bolsheviks	9·8	million votes
Non-Russian parties (i.e.Ukrainians)	7·6	million votes
Mensheviks	1·4	million votes
Other parties	4	million votes

0   1000
Yards

NICHOLAS STATION

STATE BANK

ELECTRICAL STATION

TSARSKOYE SELO STATION

HEAD POST OFFICE

WARSAW STATION

BALTIC STATION

Section Three

THE SOVIET UNION

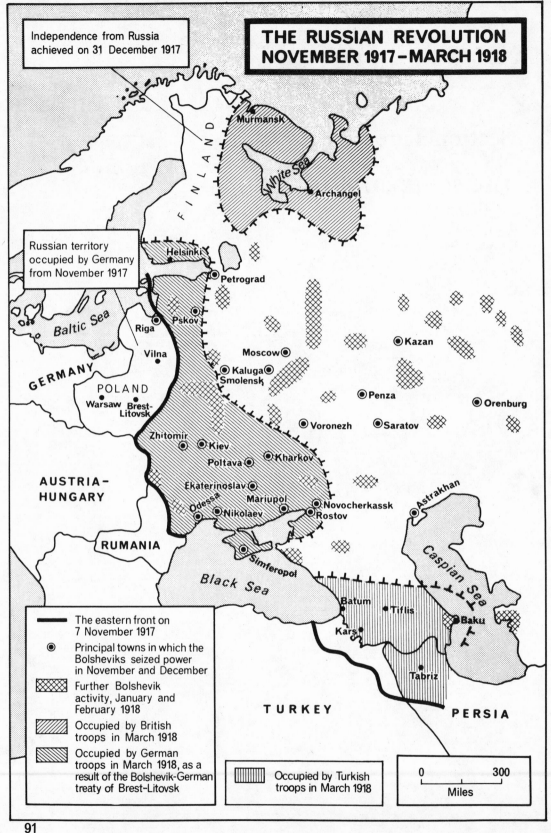

Independence from Russia
achieved on 31 December 1917

Russian territory
occupied by Germany
from November 1917

Murmansk

White Sea

Archangel

FINLAND

Helsinki

Petrograd

Baltic Sea

Riga   **Pskov**

Vilna

Moscow   **Kazan**

GERMANY

Kaluga
Smolensk

POLAND

Warsaw   **Brest-**
             Litovsk

Penza   **Orenburg**

Zhitomir

Kiev   **Voronezh**   **Saratov**

Poltava   **Kharkov**

AUSTRIA-
HUNGARY

Ekaterinoslav

Odessa   **Mariupol**   **Astrakhan**
Nikolaev   **Novocherkassk**
               Rostov

RUMANIA

Simferopol

Caspian Sea

Black Sea

Batum   **Tiflis**

Baku

Kars

TURKEY

Tabriz

PERSIA

The eastern front on
7 November 1917

Principal towns in which the
Bolsheviks seized power
in November and December

Further Bolshevik
activity, January and
February 1918

Occupied by British
troops in March 1918

Occupied by German
troops in March 1918, as a
result of the Bolshevik-German
treaty of Brest-Litovsk

Occupied by Turkish
troops in March 1918

0   300
Miles

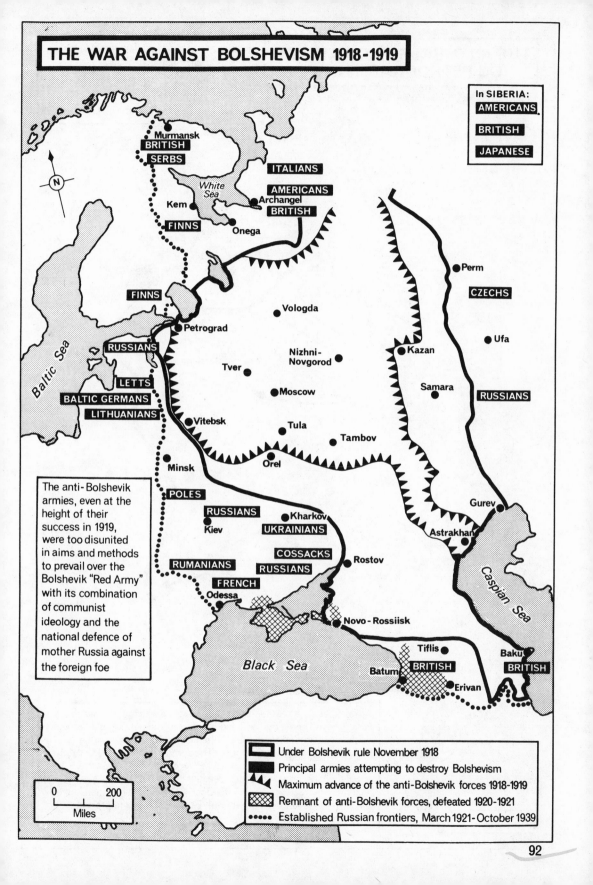

THE WAR AGAINST BOLSHEVISM 1918-1919

In SIBERIA:
AMERICANS
BRITISH
JAPANESE

N

Murmansk
BRITISH
SERBS

ITALIANS

White Sea

AMERICANS
Archangel
BRITISH

Kem

FINNS

Onega

Perm

CZECHS

FINNS

Vologda

Ufa

Petrograd

Kazan

RUSSIANS

Nizhni-
Novgorod

Tver

Samara

Baltic Sea

LETTS

Moscow

RUSSIANS

BALTIC GERMANS
LITHUANIANS

Vitebsk

Tula

Tambov

Minsk

Orel

POLES

The anti-Bolshevik
armies, even at the
height of their
success in 1919,
were too disunited
in aims and methods
to prevail over the
Bolshevik "Red Army"
with its combination
of communist
ideology and the
national defence of
mother Russia against
the foreign foe

RUSSIANS

Kiev

Kharkov

UKRAINIANS

Gurev

COSSACKS

Astrakhan

RUMANIANS

RUSSIANS

Rostov

FRENCH

Odessa

Novo-Rossiisk

Caspian Sea

Tiflis

Baku

BRITISH

BRITISH

Batum

Erivan

Black Sea

0   200
Miles

☐	Under Bolshevik rule November 1918
■	Principal armies attempting to destroy Bolshevism
◤◤◤	Maximum advance of the anti-Bolshevik forces 1918-1919
▨	Remnant of anti-Bolshevik forces, defeated 1920-1921
••••	Established Russian frontiers, March 1921-October 1939

92

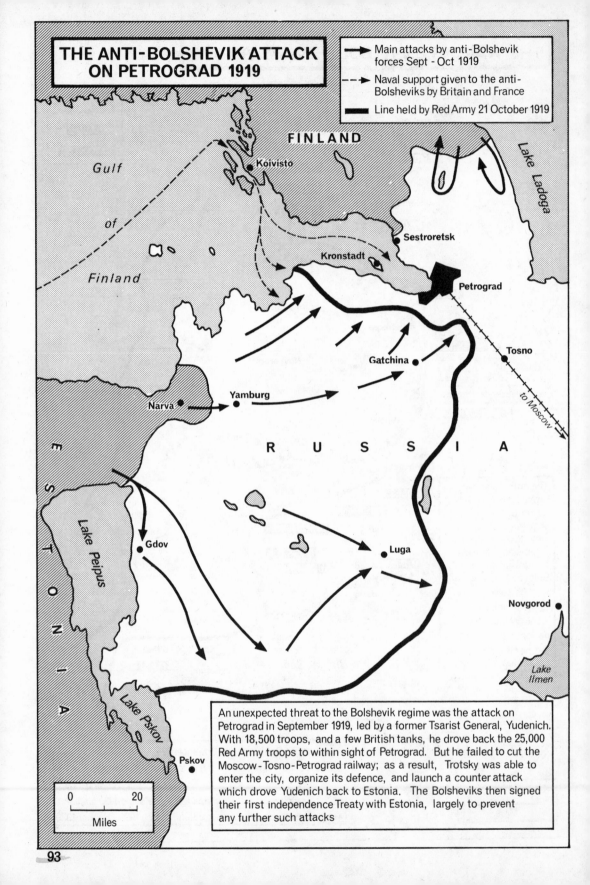

THE ANTI-BOLSHEVIK ATTACK ON PETROGRAD 1919

→ Main attacks by anti-Bolshevik forces Sept - Oct 1919

╌╌→ Naval support given to the anti-Bolsheviks by Britain and France

▬ Line held by Red Army 21 October 1919

FINLAND

Gulf

of

Finland

Koivisto

Sestroretsk

Kronstadt

Petrograd

Lake Ladoga

Gatchina

Tosno

to Moscow

Yamburg

Narva

R U S S I A

E
S
T
O
N
I
A

Lake Peipus

Gdov

Luga

Novgorod

Lake Ilmen

Lake Pskov

Pskov

An unexpected threat to the Bolshevik regime was the attack on Petrograd in September 1919, led by a former Tsarist General, Yudenich. With 18,500 troops, and a few British tanks, he drove back the 25,000 Red Army troops to within sight of Petrograd. But he failed to cut the Moscow - Tosno - Petrograd railway; as a result, Trotsky was able to enter the city, organize its defence, and launch a counter attack which drove Yudenich back to Estonia. The Bolsheviks then signed their first independence Treaty with Estonia, largely to prevent any further such attacks

0   20

Miles

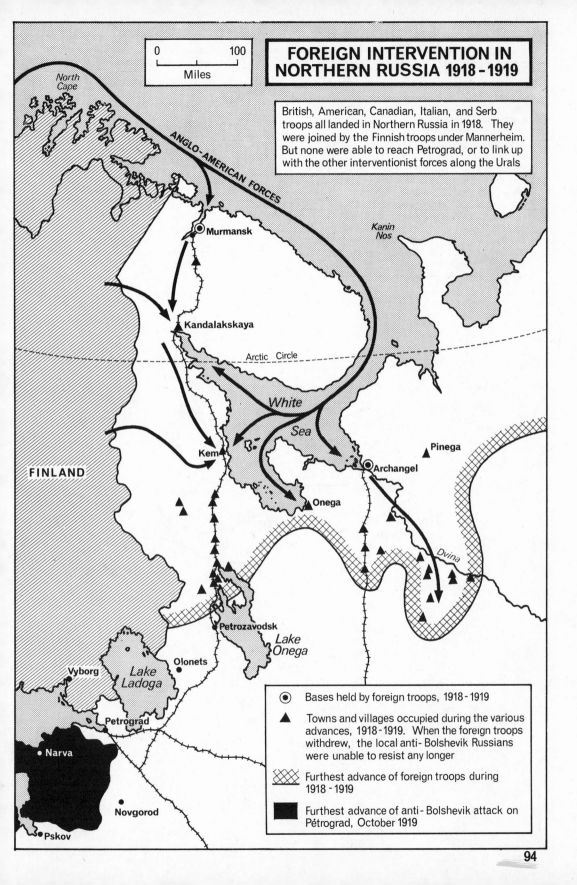

FOREIGN INTERVENTION IN NORTHERN RUSSIA 1918-1919

0   100
Miles

British, American, Canadian, Italian, and Serb troops all landed in Northern Russia in 1918. They were joined by the Finnish troops under Mannerheim. But none were able to reach Petrograd, or to link up with the other interventionist forces along the Urals

North Cape

ANGLO-AMERICAN FORCES

Kanin Nos

Murmansk

Kandalakskaya

Arctic Circle

White

Sea

Pinega

Kem

Archangel

FINLAND

Onega

Dvina

Petrozavodsk

Lake
Onega

Olonets

Vyborg

Lake
Ladoga

Petrograd

Narva

Novgorod

Pskov

⊙   Bases held by foreign troops, 1918-1919

▲   Towns and villages occupied during the various advances, 1918-1919. When the foreign troops withdrew, the local anti-Bolshevik Russians were unable to resist any longer

▨   Furthest advance of foreign troops during 1918-1919

█   Furthest advance of anti-Bolshevik attack on Pétrograd, October 1919

MAKHNO AND THE ANARCHISTS 1917-1920

Nestor Makhno, the Ukrainian anarchist, was imprisoned for terrorism in 1907, at the age of eighteen. Released in February 1917, he organized a peasant army, and established control over a large area of southern Russia. He defeated the Austrians at Dibrivki (Sept 1918) and the Ukrainian nationalists at Ekaterinoslav (Nov 1918). In 1919 he allied with the Bolsheviks, defeating two anti-Bolshevik armies, Denikin's at Peregonovka (Sept 1919) and Wrangel's in the Crimea (June 1920). Makhno himself was then attacked continuously by the Bolsheviks and fled (November 1920) via Rumania to France, where he died in 1935

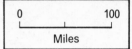

- ◉ Centres of the Confederation of Anarchist Organizations (Nabat), 1918
- ⊘ Anarchist conferences, with dates
- ◕ Makhno's Headquarters 1918-1920
- → Makhno's principal military activities

```
0                    100
|_____|
        Miles
```

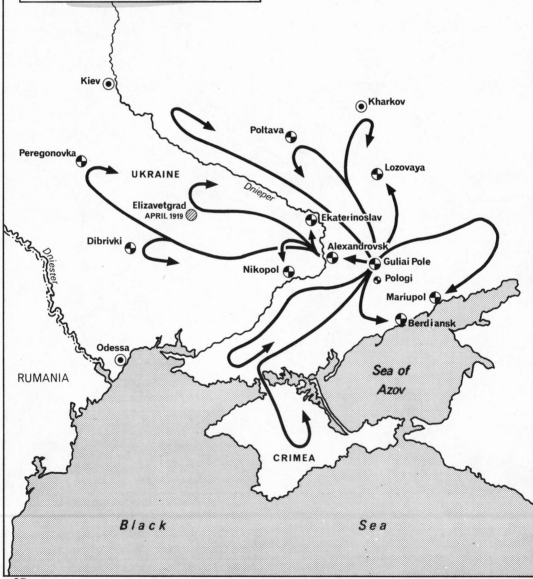

Kursk
NOV. 1918

Kiev

Kharkov

Poltava

UKRAINE

Peregonovka

Lozovaya

Dnieper

Elizavetgrad
APRIL 1919

Ekaterinoslav

Dibrivki

Alexandrovsk

Guliai Pole

Nikopol

Pologi

Mariupol

Berdiansk

Odessa

Dniester

RUMANIA

Sea of Azov

CRIMEA

Black   Sea

THE RUSSO-POLISH WAR 1920

Legend:

— Poland's established frontiers, June 1920

······ The eastern extent of Polish conquests, April, May and June 1920

← Russian attacks following the Polish occupation of Kiev in June 1920

Polish lines of defence, August 1920

◔ The 'Miracle of the Vistula'. Russian armies were defeated; they retreated to Russia

Seized by Poland from Lithuania, October 1920

Annexed by Poland from Russia, Treaty of Riga, March 1921

– – Poland's eastern frontier from 1921 to 1939

ESTONIA

LATVIA

LITHUANIA

Vilna

RUSSIA

Minsk

Baltic Sea

DANZIG

EAST PRUSSIA

Vistula

Grodno

Bialystok

Pinsk

Plotsk

Poznan

Warsaw

P O L A N D

Radom

Lublin

Kholm

Kiev

GERMANY

GERMANY

Vistula

Lvov

Cracow

C Z E C H O S L O V A K I A

Kamenets Podolsk

0   100
Miles

HUNGARY

RUMANIA

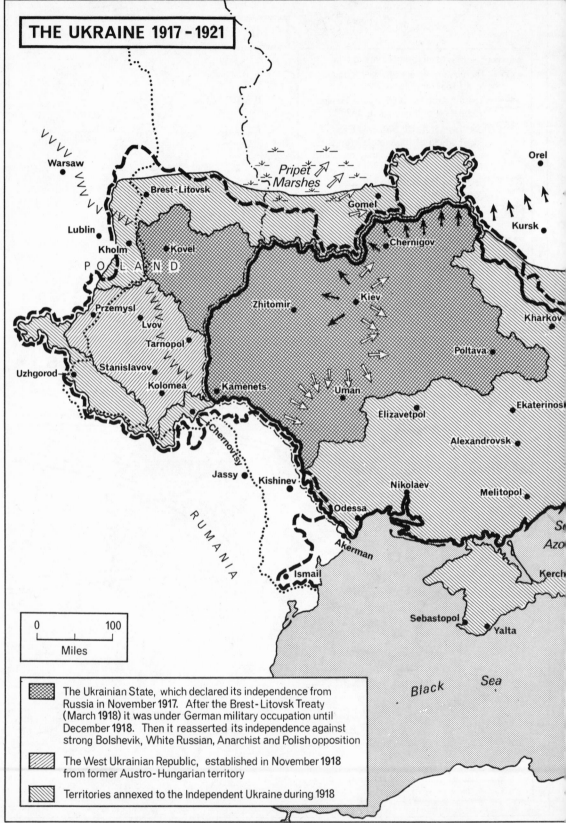

THE UKRAINE 1917 - 1921

Warsaw

Orel

Brest-Litovsk

Pripet
Marshes

Gomel

Kursk

Lublin

Chernigov

Kholm

Kovel

P O L A N D

Przemysl

Zhitomir

Kiev

Kharkov

Lvov

Tarnopol

Poltava

Uzhgorod

Stanislavov

Kamenets

Uman

Kolomea

Elizavetpol

Ekaterinos

Chernovtsy

Alexandrovsk

Jassy

Kishinev

Nikolaev

Melitopol

R U M A N I A

Odessa

Akerman

Se
Azo

Ismail

Kerch

Sebastopol

Yalta

0   100

Miles

Black   Sea

The Ukrainian State, which declared its independence from
Russia in November 1917. After the Brest-Litovsk Treaty
(March 1918) it was under German military occupation until
December 1918. Then it reasserted its independence against
strong Bolshevik, White Russian, Anarchist and Polish opposition

The West Ukrainian Republic, established in November 1918
from former Austro-Hungarian territory

Territories annexed to the Independent Ukraine during 1918

Legend:

- ▬ ▬ ▬ Territory claimed by the Ukrainian nationalists as part of the "ethnographic" Ukraine
- ▬▬▬ Boundary of the Ukrainian Soviet Socialist Republic **1921**
- ▬ · ▬ · Western boundary of the Soviet Union **1921-1939**
- ·········· Western boundary of the Soviet Union since **1945**

- ↟↟↟ Furthest northern advance of Denikin's anti-Bolshevik armies, November **1919**. Denikin's Great Russian policies failed to gain him much Ukrainian support
- ₩₩₩ Furthest eastern advance of the Polish Army in June **1920**
- ∧∧∧ Furthest western advance of the Red Army by August **1920**

Voronezh

Buturlinovka

Lugansk

Taganrog

Rostov

Mariupol

Astrakhan

Caspian

Sea

Ekaterinodar

Stavropol

Armavir

Novorossiisk

Mineralnye Vody

Mozdok

Tuapse

Sochi

Causasus

Batum

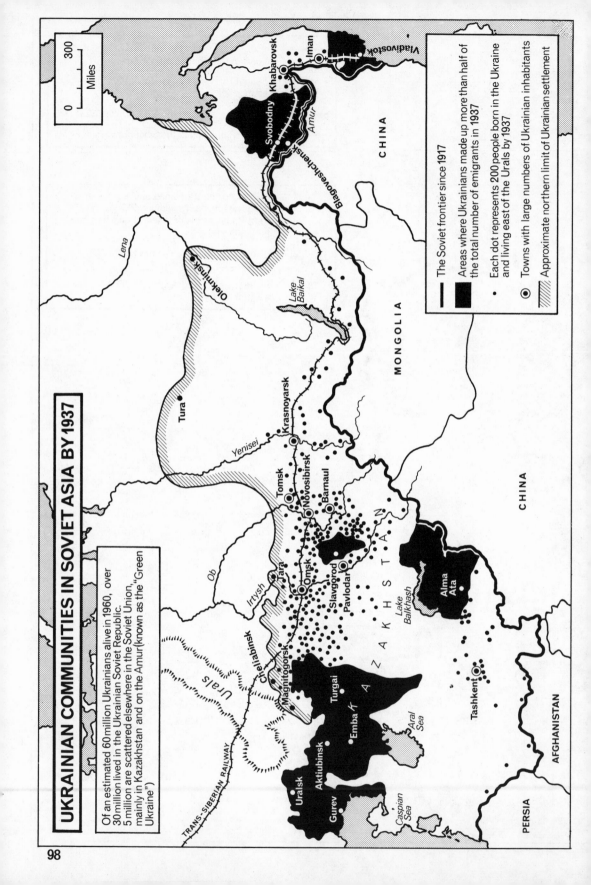

UKRAINIAN COMMUNITIES IN SOVIET ASIA BY 1937

Of an estimated 60 million Ukrainians alive in 1960, over 30 million lived in the Ukrainian Soviet Republic. 5 million are scattered elsewhere in the Soviet Union, mainly in Kazakhstan and on the Amur (known as the "Green Ukraine")

Legend:
- The Soviet frontier since 1917
- Areas where Ukrainians made up more than half of the total number of emigrants in 1937
- Each dot represents 200 people born in the Ukraine and living east of the Urals by 1937
- Towns with large numbers of Ukrainian inhabitants
- Approximate northern limit of Ukrainian settlement

Scale: 0 — 300 Miles

Labels: Vladivostok, Iman, Khabarovsk, Svobodny, Blagoveshchensk, Amur, CHINA, MONGOLIA, Olekminsk, Lena, Lake Baikal, Tura, Yenisei, Krasnoyarsk, Tomsk, Novosibirsk, Barnaul, Tara, Omsk, Slavgorod, Pavlodar, Ob, Irtysh, KAZAKHSTAN, Lake Balkhash, Alma Ata, Cheliabinsk, Magnitogorsk, Urals, Turgai, Emba R., Aral Sea, Tashkent, Uralsk, Aktiubinsk, Gurev, Caspian Sea, TRANS-SIBERIAN RAILWAY, PERSIA, AFGHANISTAN

98

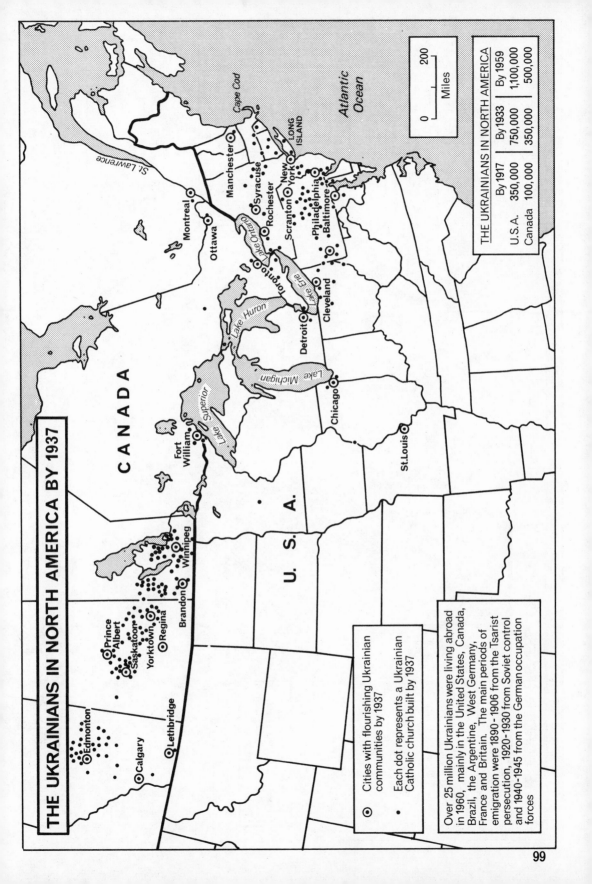

THE UKRAINIANS IN NORTH AMERICA BY 1937

THE UKRAINIANS IN NORTH AMERICA

	By 1917	By 1933	By 1959
U.S.A.	350,000	750,000	1,100,000
Canada	100,000	350,000	500,000

⊙ Cities with flourishing Ukrainian communities by 1937

• Each dot represents a Ukrainian Catholic church built by 1937

Over 25 million Ukrainians were living abroad in 1960, mainly in the United States, Canada, Brazil, the Argentine, West Germany, France and Britain. The main periods of emigration were 1890 - 1906 from the Tsarist persecution, 1920-1930 from Soviet control and 1940-1945 from the German occupation forces

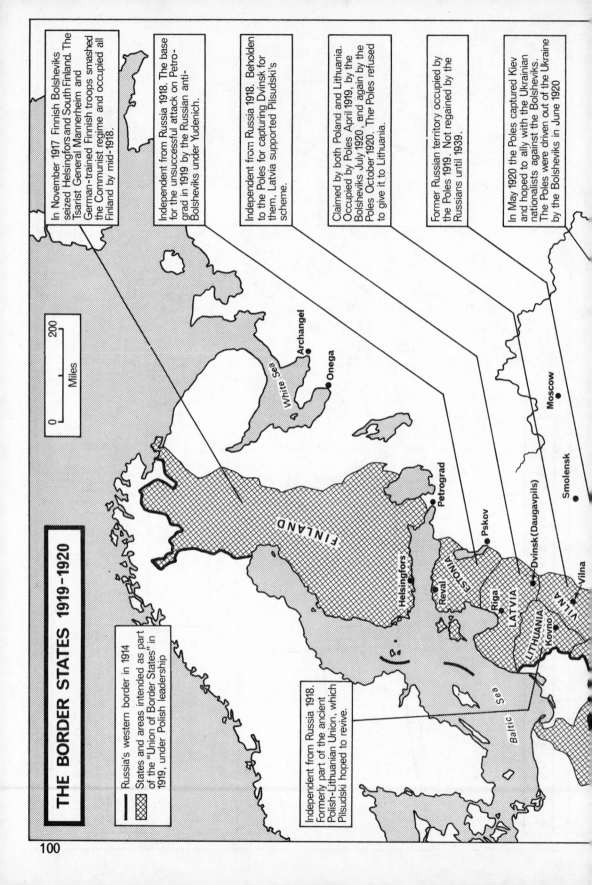

THE BORDER STATES 1919–1920

In November 1917 Finnish Bolsheviks seized Helsingfors and South Finland. The Tsarist General Mannerheim and German-trained Finnish troops smashed the Communist regime and occupied all Finland by mid-1918.

Independent from Russia 1918. The base for the unsuccessful attack on Petrograd in 1919 by the Russian anti-Bolsheviks under Yudenich.

Independent from Russia 1918. Beholden to the Poles for capturing Dvinsk for them. Latvia supported Pilsudski's scheme.

Claimed by both Poland and Lithuania. Occupied by Poles April 1919, by the Bolsheviks July 1920, and again by the Poles October 1920. The Poles refused to give it to Lithuania.

Former Russian territory occupied by the Poles 1919. Not regained by the Russians until 1939.

In May 1920 the Poles captured Kiev and hoped to ally with the Ukrainian nationalists against the Bolsheviks. The Poles were driven out of the Ukraine by the Bolsheviks in June 1920.

Independent from Russia 1918. Formerly part of the ancient Polish-Lithuanian Union, which Pilsudski hoped to revive.

Russia's western border in 1914

States and areas intended as part of the "Union of Border States" in 1919, under Polish leadership

200

0

Miles

White Sea

Archangel

Onega

Baltic Sea

FINLAND

Helsingfors

Reval

ESTONIA

Petrograd

Pskov

Riga

LATVIA

Dvinsk (Daugavpils)

Vilna

VILNA

LITHUANIA

Kovno

Moscow

Smolensk

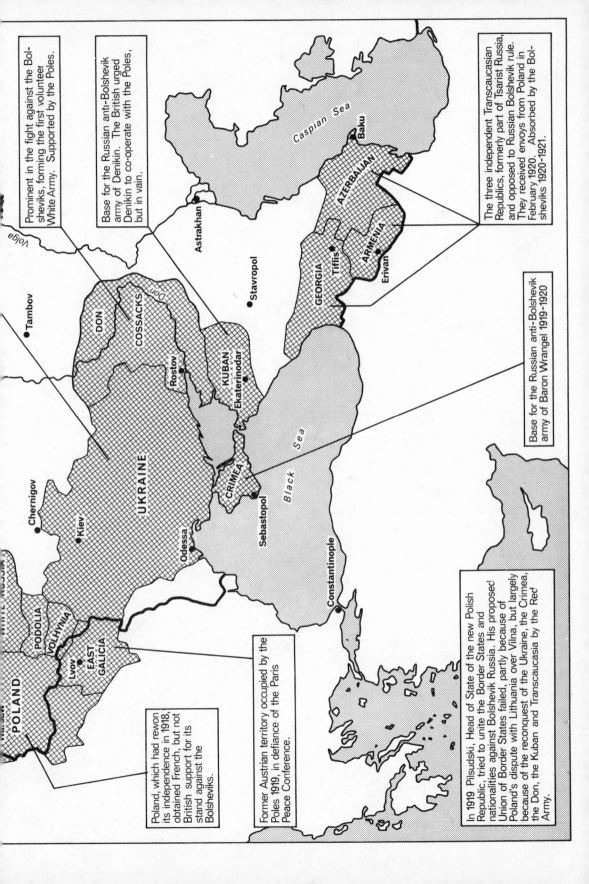

Prominent in the fight against the Bolsheviks, forming the first volunteer White Army. Supported by the Poles.

Base for the Russian anti-Bolshevik army of Denikin. The British urged Denikin to co-operate with the Poles, but in vain.

The three independent Transcaucasian Republics, formerly part of Tsarist Russia, and opposed to Russian Bolshevik rule. They received envoys from Poland in February 1920. Absorbed by the Bolsheviks 1920-1921.

Base for the Russian anti-Bolshevik army of Baron Wrangel 1919-1920.

Volga

Caspian Sea

Baku

AZERBAIJAN

ARMENIA

GEORGIA

Tiflis

Erivan

• Astrakhan

• Stavropol

• Tambov

DON

COSSACKS

Don

Rostov

KUBAN

Ekaterinodar

WHITE RUSSIA

Chernigov
•

Kiev
•

UKRAINE

CRIMEA

Sebastopol

Odessa

Black Sea

Constantinople

POLAND

PODOLIA

VOLHYNIA

Lvov
•

EAST
GALICIA

Poland, which had rewon its independence in 1918, obtained French, but not British support for its stand against the Bolsheviks.

Former Austrian territory occupied by the Poles 1919, in defiance of the Paris Peace Conference.

In 1919 Pilsudski, Head of State of the new Polish Republic, tried to unite the Border States and nationalities against Bolshevik Russia. His proposed Union of Border States failed, partly because of Poland's dispute with Lithuania over Vilna, but largely because of the reconquest of the Ukraine, the Crimea, the Don, the Kuban and Transcaucasia by the Red Army.

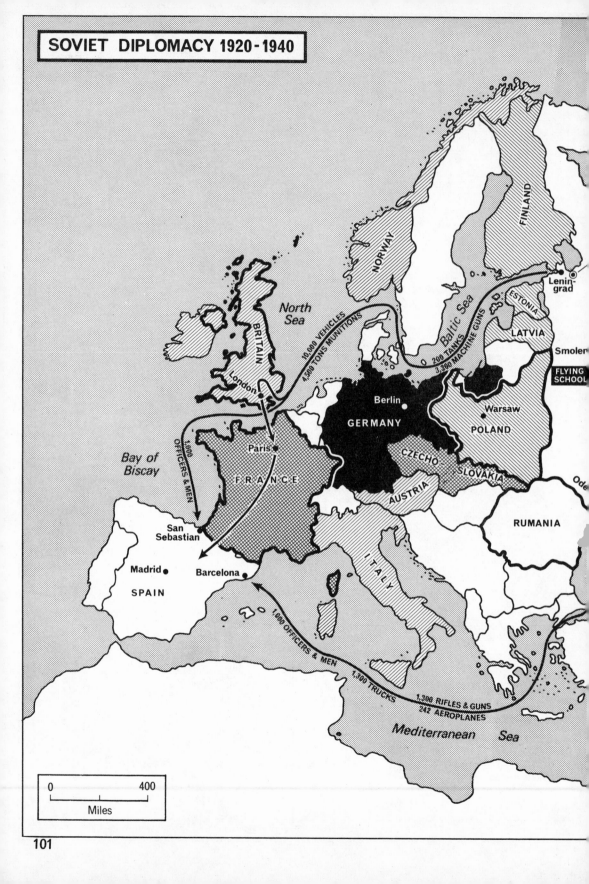

SOVIET DIPLOMACY 1920-1940

North Sea

NORWAY

FINLAND

Lenin-grad

Baltic Sea

ESTONIA

LATVIA

Smoler

FLYING SCHOOL

10,000 VEHICLES

4,500 TONS MUNITIONS

200 TANKS

3,300 MACHINE GUNS

BRITAIN

London

Berlin

GERMANY

Warsaw

POLAND

Bay of Biscay

1,000 OFFICERS & MEN

Paris

FRANCE

CZECHO

SLOVAKIA

AUSTRIA

RUMANIA

Ode

San Sebastian

Madrid

Barcelona

SPAIN

ITALY

1,000 OFFICERS & MEN

1,300 TRUCKS

1,300 RIFLES & GUNS

242 AEROPLANES

Mediterranean Sea

0   400

Miles

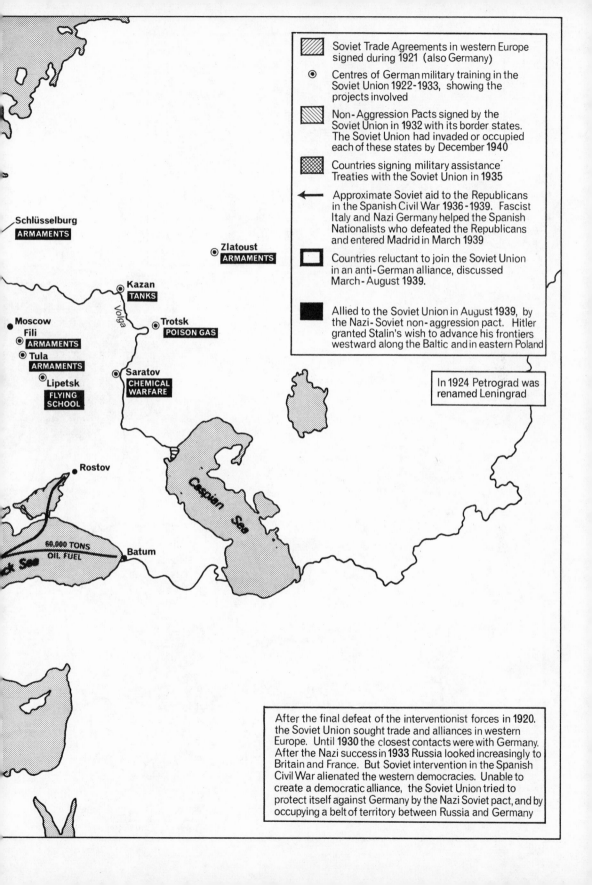

Soviet Trade Agreements in western Europe signed during 1921 (also Germany)

⊙ Centres of German military training in the Soviet Union 1922-1933, showing the projects involved

Non-Aggression Pacts signed by the Soviet Union in 1932 with its border states. The Soviet Union had invaded or occupied each of these states by December 1940

Countries signing military assistance Treaties with the Soviet Union in 1935

← Approximate Soviet aid to the Republicans in the Spanish Civil War 1936-1939. Fascist Italy and Nazi Germany helped the Spanish Nationalists who defeated the Republicans and entered Madrid in March 1939

Countries reluctant to join the Soviet Union in an anti-German alliance, discussed March-August 1939.

Allied to the Soviet Union in August 1939, by the Nazi-Soviet non-aggression pact. Hitler granted Stalin's wish to advance his frontiers westward along the Baltic and in eastern Poland

In 1924 Petrograd was renamed Leningrad

Schlüsselburg
ARMAMENTS

⊙ **Zlatoust**
ARMAMENTS

Kazan
TANKS

Volga

Moscow
Fili
⊙ ARMAMENTS

⊙ **Tula**
ARMAMENTS

⊙ **Lipetsk**
FLYING SCHOOL

⊙ **Trotsk**
POISON GAS

⊙ **Saratov**
CHEMICAL WARFARE

Rostov

Caspian Sea

60,000 TONS OIL FUEL

Batum

Black Sea

After the final defeat of the interventionist forces in 1920, the Soviet Union sought trade and alliances in western Europe. Until 1930 the closest contacts were with Germany. After the Nazi success in 1933 Russia looked increasingly to Britain and France. But Soviet intervention in the Spanish Civil War alienated the western democracies. Unable to create a democratic alliance, the Soviet Union tried to protect itself against Germany by the Nazi Soviet pact, and by occupying a belt of territory between Russia and Germany

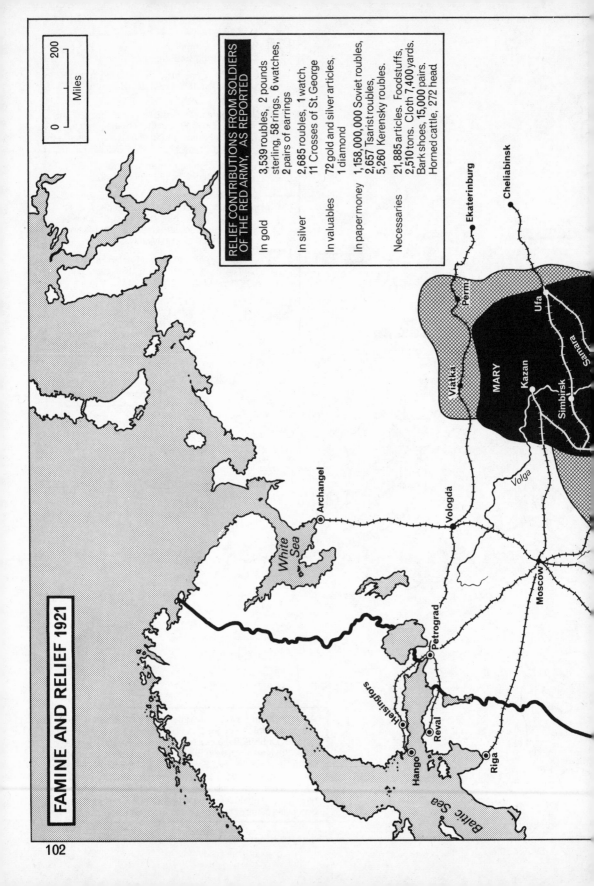

FAMINE AND RELIEF 1921

RELIEF CONTRIBUTIONS FROM SOLDIERS OF THE RED ARMY, AS REPORTED

In gold	3,539 roubles, 2 pounds sterling, 58 rings, 6 watches, 2 pairs of earrings
In silver	2,685 roubles, 1 watch, 11 Crosses of St. George
In valuables	72 gold and silver articles, 1 diamond
In paper money	1,158,000,000 Soviet roubles, 2,657 Tsarist roubles, 5,260 Kerensky roubles.
Necessaries	21,885 articles. Foodstuffs, 2,510 tons. Cloth 7,400 yards. Bark shoes, 15,000 pairs. Horned cattle, 272 head

0   200
Miles

White Sea

Baltic Sea

Volga

Archangel
Vologda
Petrograd
Helsingfors
Reval
Hango
Riga
Moscow
Ekaterinburg
Cheliabinsk
Perm
Viatka
MARY
Kazan
Ufa
Simbirsk
Samara

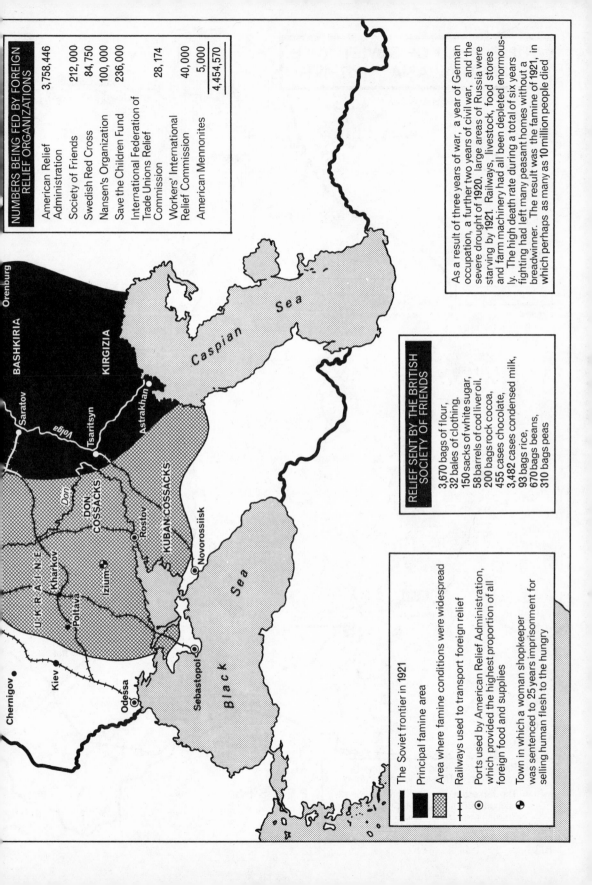

NUMBERS BEING FED BY FOREIGN RELIEF ORGANIZATIONS

American Relief Administration	3,758,446
Society of Friends	212,000
Swedish Red Cross	84,750
Nansen's Organization	100,000
Save the Children Fund	236,000
International Federation of Trade Unions Relief Commission	28,174
Workers' International Relief Commission	40,000
American Mennonites	5,000
	4,454,570

As a result of three years of war, a year of German occupation, a further two years of civil war, and the severe drought of 1920, large areas of Russia were starving by 1921. Railways, livestock, food stores and farm machinery had all been depleted enormously. The high death rate during a total of six years fighting had left many peasant homes without a breadwinner. The result was the famine of 1921, in which perhaps as many as 10 million people died

RELIEF SENT BY THE BRITISH SOCIETY OF FRIENDS

3,670 bags of flour,
32 bales of clothing.
150 sacks of white sugar,
58 barrels of cod liver oil,
200 bags rock cocoa,
455 cases chocolate,
3,482 cases condensed milk,
93 bags rice,
670 bags beans,
310 bags peas

The Soviet frontier in 1921

Principal famine area

Area where famine conditions were widespread

Railways used to transport foreign relief

⊙ Ports used by American Relief Administration, which provided the highest proportion of all foreign food and supplies

● Town in which a woman shopkeeper was sentenced to 25 years imprisonment for selling human flesh to the hungry

Orenburg

BASHKIRIA

KIRGIZIA

Caspian Sea

Saratov

Volga

Tsaritsyn

Astrakhan

Don

DON COSSACKS

Rostov

KUBAN COSSACKS

U K R A I N E

Kharkov

Izium

Poltava

Novorossiisk

Black Sea

Kiev

Odessa

Sebastopol

Chernigov

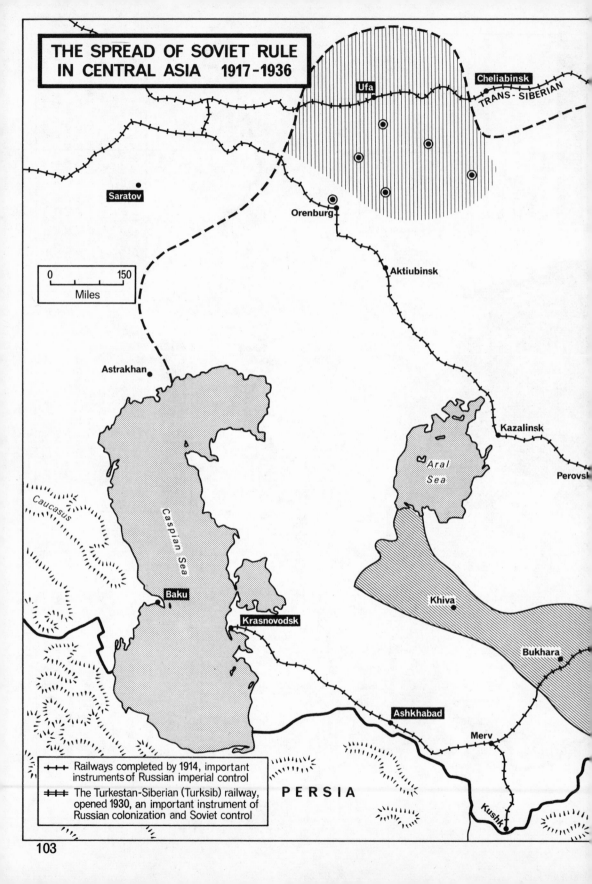

THE SPREAD OF SOVIET RULE
IN CENTRAL ASIA   1917-1936

Cheliabinsk

TRANS-SIBERIAN

Ufa

Saratov

Orenburg

0   150
Miles

Aktiubinsk

Astrakhan

Kazalinsk

Aral Sea

Perovsk

Caucasus

Caspian Sea

Khiva

Bukhara

Baku

Krasnovodsk

Ashkhabad

Merv

PERSIA

Kushk

Railways completed by 1914, important
instruments of Russian imperial control

The Turkestan-Siberian (Turksib) railway,
opened 1930, an important instrument of
Russian colonization and Soviet control

103

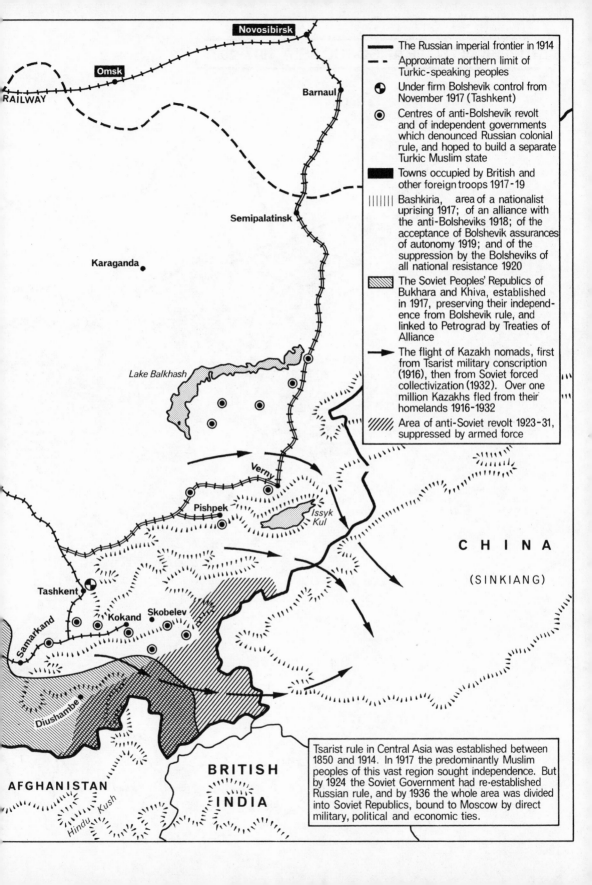

Novosibirsk

Omsk

RAILWAY

Barnaul

The Russian imperial frontier in 1914

Approximate northern limit of Turkic-speaking peoples

Under firm Bolshevik control from November 1917 (Tashkent)

Centres of anti-Bolshevik revolt and of independent governments which denounced Russian colonial rule, and hoped to build a separate Turkic Muslim state

Towns occupied by British and other foreign troops 1917-19

Bashkiria, area of a nationalist uprising 1917; of an alliance with the anti-Bolsheviks 1918; of the acceptance of Bolshevik assurances of autonomy 1919; and of the suppression by the Bolsheviks of all national resistance 1920

The Soviet Peoples' Republics of Bukhara and Khiva, established in 1917, preserving their independence from Bolshevik rule, and linked to Petrograd by Treaties of Alliance

The flight of Kazakh nomads, first from Tsarist military conscription (1916), then from Soviet forced collectivization (1932). Over one million Kazakhs fled from their homelands 1916-1932

Area of anti-Soviet revolt 1923-31, suppressed by armed force

Semipalatinsk

Karaganda

Lake Balkhash

Verny

Pishpek

Issyk Kul

C H I N A

(SINKIANG)

Tashkent

Samarkand

Kokand

Skobelev

Diushambe

AFGHANISTAN

Hindu Kush

BRITISH

INDIA

Tsarist rule in Central Asia was established between 1850 and 1914. In 1917 the predominantly Muslim peoples of this vast region sought independence. But by 1924 the Soviet Government had re-established Russian rule, and by 1936 the whole area was divided into Soviet Republics, bound to Moscow by direct military, political and economic ties.

INDEPENDENT TRANSCAUCASIA 1917-1921

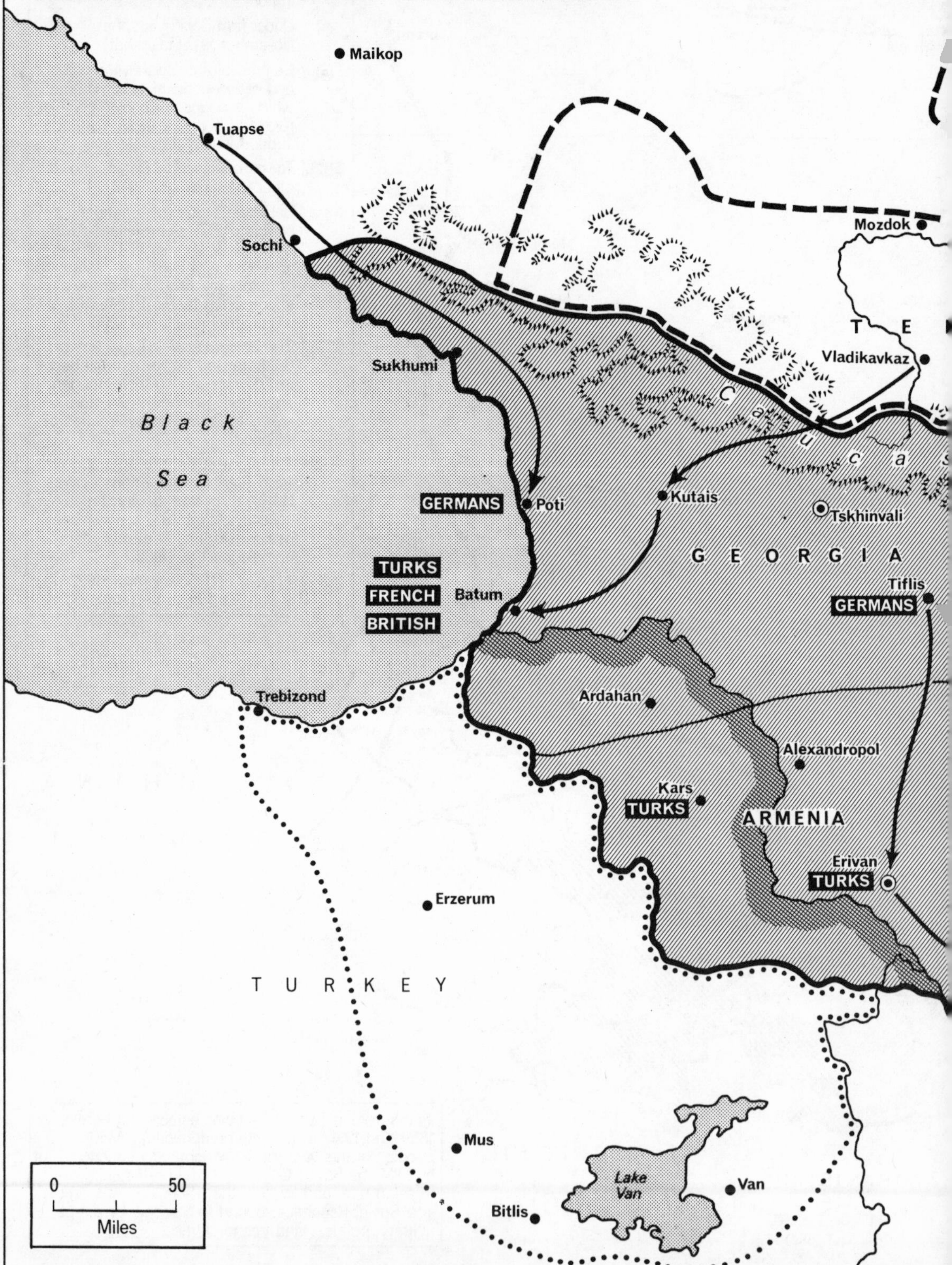

● Maikop

● Tuapse

● Sochi

Black Sea

● Sukhumi

GERMANS ● Poti

● Kutais

● Mozdok

● Vladikavkaz

T E

⊙ Tskhinvali

G E O R G I A

● Tiflis

GERMANS

TURKS
FRENCH
BRITISH ● Batum

● Trebizond

● Ardahan

● Alexandropol

● Kars
TURKS

A R M E N I A

Erivan ⊙
TURKS

● Erzerum

T U R K E Y

● Mus

Lake Van

● Van

● Bitlis

0	50

Miles

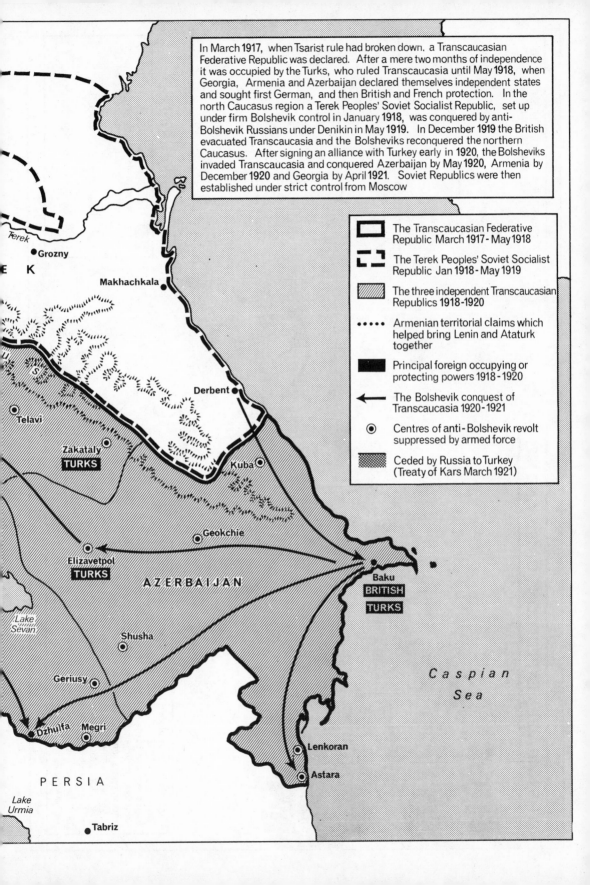

In March 1917, when Tsarist rule had broken down, a Transcaucasian Federative Republic was declared. After a mere two months of independence it was occupied by the Turks, who ruled Transcaucasia until May 1918, when Georgia, Armenia and Azerbaijan declared themselves independent states and sought first German, and then British and French protection. In the north Caucasus region a Terek Peoples' Soviet Socialist Republic, set up under firm Bolshevik control in January 1918, was conquered by anti-Bolshevik Russians under Denikin in May 1919. In December 1919 the British evacuated Transcaucasia and the Bolsheviks reconquered the northern Caucasus. After signing an alliance with Turkey early in 1920, the Bolsheviks invaded Transcaucasia and conquered Azerbaijan by May 1920, Armenia by December 1920 and Georgia by April 1921. Soviet Republics were then established under strict control from Moscow

The Transcaucasian Federative Republic March 1917 - May 1918

The Terek Peoples' Soviet Socialist Republic Jan 1918 - May 1919

The three independent Transcaucasian Republics 1918-1920

••••• Armenian territorial claims which helped bring Lenin and Ataturk together

Principal foreign occupying or protecting powers 1918-1920

← The Bolshevik conquest of Transcaucasia 1920-1921

◉ Centres of anti-Bolshevik revolt suppressed by armed force

Ceded by Russia to Turkey (Treaty of Kars March 1921)

Terek
●Grozny

E K

Makhachkala

●Telavi

Derbent ●

Zakataly ◉
TURKS

Kuba ◉

◉Geokchie

Elizavetpol ◉
TURKS

A Z E R B A I J A N

Baku ●
BRITISH
TURKS

*Lake
Sevan*

Shusha ◉

*C a s p i a n
S e a*

Geriusy ◉

Dzhulfa ● Megri ●

Lenkoran ●

Astara ◉

P E R S I A

*Lake
Urmia*

●Tabriz

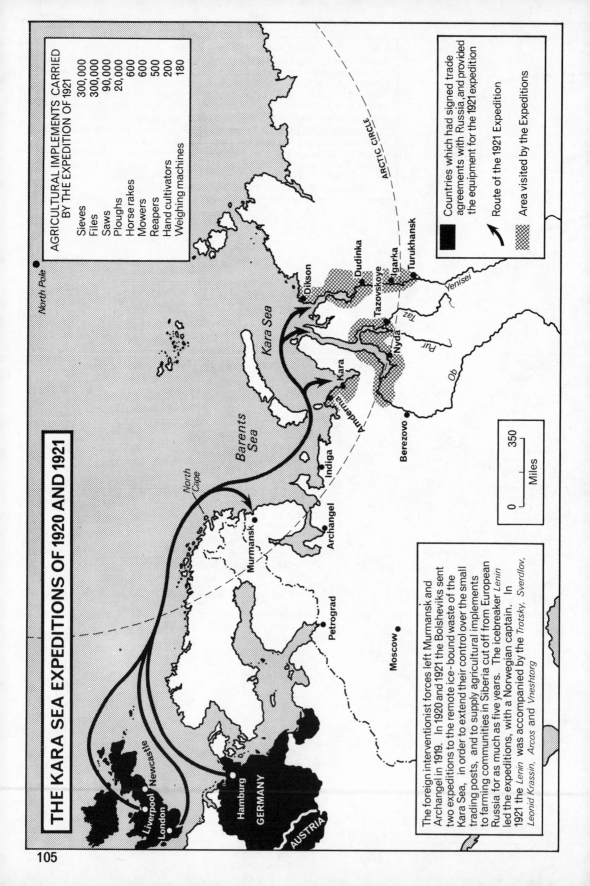

THE KARA SEA EXPEDITIONS OF 1920 AND 1921

AGRICULTURAL IMPLEMENTS CARRIED
BY THE EXPEDITION OF 1921

Sieves	300,000
Files	300,000
Saws	90,000
Ploughs	20,000
Horse rakes	600
Mowers	600
Reapers	500
Hand cultivators	200
Weighing machines	180

Countries which had signed trade
agreements with Russia, and provided
the equipment for the 1921 expedition

Route of the 1921 Expedition

Area visited by the Expeditions

North Pole

ARCTIC CIRCLE

Turukhansk

Igarka

Dudinka

Dikson

Tazovskoye

Nyda

Yenisei

Taz

Pur

Ob

Kara Sea

Kara

Amderma

Berezovo

Barents Sea

Indiga

North Cape

Archangel

Murmansk

0   350
Miles

Petrograd

Moscow

Newcastle

Liverpool

London

Hamburg

GERMANY

AUSTRIA

The foreign interventionist forces left Murmansk and
Archangel in 1919. In 1920 and 1921 the Bolsheviks sent
two expeditions to the remote ice-bound waste of the
Kara Sea, in order to extend their control over the small
trading posts, and to supply agricultural implements
to farming communities in Siberia cut off from European
Russia for as much as five years. The icebreaker *Lenin*
led the expeditions, with a Norwegian captain. In
1921 the *Lenin* was accompanied by the *Trotsky*, *Sverdlov*,
Leonid Krassin, *Arcos* and *Vneshtorg*.

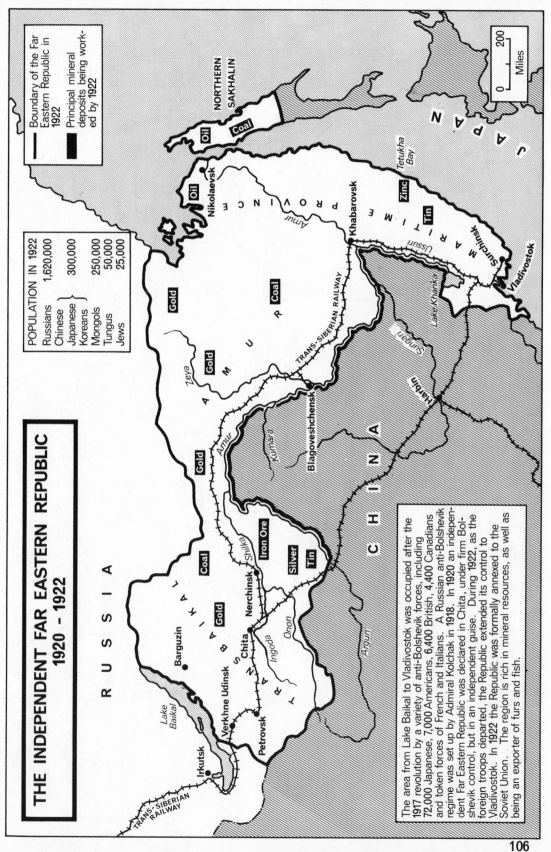

THE INDEPENDENT FAR EASTERN REPUBLIC
1920 - 1922

Boundary of the Far Eastern Republic in 1922	Principal mineral deposits being work- ed by 1922

POPULATION IN 1922

Russians	1,620,000
Chinese	300,000
Japanese }	250,000
Koreans	50,000
Mongols	
Tungus	25,000
Jews	

0 — 200 Miles

JAPAN

NORTHERN SAKHALIN

Oil

Coal

Oil

Nikolaevsk

Tetukha Bay

Zinc

Khabarovsk

Tin

M A R I T I M E   P R O V I N C E

Surchinsk

Amur

Vladivostok

Ussuri

Gold

Coal

A   M   U   R

Lake Khanka

Zeya

Sungari

Gold

Harbin

Gold

Amur

Blagoveshchensk

Kumara

C H I N A

R U S S I A

Coal

Iron Ore

Shilka

Silver

Tin

Barguzin

Gold

Nerchinsk

Lake Baikal

B A I K A L

Chita

Argun

Onon

Verkhne Udinsk

Ingoda

T R A N S

Petrovsk

Irkutsk

TRANS-SIBERIAN RAILWAY

TRANS-SIBERIAN RAILWAY

The area from Lake Baikal to Vladivostok was occupied after the 1917 revolution by a variety of anti-Bolshevik forces, including 72,000 Japanese, 7,000 Americans, 6,400 British, 4,400 Canadians and token forces of French and Italians. A Russian anti-Bolshevik regime was set up by Admiral Kolchak in 1918. In 1920 an independent Far Eastern Republic was declared in Chita, under firm Bolshevik control, but in an independent guise. During 1922, as the foreign troops departed, the Republic extended its control to Vladivostok. In 1922 the Republic was formally annexed to the Soviet Union. The region is rich in mineral resources, as well as being an exporter of furs and fish.

106

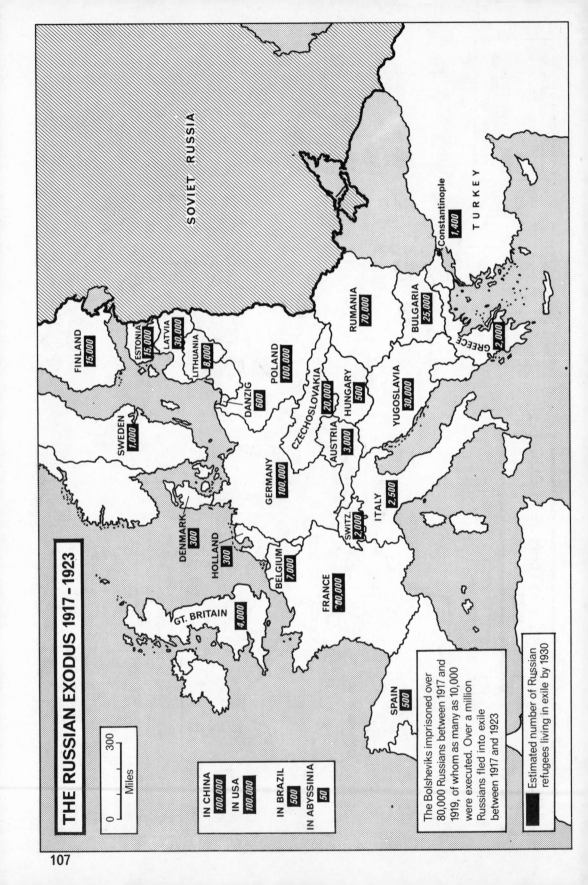

THE RUSSIAN EXODUS 1917–1923

SOVIET RUSSIA

TURKEY

Constantinople
1,400

FINLAND
15,000

ESTONIA
15,000

LATVIA
30,000

LITHUANIA
8,000

RUMANIA
70,000

BULGARIA
25,000

SWEDEN
1,000

POLAND
100,000

DANZIG
500

CZECHOSLOVAKIA
20,000

HUNGARY
500

YUGOSLAVIA
30,000

GREECE
2,000

AUSTRIA
3,000

DENMARK
300

HOLLAND
300

GERMANY
100,000

SWITZ.
2,000

ITALY
2,500

BELGIUM
7,000

FRANCE
200,000

GT. BRITAIN
4,000

SPAIN
500

0	300

Miles

IN CHINA
100,000

IN USA
100,000

IN BRAZIL
500

IN ABYSSINIA
50

The Bolsheviks imprisoned over 80,000 Russians between 1917 and 1919, of whom as many as 10,000 were executed. Over a million Russians fled into exile between 1917 and 1923

Estimated number of Russian refugees living in exile by 1930

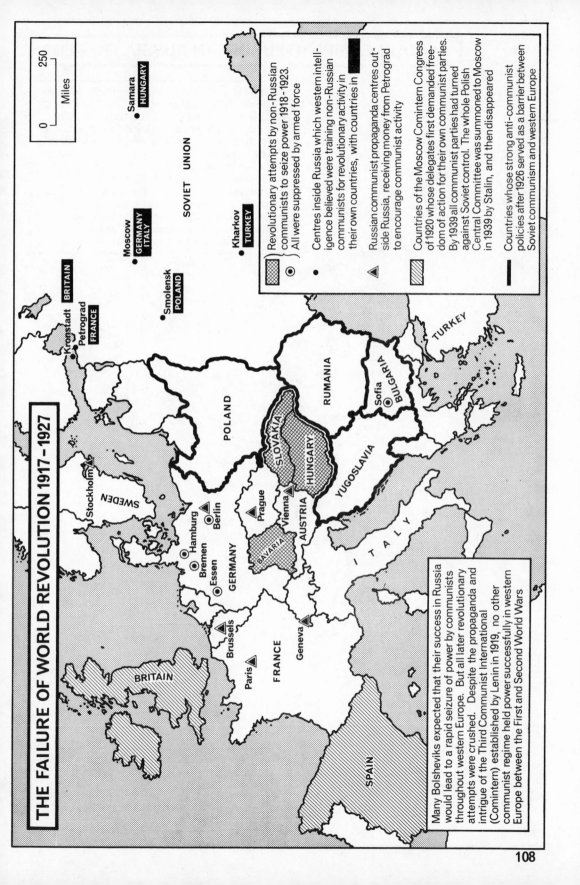

THE FAILURE OF WORLD REVOLUTION 1917–1927

0 250	
Miles	

Legend:

- Revolutionary attempts by non-Russian communists to seize power 1918-1923. All were suppressed by armed force

- Centres inside Russia which western intelligence believed were training non-Russian communists for revolutionary activity in their own countries, with countries in

- Russian communist propaganda centres outside Russia, receiving money from Petrograd to encourage communist activity

- Countries of the Moscow Comintern Congress of 1920 whose delegates first demanded freedom of action for their own communist parties. By 1939 all communist parties had turned against Soviet control. The whole Polish Central Committee was summoned to Moscow in 1939 by Stalin, and then disappeared

- Countries whose strong anti-communist policies after 1926 served as a barrier between Soviet communism and western Europe

Many Bolsheviks expected that their success in Russia would lead to a rapid seizure of power by communists throughout western Europe. But all later revolutionary attempts were crushed. Despite the propaganda and intrigue of the Third Communist International (Comintern) established by Lenin in 1919, no other communist regime held power successfully in western Europe between the First and Second World Wars

Place names and labels on map:

Samara HUNGARY

Moscow GERMANY ITALY

Smolensk POLAND

Kharkov TURKEY

SOVIET UNION

Kronstadt BRITAIN
Petrograd FRANCE

SWEDEN
Stockholm

Hamburg
Bremen
Berlin
Essen
Prague
GERMANY
Vienna
BAVARIA
AUSTRIA
SLOVAKIA
HUNGARY
YUGOSLAVIA

POLAND

RUMANIA

Sofia BULGARIA

Brussels
Paris
FRANCE
Geneva

ITALY

TURKEY

BRITAIN

SPAIN

LABOUR CAMPS IN EUROPEAN RUSSIA 1917-1936

Barents Sea

NORWAY

In February 1917 a spontaneous amnesty led to the release of all Tsarist political prisoners and exiles. Many returned from the remote corners of Russia to play a prominent part in the Bolshevik revolution. But the Bolsheviks themselves soon began sending their opponents and critics to forced labour camps (Corrective Labour Colonies). By 1930 there were an estimated minimum of 750,000 prisoners employed by the CHEKA (later OGPU), the Soviet political and security Police. Conditions were as bad as they had been in Tsarist times for political prisoners sent to the Kara Mines, and were far worse than for the majority of Tsarist exiles

Kanin Nos

Murmansk

Lake Imandra

KOLA

Kandalakskaya

PENINSULA

Kovda

ARCTIC CIRCLE

FINLAND

Lake Top

White Sea

Ukhta

Solovetski Island

Kem **Kem**

Archangel

Onega Bay

KARELIA

Onega

Onega

Lake Seg

Lake Vyg

Northern Dvina

Lake Onega

Petrozavodsk

Svir

Lake Ladoga

Svirstroi

⊙ Forced labour camps set up in Northern European Russia 1917-1936

━━ The Belomor (White Sea) canal, built almost entirely by forced labour, in conditions of extreme hardship

Leningrad   **Volkhov**

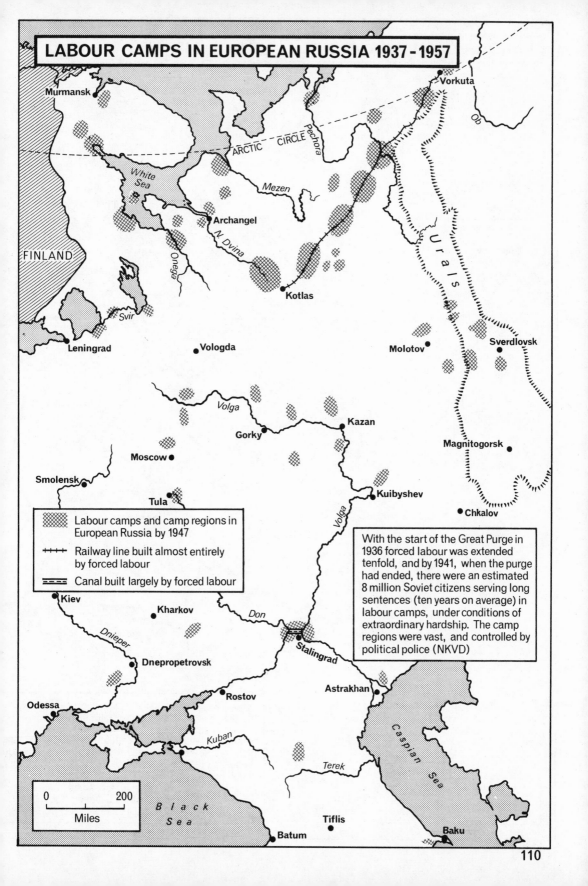

LABOUR CAMPS IN EUROPEAN RUSSIA 1937 - 1957

Murmansk

Vorkuta

ARCTIC CIRCLE

Pechora

Ob

White
Sea

Mezen

Urals

Archangel

N Dvina

FINLAND

Onega

Kotlas

Svir

Leningrad

Vologda

Molotov

Sverdlovsk

Volga

Gorky

Kazan

Magnitogorsk

Moscow

Smolensk

Tula

Kuibyshev

Chkalov

Labour camps and camp regions in
European Russia by 1947

Railway line built almost entirely
by forced labour

Canal built largely by forced labour

Kiev

Kharkov

Don

With the start of the Great Purge in
1936 forced labour was extended
tenfold, and by 1941, when the purge
had ended, there were an estimated
8 million Soviet citizens serving long
sentences (ten years on average) in
labour camps, under conditions of
extraordinary hardship. The camp
regions were vast, and controlled by
political police (NKVD)

Dnieper

Stalingrad

Dnepropetrovsk

Astrakhan

Odessa

Rostov

Caspian
Sea

Kuban

0   200

Miles

Black
Sea

Terek

Tiflis

Baku

Batum

110

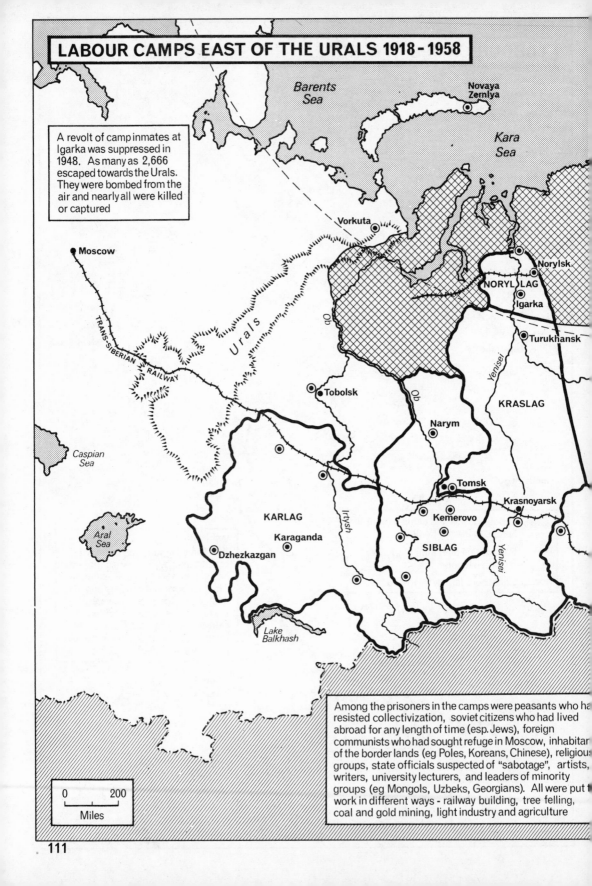

LABOUR CAMPS EAST OF THE URALS 1918-1958

Barents Sea

Kara Sea

Novaya Zemlya

A revolt of camp inmates at Igarka was suppressed in 1948. As many as 2,666 escaped towards the Urals. They were bombed from the air and nearly all were killed or captured

Vorkuta

Norylsk

NORYLLAG

Igarka

Turukhansk

Moscow

Ob

U r a l s

Ob

Yenisei

TRANS-SIBERIAN RAILWAY

Tobolsk

Narym

KRASLAG

Caspian Sea

Tomsk

Krasnoyarsk

KARLAG

Kemerovo

Irtysh

Yenisei

SIBLAG

Karaganda

Aral Sea

Dzhezkazgan

Lake Balkhash

| 0 | 200 |
Miles

Among the prisoners in the camps were peasants who ha[d] resisted collectivization, soviet citizens who had lived abroad for any length of time (esp. Jews), foreign communists who had sought refuge in Moscow, inhabitan[ts] of the border lands (eg Poles, Koreans, Chinese), religiou[s] groups, state officials suspected of "sabotage", artists, writers, university lecturers, and leaders of minority groups (eg Mongols, Uzbeks, Georgians). All were put t[o] work in different ways - railway building, tree felling, coal and gold mining, light industry and agriculture

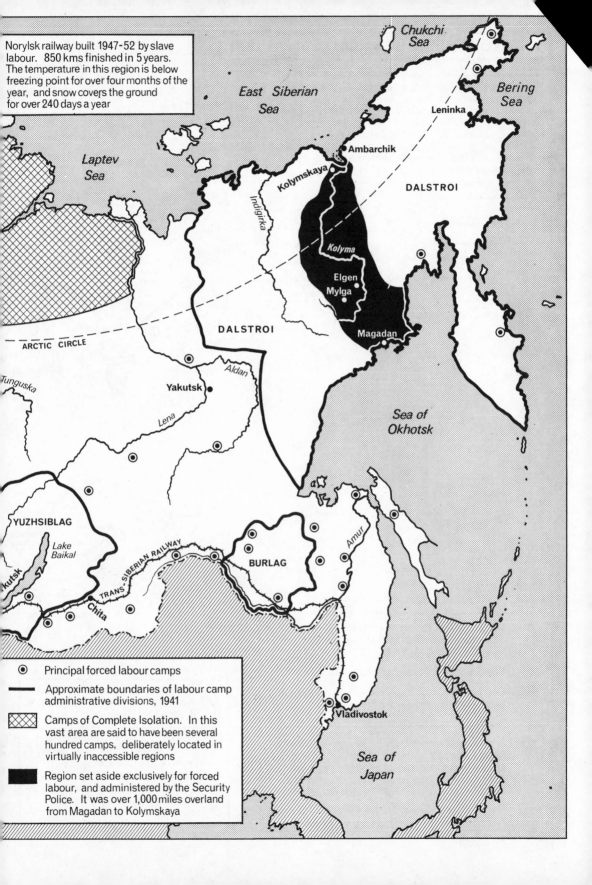

Norylsk railway built 1947-52 by slave labour. 850 kms finished in 5 years. The temperature in this region is below freezing point for over four months of the year, and snow covers the ground for over 240 days a year

Chukchi Sea

East Siberian Sea

Bering Sea

Leninka

Laptev Sea

Ambarchik

Kolymskaya

DALSTROI

Indigirka

Kolyma

Elgen
Mylga

Tunguska

ARCTIC CIRCLE

Aldan

DALSTROI

Magadan

Yakutsk

Lena

Sea of Okhotsk

YUZHSIBLAG

Lake Baikal

Amur

BURLAG

TRANS-SIBERIAN RAILWAY

kutsk

Chita

Vladivostok

Sea of Japan

⊙ Principal forced labour camps

── Approximate boundaries of labour camp administrative divisions, 1941

⧄ Camps of Complete Isolation. In this vast area are said to have been several hundred camps, deliberately located in virtually inaccessible regions

■ Region set aside exclusively for forced labour, and administered by the Security Police. It was over 1,000 miles overland from Magadan to Kolymskaya

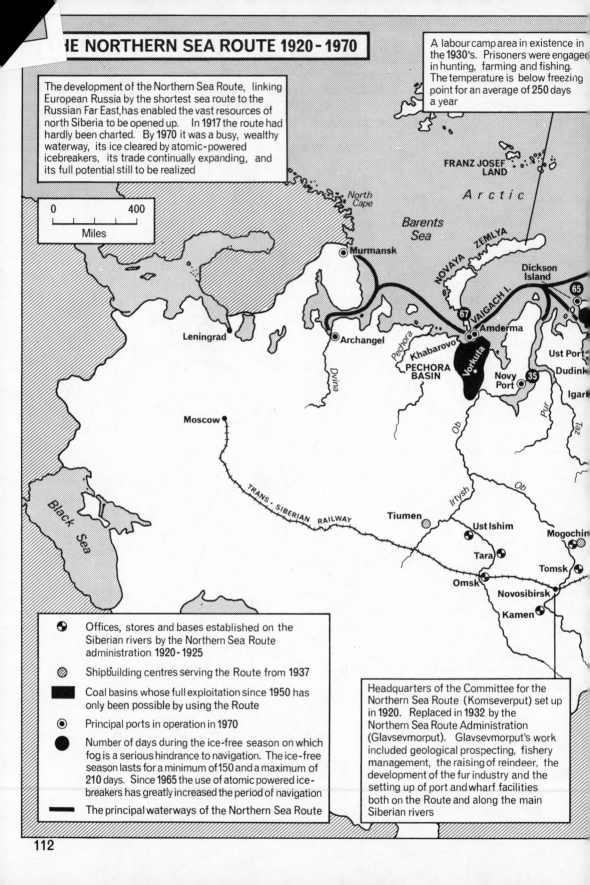

HE NORTHERN SEA ROUTE 1920-1970

A labour camp area in existence in the 1930's. Prisoners were engaged in hunting, farming and fishing. The temperature is below freezing point for an average of 250 days a year

The development of the Northern Sea Route, linking European Russia by the shortest sea route to the Russian Far East, has enabled the vast resources of north Siberia to be opened up. In 1917 the route had hardly been charted. By 1970 it was a busy, wealthy waterway, its ice cleared by atomic-powered icebreakers, its trade continually expanding, and its full potential still to be realized

FRANZ JOSEF LAND

Arctic

North Cape

Barents Sea

NOVAYA ZEMLYA

Murmansk

Dickson Island

65

67 VAIGACH I.

Amderma

Leningrad

Archangel

Pechora

Khabarovo

Vorkuta

Ust Port

PECHORA BASIN

Novy Port

Dudink

Dvina

Moscow

Ob

Pur

Igar

Taz

TRANS-SIBERIAN RAILWAY

Irtysh

Ob

Tiumen

Ust Ishim

Mogochin

Tara

Tomsk

Black Sea

Omsk

Novosibirsk

Kamen

0   400
Miles

◔ Offices, stores and bases established on the Siberian rivers by the Northern Sea Route administration 1920-1925

▨ Shipbuilding centres serving the Route from 1937

▬ Coal basins whose full exploitation since 1950 has only been possible by using the Route

◉ Principal ports in operation in 1970

● Number of days during the ice-free season on which fog is a serious hindrance to navigation. The ice-free season lasts for a minimum of 150 and a maximum of 210 days. Since 1965 the use of atomic powered ice-breakers has greatly increased the period of navigation

▬ The principal waterways of the Northern Sea Route

Headquarters of the Committee for the Northern Sea Route (Komseverput) set up in 1920. Replaced in 1932 by the Northern Sea Route Administration (Glavsevmorput). Glavsevmorput's work included geological prospecting, fishery management, the raising of reindeer, the development of the fur industry and the setting up of port and wharf facilities both on the Route and along the main Siberian rivers

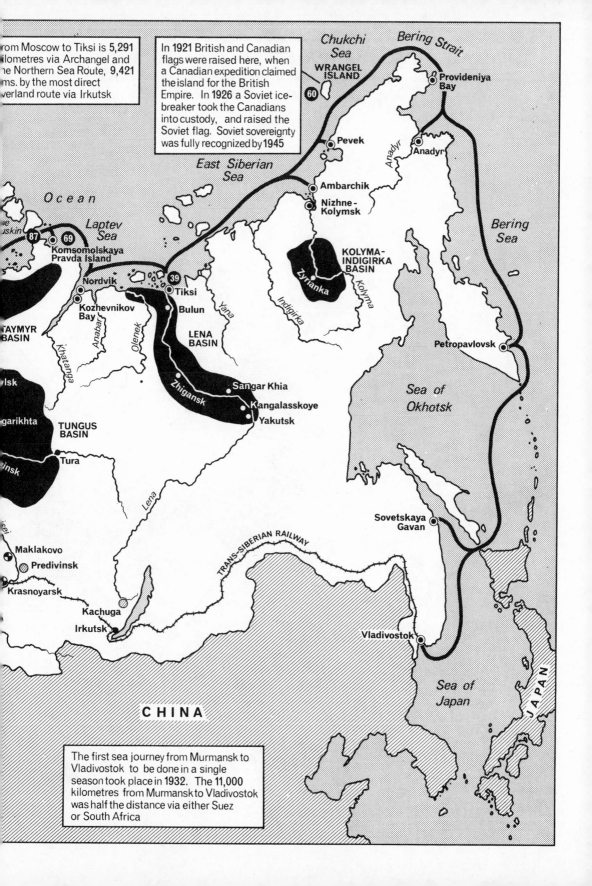

rom Moscow to Tiksi is **5,291** ilometres via Archangel and he Northern Sea Route, **9,421** ms. by the most direct verland route via Irkutsk

In **1921** British and Canadian flags were raised here, when a Canadian expedition claimed the island for the British Empire. In **1926** a Soviet ice-breaker took the Canadians into custody, and raised the Soviet flag. Soviet sovereignty was fully recognized by **1945**

Chukchi Sea

Bering Strait

WRANGEL ISLAND

60

Provideniya Bay

East Siberian Sea

Pevek

Anadyr

Anadyr

Ocean

Ambarchik

Bering Sea

Nizhne-Kolymsk

Laptev Sea

uskin

87

69

Komsomolskaya Pravda Island

KOLYMA-INDIGIRKA BASIN

Zyrianka

Kolyma

Nordvik

39

Tiksi

AYMYR BASIN

Kozhevnikov Bay

Anabar

Olenek

Bulun

Yana

Indigirka

Petropavlovsk

Khatanga

LENA BASIN

lsk

Zhigansk

Sangar Khia

Sea of Okhotsk

garikhta

TUNGUS BASIN

Kangalasskoye

Yakutsk

Tura

Lena

insk

Maklakovo

TRANS-SIBERIAN RAILWAY

Sovetskaya Gavan

Predivinsk

el

Krasnoyarsk

Kachuga

Irkutsk

Vladivostok

J A P A N

C H I N A

Sea of Japan

The first sea journey from Murmansk to Vladivostok to be done in a single season took place in **1932**. The **11,000** kilometres from Murmansk to Vladivostok was half the distance via either Suez or South Africa

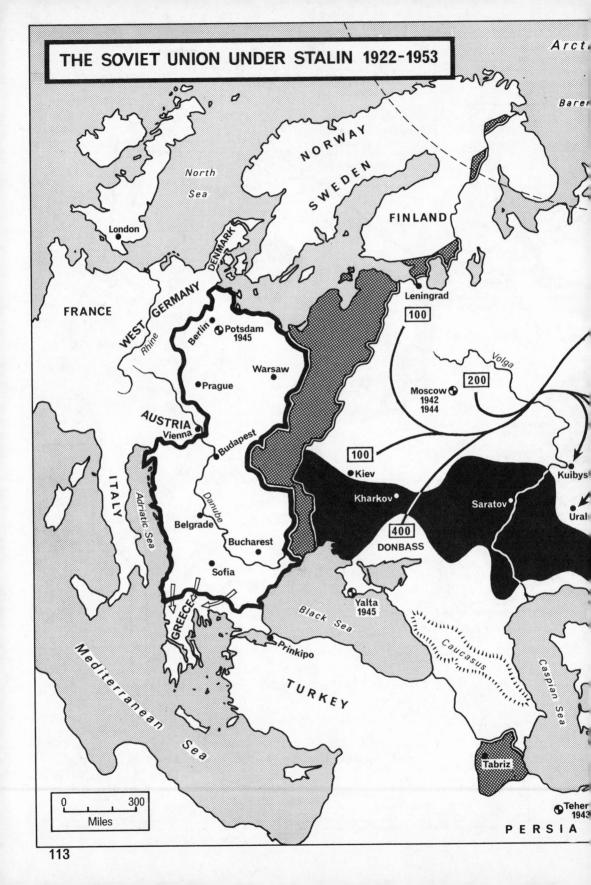

THE SOVIET UNION UNDER STALIN 1922-1953

Arct

Baren

North Sea

NORWAY

SWEDEN

FINLAND

London

FRANCE

WEST GERMANY

DENMARK

Rhine

Berlin

⊕ Potsdam
1945

Warsaw

Leningrad

100

Prague

Volga

Moscow ⊕
1942
1944

200

AUSTRIA
Vienna

Budapest

ITALY

Adriatic Sea

Danube

100

Kiev

Kharkov

Saratov

Kuibys

Belgrade

Bucharest

400

DONBASS

Ural

Sofia

GREECE

Yalta
1945

Black Sea

Caucasus

Caspian Sea

Prinkipo

TURKEY

Mediterranean Sea

Tabriz

⊕ Teher
1943

0   300

Miles

PERSIA

113

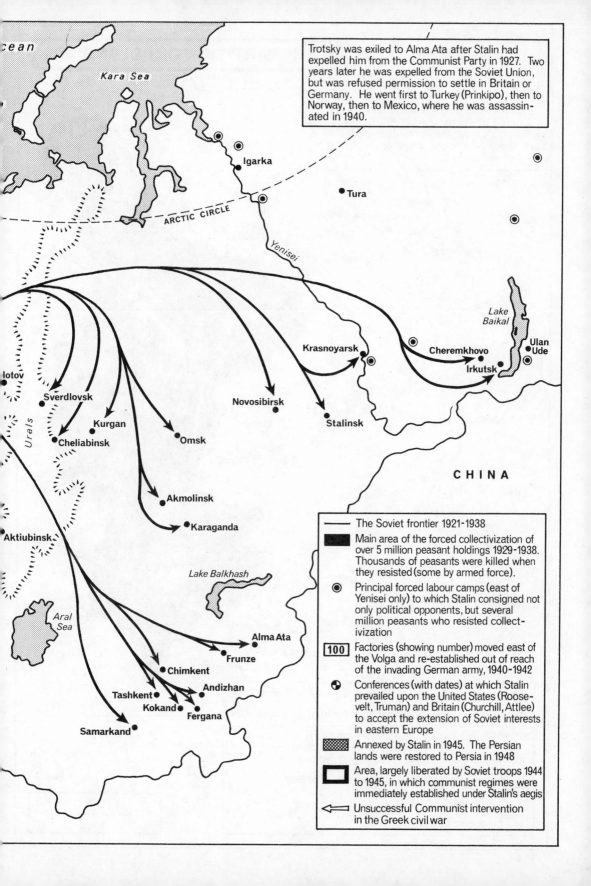

Trotsky was exiled to Alma Ata after Stalin had
expelled him from the Communist Party in 1927. Two
years later he was expelled from the Soviet Union,
but was refused permission to settle in Britain or
Germany. He went first to Turkey (Prinkipo), then to
Norway, then to Mexico, where he was assassin-
ated in 1940.

Kara Sea

⊙cean

Igarka

ARCTIC CIRCLE

Tura

Yenisei

Lake
Baikal

Krasnoyarsk
Cheremkhovo
Ulan
Ude
Irkutsk

lotov
Sverdlovsk

Kurgan
Cheliabinsk

Urals

Novosibirsk

Stalinsk

Omsk

CHINA

Akmolinsk

Aktiubinsk

Karaganda

Lake Balkhash

Aral
Sea

Alma Ata
Frunze

Chimkent

Andizhan

Tashkent

Kokand
Fergana

Samarkand

The Soviet frontier 1921-1938

Main area of the forced collectivization of
over 5 million peasant holdings 1929-1938.
Thousands of peasants were killed when
they resisted (some by armed force).

Principal forced labour camps (east of
Yenisei only) to which Stalin consigned not
only political opponents, but several
million peasants who resisted collectivization

| 100 | Factories (showing number) moved east of
the Volga and re-established out of reach
of the invading German army, 1940-1942

Conferences (with dates) at which Stalin
prevailed upon the United States (Roose-
velt, Truman) and Britain (Churchill, Attlee)
to accept the extension of Soviet interests
in eastern Europe

Annexed by Stalin in 1945. The Persian
lands were restored to Persia in 1948

Area, largely liberated by Soviet troops 1944
to 1945, in which communist regimes were
immediately established under Stalin's aegis

Unsuccessful Communist intervention
in the Greek civil war

THE PARTITION OF POLAND 1939

The destruction of Poland was principally a German action. 1,700,000 German troops soon defeated the 600,000 Polish soldiers. German air attack destroyed the centres of the main Polish cities. The Poles hoped to make a final stand in the Pripet marsh area, but the Russian advance destroyed all chance of further Polish resistance

Baltic Sea

LITHUANIA

Königsberg

EAST PRUSSIA

Vilna

Suvalki

Minsk

Augustov

Grodno

Lomza

Bialystok

RUSSIA

Posnan

Warsaw

Brest-Litovsk

Pinsk

Pripet

Marshes

P O L A N D

Lodz

Lublin

SOVIET

GERMANY

Lutsk

Sokal

Rovno

Tarnov

Cracow

Yaroslav

Lvov

Tarnopol

Przemysl

Stanislavov

Kamenets Podolsk

SLOVAKIA

HUNGARY

RUMANIA

Legend:
- German advance against Poland from 3 September 1939
- Russian advance against Poland from 17 September 1939
- Dividing line between the German and Russian zones of occupation, agreed upon in advance by the Russo-German Pact of 23 August 1939
- Annexed by the Soviet Union in October 1939
- Annexed by Germany
- Annexed by Lithuania

0   100

Miles

114

THE RUSSO – FINNISH WAR 1939 – 1940

Atlantic
Ocean

NORWAY

Russian fears of Germany and German influence led to the invasion of Finland in November 1939. The Finns had been independent from Russia for 22 years, and fought tenaciously to preserve their independence. French and British volunteers fought on the Finnish side. In March 1940 the Finns agreed to the Treaty of Moscow and the war was over. Russia gained territory around Leningrad and further protection for the Leningrad to Murmansk railway

Petsamo

Murmansk

Kandalaksha

WAR DEAD	
Finnish	30,000
Russian	80,000

Salla

SWEDEN

Kemijaervi

Tornea

Kem

```
0          100
    Miles
```

Suomussalmi

Kajaani

S O V I E T

Lake
Onega

Vaasa

FINLAND

Tampere

Lake
Ladoga

U N I O N

Vyborg

Abo

Helsinki

Gulf of Finland

Leningrad

Hangö

Tallin

Stockholm

ESTONIA

Baltic
Sea

Gulf of Bothnia

▨	Occupied by Russia in October 1939
←	Russian attacks on Finland in November 1939
⊏⊐	The Mannerheim Line defences, broken by Russian assaults by land, sea and air
■	Finnish territory ceded to Russia by the Treaty of Moscow
▨	Russia granted access to the Norwegian border by Finland
⊙	Russia given a thirty-year lease on the strategic Hangö Peninsula

LATVIA

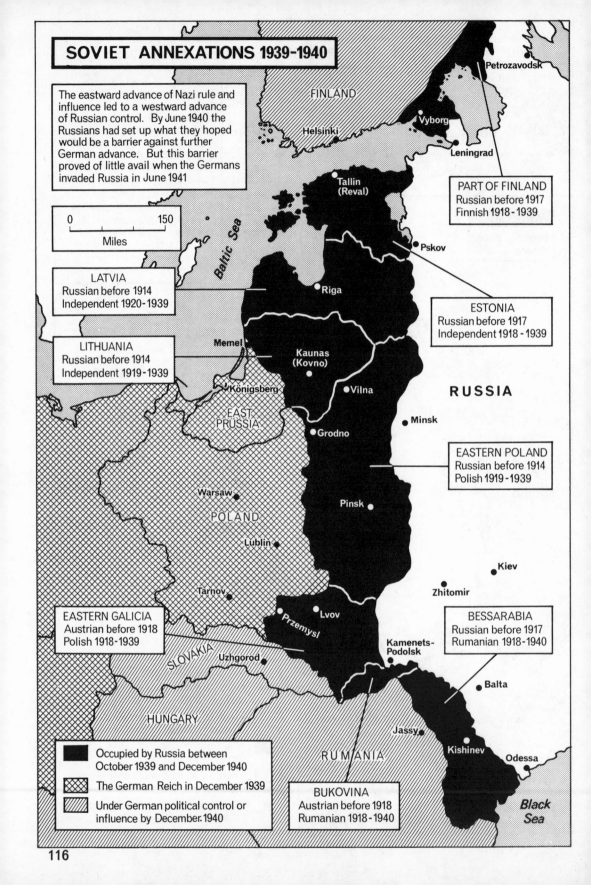

SOVIET ANNEXATIONS 1939-1940

The eastward advance of Nazi rule and
influence led to a westward advance
of Russian control. By June 1940 the
Russians had set up what they hoped
would be a barrier against further
German advance. But this barrier
proved of little avail when the Germans
invaded Russia in June 1941

0 ——— 150
Miles

FINLAND

Helsinki

Vyborg

Leningrad

Tallin
(Reval)

PART OF FINLAND
Russian before 1917
Finnish 1918 - 1939

Pskov

Baltic Sea

Riga

LATVIA
Russian before 1914
Independent 1920-1939

ESTONIA
Russian before 1917
Independent 1918 - 1939

Memel

Kaunas
(Kovno)

LITHUANIA
Russian before 1914
Independent 1919-1939

Königsberg

EAST
PRUSSIA

Vilna

RUSSIA

Minsk

Grodno

Warsaw

POLAND

EASTERN POLAND
Russian before 1914
Polish 1919-1939

Pinsk

Lublin

Kiev

Tarnov

Zhitomir

EASTERN GALICIA
Austrian before 1918
Polish 1918-1939

Przemysl

Lvov

BESSARABIA
Russian before 1917
Rumanian 1918-1940

Kamenets-
Podolsk

SLOVAKIA

Uzhgorod

Balta

HUNGARY

Jassy

RUMANIA

Kishinev

Odessa

Occupied by Russia between
October 1939 and December 1940

The German Reich in December 1939

Under German political control or
influence by December 1940

BUKOVINA
Austrian before 1918
Rumanian 1918-1940

Black
Sea

EUROPE ON 22 JUNE 1941

Archangel

NORWAY

SWEDEN

FINLAND

Hango

Leningrad

DENMARK

Riga

Kovno

Moscow

Vilna

BRITAIN

EIRE

HOLLAND

London

Danzig

Berlin

Warsaw

Brest-Litovsk

SOVIET UNION

GREATER GERMANY

BELGIUM

Cologne

Cracow

Lvov

FRANCE

Prague

SLOVAKIA

Munich

SWITZ.

Vienna

HUNGARY

Kishinev

Odessa

RUMANIA

SPAIN

ITALY

YUGOSLAVIA

BULGARIA

ALBANIA

TURKEY

GREECE

The German Reich on 22 June 1941, the day of the German invasion of Russia

Countries under German rule or influence by June 1941

Neutral countries

Great Britain, the only state at war with Germany on 21 June 1941; and the Soviet Union, to whom Britain immediately offered all possible help and alliance in the fight against Nazism

0   300

Miles

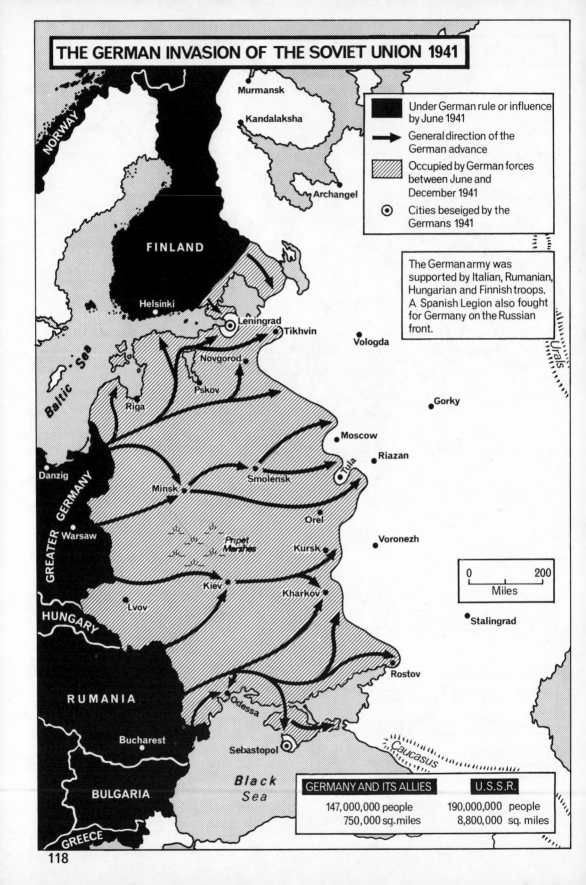

THE GERMAN INVASION OF THE SOVIET UNION 1941

Under German rule or influence by June 1941

General direction of the German advance

Occupied by German forces between June and December 1941

⊙ Cities beseiged by the Germans 1941

The German army was supported by Italian, Rumanian, Hungarian and Finnish troops. A Spanish Legion also fought for Germany on the Russian front.

NORWAY

Murmansk

Kandalaksha

Archangel

FINLAND

Helsinki

Baltic Sea

Leningrad
Tikhvin

Novgorod

Vologda

Pskov

Riga

Gorky

Moscow

Danzig

Minsk
Smolensk

Riazan

Tula

GREATER GERMANY

Warsaw

Orel

Voronezh

Pripet Marshes

Kursk

Kiev

Kharkov

HUNGARY

Lvov

Stalingrad

0   200
Miles

Rostov

RUMANIA

Odessa

Bucharest

Sebastopol

Caucasus

Black Sea

BULGARIA

GREECE

GERMANY AND ITS ALLIES	U.S.S.R.
147,000,000 people	190,000,000 people
750,000 sq. miles	8,800,000 sq. miles

Urals

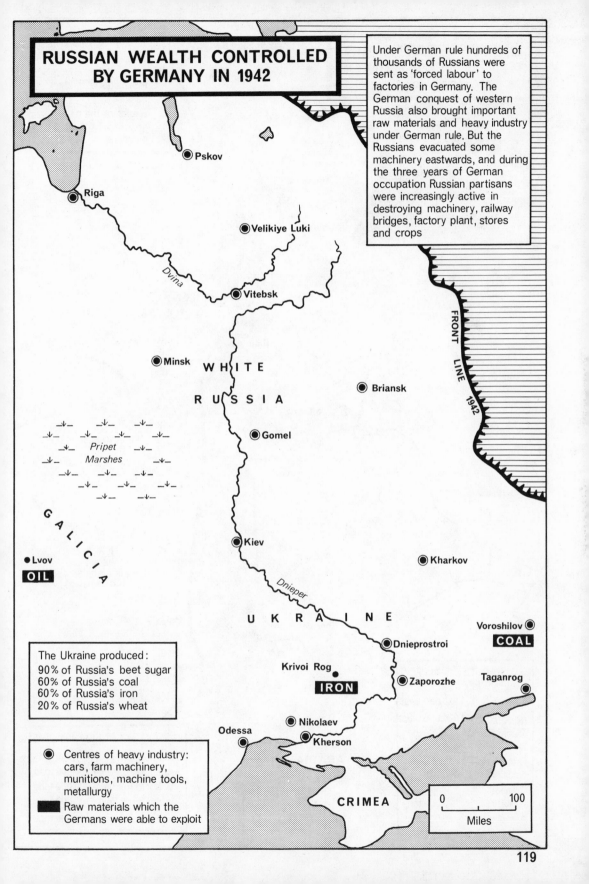

RUSSIAN WEALTH CONTROLLED BY GERMANY IN 1942

Under German rule hundreds of thousands of Russians were sent as 'forced labour' to factories in Germany. The German conquest of western Russia also brought important raw materials and heavy industry under German rule. But the Russians evacuated some machinery eastwards, and during the three years of German occupation Russian partisans were increasingly active in destroying machinery, railway bridges, factory plant, stores and crops

Pskov

Riga

Velikiye Luki

Dvina

Vitebsk

FRONT LINE 1942

Minsk

W H I T E

R U S S I A

Briansk

Gomel

Pripet
Marshes

G A L I C I A

Kiev

Lvov

OIL

Dnieper

Kharkov

U K R A I N E

Voroshilov

COAL

Dnieprostroi

Krivoi Rog

Zaporozhe

Taganrog

IRON

The Ukraine produced:
90% of Russia's beet sugar
60% of Russia's coal
60% of Russia's iron
20% of Russia's wheat

Odessa

Nikolaev

Kherson

◉ Centres of heavy industry:
cars, farm machinery,
munitions, machine tools,
metallurgy

■ Raw materials which the
Germans were able to exploit

C R I M E A

0   100

Miles

119

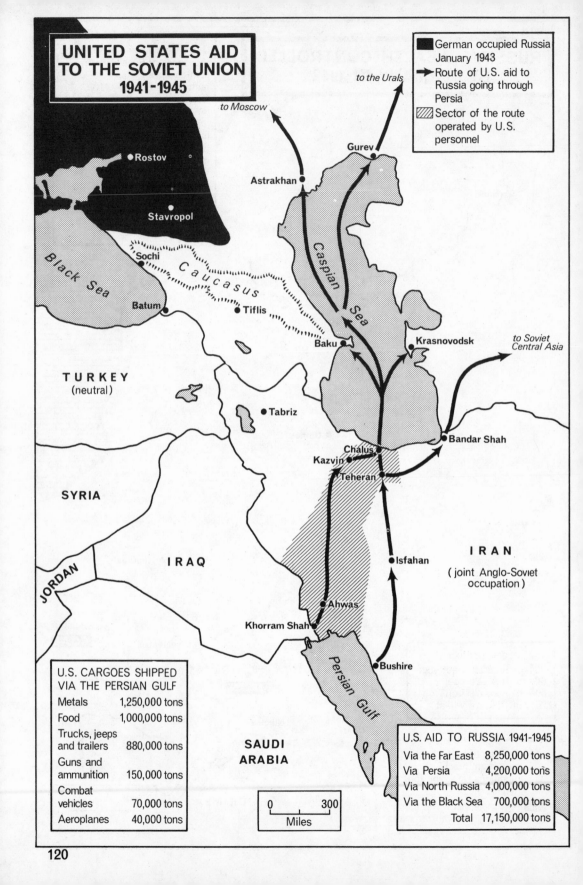

UNITED STATES AID TO THE SOVIET UNION 1941-1945

- ■ German occupied Russia January 1943
- → Route of U.S. aid to Russia going through Persia
- ▨ Sector of the route operated by U.S. personnel

Rostov

Stavropol

to Moscow

to the Urals

Gurev

Astrakhan

Black Sea

Sochi

Caucasus

Batum

Tiflis

Baku

Caspian Sea

Krasnovodsk

to Soviet Central Asia

TURKEY
(neutral)

Tabriz

Bandar Shah

Chalus

Kazvin

Teheran

SYRIA

IRAN
(joint Anglo-Soviet occupation)

Isfahan

IRAQ

JORDAN

Ahwas

Khorram Shah

Bushire

Persian Gulf

SAUDI ARABIA

U.S. CARGOES SHIPPED VIA THE PERSIAN GULF

Metals	1,250,000 tons
Food	1,000,000 tons
Trucks, jeeps and trailers	880,000 tons
Guns and ammunition	150,000 tons
Combat vehicles	70,000 tons
Aeroplanes	40,000 tons

U.S. AID TO RUSSIA 1941-1945

Via the Far East	8,250,000 tons
Via Persia	4,200,000 tons
Via North Russia	4,000,000 tons
Via the Black Sea	700,000 tons
Total	17,150,000 tons

0   300
Miles

120

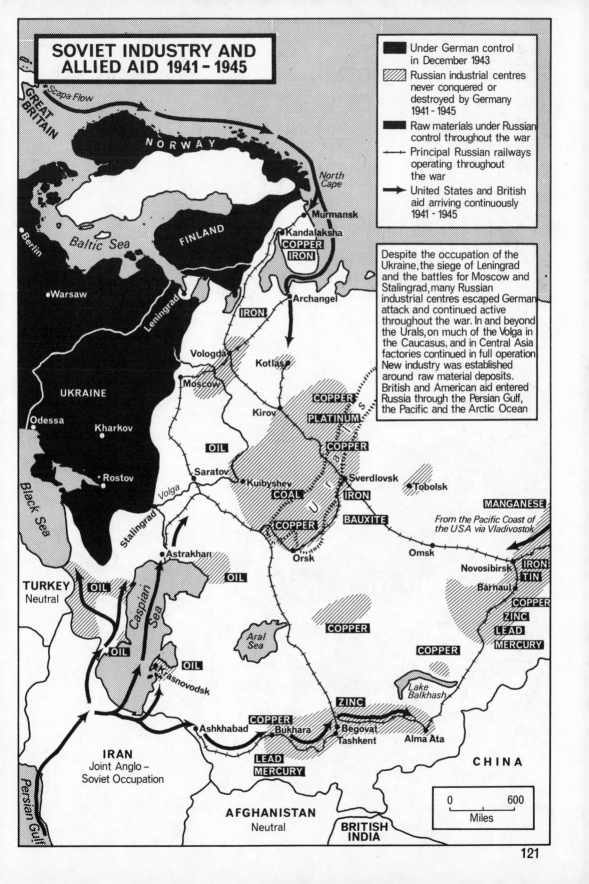

SOVIET INDUSTRY AND ALLIED AID 1941 - 1945

Legend:

- ■ Under German control in December 1943
- ▨ Russian industrial centres never conquered or destroyed by Germany 1941 - 1945
- ■ Raw materials under Russian control throughout the war
- ┼─┼ Principal Russian railways operating throughout the war
- ➤ United States and British aid arriving continuously 1941 - 1945

Despite the occupation of the Ukraine, the siege of Leningrad and the battles for Moscow and Stalingrad, many Russian industrial centres escaped German attack and continued active throughout the war. In and beyond the Urals, on much of the Volga in the Caucasus, and in Central Asia factories continued in full operation. New industry was established around raw material deposits. British and American aid entered Russia through the Persian Gulf, the Pacific and the Arctic Ocean

GREAT BRITAIN

Scapa Flow

NORWAY

North Cape

Baltic Sea

FINLAND

Berlin

Warsaw

Murmansk

Kandalaksha
COPPER
IRON

IRON

Archangel

Leningrad

Vologda

Kotlas

UKRAINE

Moscow

Kirov

COPPER

PLATINUM

COPPER

Odessa

Kharkov

OIL

Saratov

Kuibyshev

Sverdlovsk

Tobolsk

MANGANESE

From the Pacific Coast of the USA via Vladivostok

Rostov

COAL

IRON

BAUXITE

Black Sea

Volga

Stalingrad

COPPER

Orsk

Omsk

Novosibirsk
IRON
TIN

Astrakhan

OIL

Barnaul

COPPER

TURKEY
Neutral

OIL

OIL

Caspian Sea

Aral Sea

COPPER

ZINC
LEAD
MERCURY

OIL

Krasnovodsk

COPPER

Lake Balkhash

ZINC

Ashkhabad

COPPER
Bukhara

Begovat
Tashkent

Alma Ata

CHINA

IRAN
Joint Anglo – Soviet Occupation

LEAD
MERCURY

Persian Gulf

AFGHANISTAN
Neutral

BRITISH INDIA

0   600
Miles

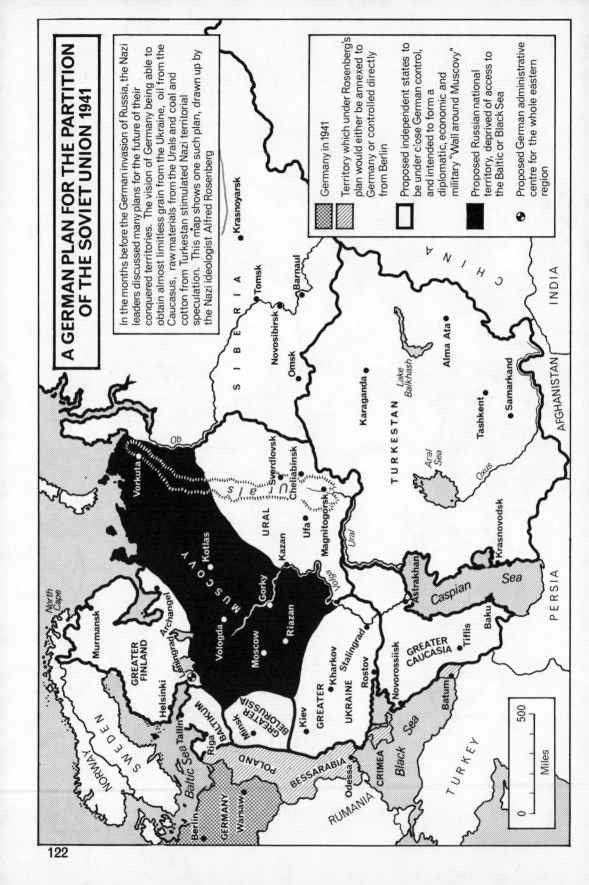

A GERMAN PLAN FOR THE PARTITION OF THE SOVIET UNION 1941

In the months before the German invasion of Russia, the Nazi leaders discussed many plans for the future of their conquered territories. The vision of Germany being able to obtain almost limitless grain from the Ukraine, oil from the Caucasus, raw materials from the Urals and coal and cotton from Turkestan stimulated Nazi territorial speculation. This map shows one such plan, drawn up by the Nazi ideologist Alfred Rosenberg

Germany in 1941

Territory which under Rosenberg's plan would either be annexed to Germany or controlled directly from Berlin

Proposed independent states to be under close German control, and intended to form a diplomatic, economic and military "Wall around Muscovy"

Proposed Russian national territory, deprived of access to the Baltic or Black Sea

Proposed German administrative centre for the whole eastern region

NORWAY

SWEDEN

North Cape

Murmansk

GREATER FINLAND

Helsinki

Archangel

Leningrad

Baltic Sea

BALTIKUM

Riga

Tallinn

Vorkuta

Ob

Vologda

Kotlas

MUSCOVY

Gorky

Moscow

Riazan

Kazan

URAL

Ufa

Magnitogorsk

Sverdlovsk

Cheliabinsk

Urals

Volga

Ural

SIBERIA

Krasnoyarsk

Tomsk

Barnaul

Novosibirsk

Omsk

Karaganda

Lake Balkhash

Alma Ata

TURKESTAN

Aral Sea

Oxus

Tashkent

Samarkand

Krasnovodsk

Caspian Sea

Astrakhan

Baku

GREATER CAUCASIA

Tiflis

Batum

CHINA

INDIA

AFGHANISTAN

PERSIA

TURKEY

Black Sea

Novorossiisk

Rostov

Stalingrad

GREATER UKRAINE

Kharkov

Kiev

CRIMEA

Odessa

BESSARABIA

RUMANIA

POLAND

GREATER BELORUSSIA

Minsk

Warsaw

GERMANY

Berlin

0   500

Miles

122

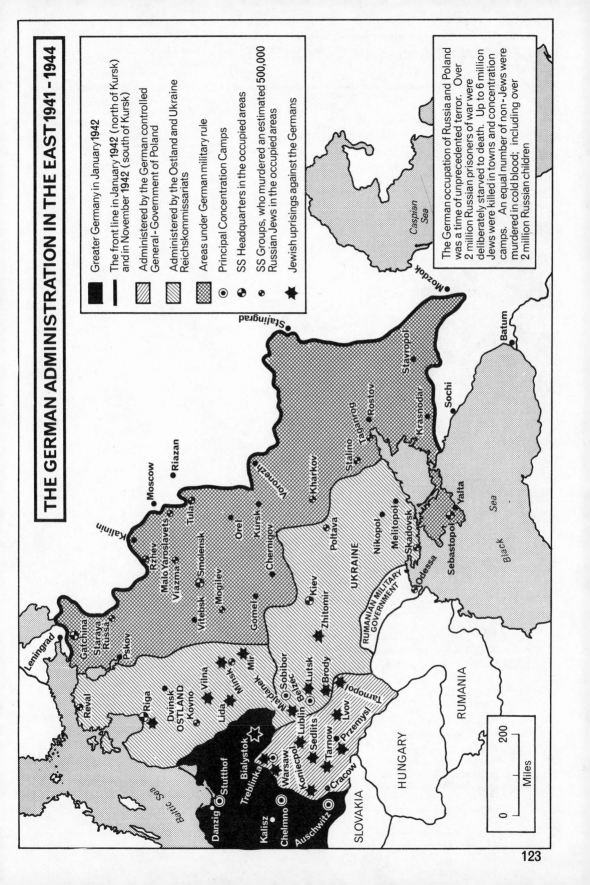

THE GERMAN ADMINISTRATION IN THE EAST 1941–1944

Greater Germany in January 1942

The front line in January 1942 (north of Kursk) and in November 1942 (south of Kursk)

Administered by the German controlled General-Government of Poland

Administered by the Ostland and Ukraine Reichskommissariats

Areas under German military rule

Principal Concentration Camps

SS Headquarters in the occupied areas

SS Groups, who murdered an estimated 500,000 Russian Jews in the occupied areas

Jewish uprisings against the Germans

The German occupation of Russia and Poland was a time of unprecedented terror. Over 2 million Russian prisoners of war were deliberately starved to death. Up to 6 million Jews were killed in towns and concentration camps. An equal number of non-Jews were murdered in cold blood; including over 2 million Russian children

Miles

0   200

123

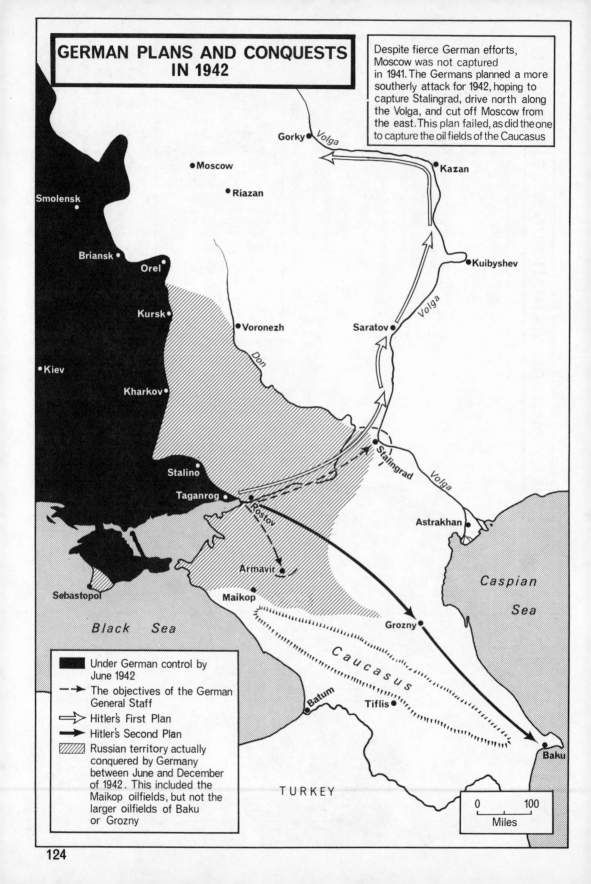

GERMAN PLANS AND CONQUESTS IN 1942

Despite fierce German efforts, Moscow was not captured in 1941. The Germans planned a more southerly attack for 1942, hoping to capture Stalingrad, drive north along the Volga, and cut off Moscow from the east. This plan failed, as did the one to capture the oil fields of the Caucasus

Gorky

Volga

Moscow

Kazan

Riazan

Smolensk

Kuibyshev

Brunsk

Orel

Volga

Kursk

Voronezh

Saratov

Don

Kiev

Kharkov

Stalingrad

Volga

Stalino

Astrakhan

Taganrog

Rostov

Caspian

Armavir

Sea

Sebastopol

Maikop

Grozny

Black Sea

Caucasus

Baku

Batum

Tiflis

TURKEY

Legend:

■ Under German control by June 1942

--→ The objectives of the German General Staff

⇨ Hitler's First Plan

➙ Hitler's Second Plan

▨ Russian territory actually conquered by Germany between June and December of 1942. This included the Maikop oilfields, but not the larger oilfields of Baku or Grozny

0   100
Miles

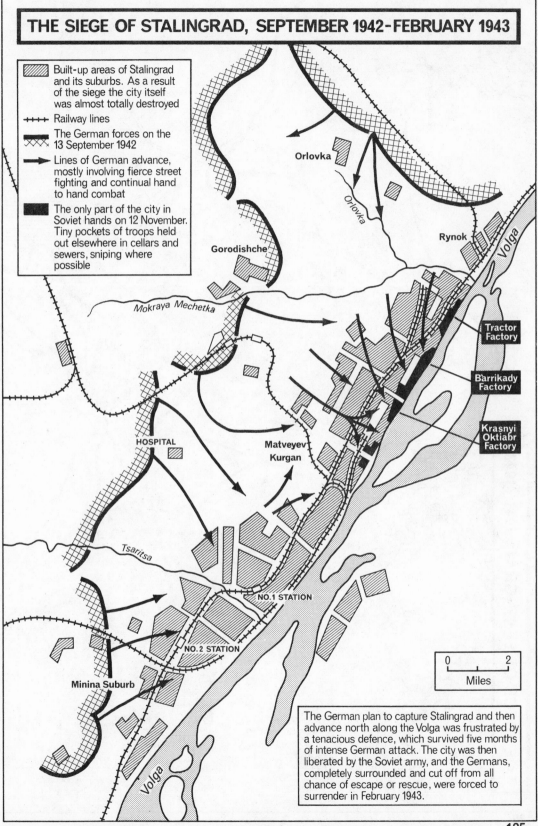

THE SIEGE OF STALINGRAD, SEPTEMBER 1942-FEBRUARY 1943

Built-up areas of Stalingrad and its suburbs. As a result of the siege the city itself was almost totally destroyed

++++ Railway lines

The German forces on the 13 September 1942

Lines of German advance, mostly involving fierce street fighting and continual hand to hand combat

The only part of the city in Soviet hands on 12 November. Tiny pockets of troops held out elsewhere in cellars and sewers, sniping where possible

Orlovka

Orlovka

Rynok

Volga

Gorodishche

Mokraya Mechetka

Tractor Factory

Barrikady Factory

Krasnyi Oktiabr Factory

HOSPITAL

Matveyev Kurgan

Tsaritsa

NO.1 STATION

NO.2 STATION

0   2
Miles

Minina Suburb

Volga

The German plan to capture Stalingrad and then advance north along the Volga was frustrated by a tenacious defence, which survived five months of intense German attack. The city was then liberated by the Soviet army, and the Germans, completely surrounded and cut off from all chance of escape or rescue, were forced to surrender in February 1943.

125

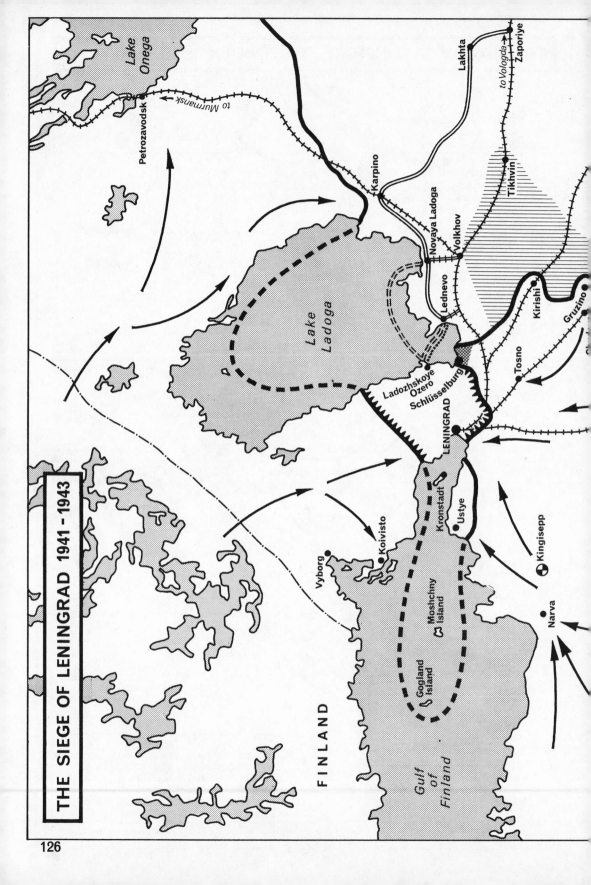

THE SIEGE OF LENINGRAD 1941–1943

Lake Onega

to Murmansk

Petrozavodsk

Karpino

Lakhta

Zaporiye

to Vologda

Tikhvin

Novaya Ladoga

Volkhov

Lednevo

Lake Ladoga

Kirishi

Gruzino

Ladozhskoye Ozero

Tosno

Schlüsselburg

LENINGRAD

Kronstadt

Ustye

Koivisto

Kingisepp

Vyborg

Moshchny Island

Gogland Island

Narva

FINLAND

Gulf of Finland

126

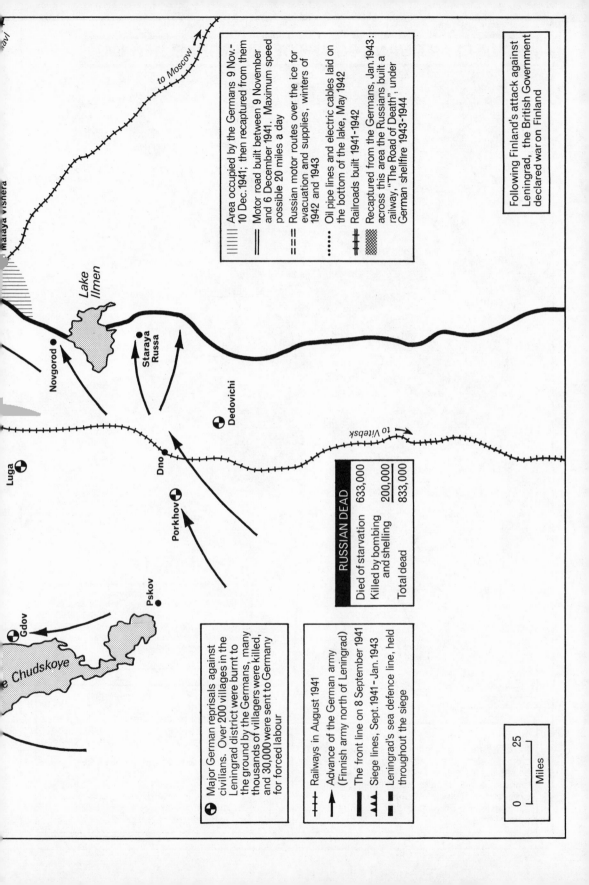

to Moscow

Malaya Vishera

Lake Ilmen

Novgorod ●

Staraya ● Russa

Dedovichi ⊕

Dno ●

to Vitebsk

Luga ⊕

Porkhov ⊕

Pskov ●

Gdov ⊕

e Chudskoye

|||||||| Area occupied by the Germans 9 Nov.-10 Dec.1941; then recaptured from them

═══ Motor road built between 9 November and 6 December 1941. Maximum speed possible 20 miles a day

≡≡≡ Russian motor routes over the ice for evacuation and supplies, winters of 1942 and 1943

∙∙∙∙∙ Oil pipe lines and electric cables laid on the bottom of the lake, May 1942

┿┿┿ Railroads built 1941-1942

╫╫╫ Recaptured from the Germans, Jan.1943: across this area the Russians built a railway, "The Road of Death", under German shellfire 1943-1944

Following Finland's attack against Leningrad, the British Government declared war on Finland

RUSSIAN DEAD	
Died of starvation	633,000
Killed by bombing and shelling	200,000
Total dead	833,000

⊕ Major German reprisals against civilians. Over 200 villages in the Leningrad district were burnt to the ground by the Germans, many thousands of villagers were killed, and 30,000 were sent to Germany for forced labour

┿┿┿ Railways in August 1941

↑ Advance of the German army (Finnish army north of Leningrad)

▌ The front line on 8 September 1941

▲▲▲ Siege lines, Sept. 1941 - Jan.1943

▬ ▬ Leningrad's sea defence line, held throughout the siege

0   25
Miles

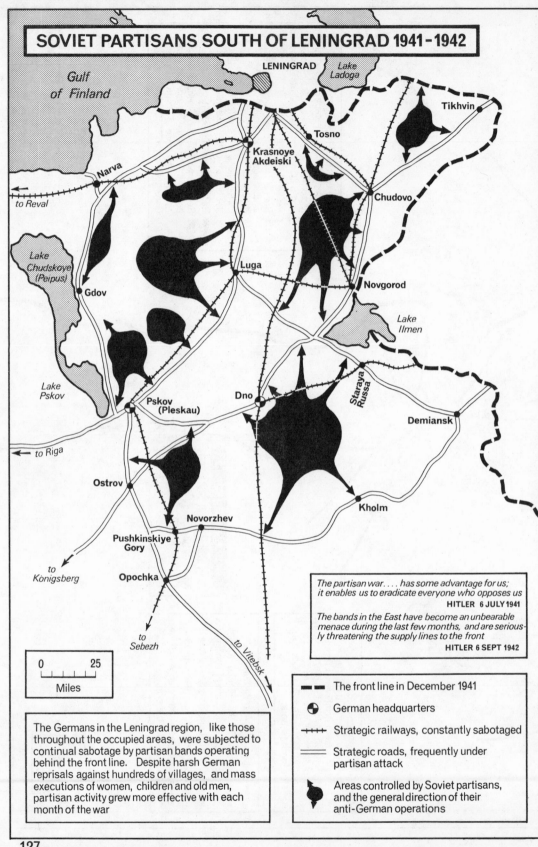

SOVIET PARTISANS SOUTH OF LENINGRAD 1941-1942

Gulf
of Finland

LENINGRAD

Lake
Ladoga

Tikhvin

Narva

Tosno

to Reval

Krasnoye
Akdeiski

Chudovo

Lake
Chudskoye
(Peipus)

Gdov

Luga

Novgorod

Lake
Ilmen

Lake
Pskov

Dno

Staraya
Russa

Demiansk

Pskov
(Pleskau)

Kholm

to Riga

Ostrov

Novorzhev

Pushkinskiye
Gory

to
Königsberg

Opochka

to
Sebezh

to Vitebsk

The partisan war.... has some advantage for us;
it enables us to eradicate everyone who opposes us
HITLER 6 JULY 1941

The bands in the East have become an unbearable
menace during the last few months, and are serious-
ly threatening the supply lines to the front
HITLER 6 SEPT 1942

0   25

Miles

- - - The front line in December 1941

🔴 German headquarters

+++++ Strategic railways, constantly sabotaged

—— Strategic roads, frequently under
partisan attack

⬛ Areas controlled by Soviet partisans,
and the general direction of their
anti-German operations

The Germans in the Leningrad region, like those
throughout the occupied areas, were subjected to
continual sabotage by partisan bands operating
behind the front line.   Despite harsh German
reprisals against hundreds of villages, and mass
executions of women, children and old men,
partisan activity grew more effective with each
month of the war

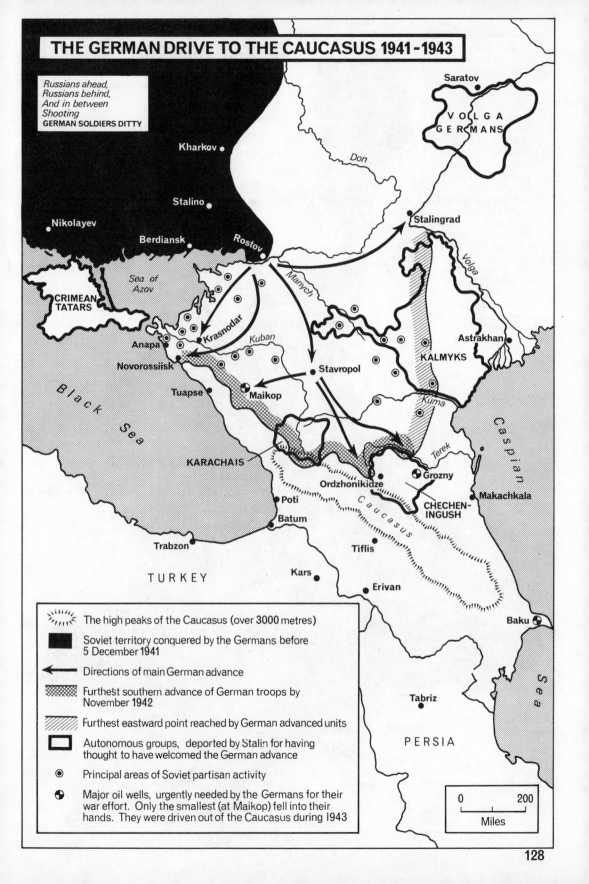

THE GERMAN DRIVE TO THE CAUCASUS 1941-1943

Russians ahead,
Russians behind,
And in between
Shooting
GERMAN SOLDIERS DITTY

Saratov

V O L G A
G E R M A N S

Kharkov

Don

Stalino

Stalingrad

Nikolayev

Berdiansk

Rostov

Volga

CRIMEAN
TATARS

Sea of
Azov

Krasnodar

Kuban

Astrakhan

Anapa

KALMYKS

Novorossiisk

Stavropol

Kuma

Tuapse

Maikop

Terek

KARACHAIS

Grozny

Ordzhonikidze

Makachkala

Poti

Caucasus

CHECHEN-
INGUSH

Batum

Trabzon

Tiflis

T U R K E Y

Kars

Erivan

Black Sea

Caspian Sea

Baku

Tabriz

P E R S I A

Legend

- The high peaks of the Caucasus (over 3000 metres)
- Soviet territory conquered by the Germans before 5 December 1941
- Directions of main German advance
- Furthest southern advance of German troops by November 1942
- Furthest eastward point reached by German advanced units
- Autonomous groups, deported by Stalin for having thought to have welcomed the German advance
- ⊙ Principal areas of Soviet partisan activity
- ⊕ Major oil wells, urgently needed by the Germans for their war effort. Only the smallest (at Maikop) fell into their hands. They were driven out of the Caucasus during 1943

0   200
Miles

128

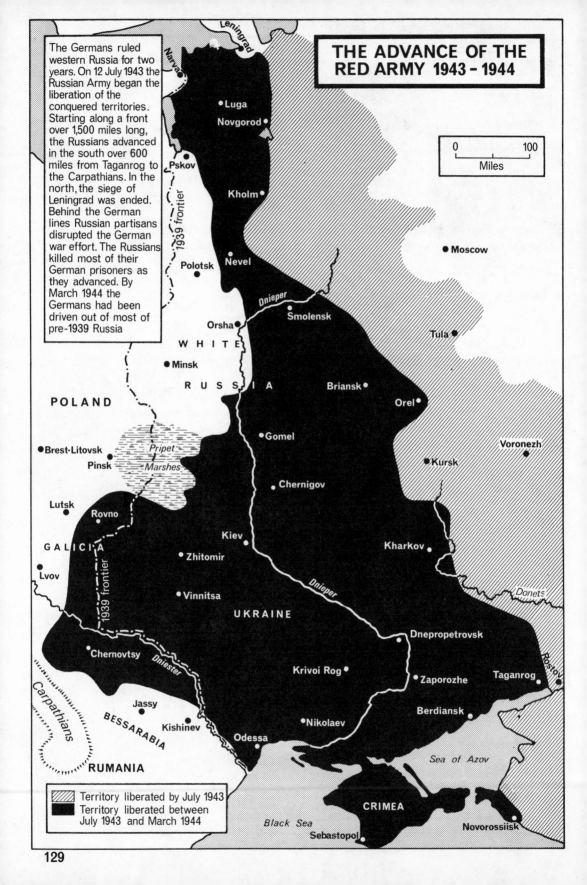

THE ADVANCE OF THE RED ARMY 1943 - 1944

The Germans ruled western Russia for two years. On 12 July 1943 the Russian Army began the liberation of the conquered territories. Starting along a front over 1,500 miles long, the Russians advanced in the south over 600 miles from Taganrog to the Carpathians. In the north, the siege of Leningrad was ended. Behind the German lines Russian partisans disrupted the German war effort. The Russians killed most of their German prisoners as they advanced. By March 1944 the Germans had been driven out of most of pre-1939 Russia

0   100
Miles

Leningrad

Narva

Luga

Novgorod

Pskov

1939 frontier

Kholm

Moscow

Polotsk

Nevel

Dnieper

Smolensk

Tula

Orsha

WHITE

Minsk

RUSSIA

Briansk

Orel

POLAND

Voronezh

Brest-Litovsk

Pinsk

Pripet
Marshes

Gomel

Kursk

Chernigov

Lutsk

Rovno

Kiev

Kharkov

GALICIA

Zhitomir

1939 frontier

Dnieper

Donets

Lvov

Vinnitsa

UKRAINE

Chernovtsy

Dniester

Dnepropetrovsk

Krivoi Rog

Zaporozhe

Taganrog

Rostov

Jassy

Berdiansk

BESSARABIA

Kishinev

Odessa

Nikolaev

Sea of Azov

RUMANIA

Carpathians

CRIMEA

Territory liberated by July 1943
Territory liberated between
July 1943 and March 1944

Black Sea

Sebastopol

Novorossiisk

129

THE DEFEAT OF GERMANY 1944–1945

EUROPEAN WAR DEAD 1939-1945

CIVILIANS

	approx.
Jews	6,000,000
Russians	3,000,000
Yugoslavs	1,280,000
Poles	1,000,000
Germans	800,000
Hungarians	280,000
Rumanians	260,000
Dutch	200,000
Greeks	140,000
French	107,000
Austrians	104,000
British	62,000
Belgians	16,000

Total civilian
dead over 13 million

0 — 400
Miles

EUROPEAN WAR DEAD 1939-1945

SOLDIERS

	approx.
Russians	7,500,000
Germans	3,500,000
Hungarians	410,000
Yugoslavs	410,000
British	400,000
Italians	330,000
Polish	320,000
Rumanians	300,000
Americans (U.S.A.)	290,000
French	210,000
Finns	85,000
Belgians	12,000
Dutch	12,000

Total military
dead over 13 million

Liberated by Soviet troops before May 1944
Liberated by British and American troops before May 1944
Soviet advances from May 1944 to May 1945
Other Allied advances, May 1944 to May 1945
Territory still in German hands when Germany surrendered unconditionally on 8 May 1945
Neutral countries

130

THE SOVIET DEPORTATION OF NATIONALITIES 1941 - 1945

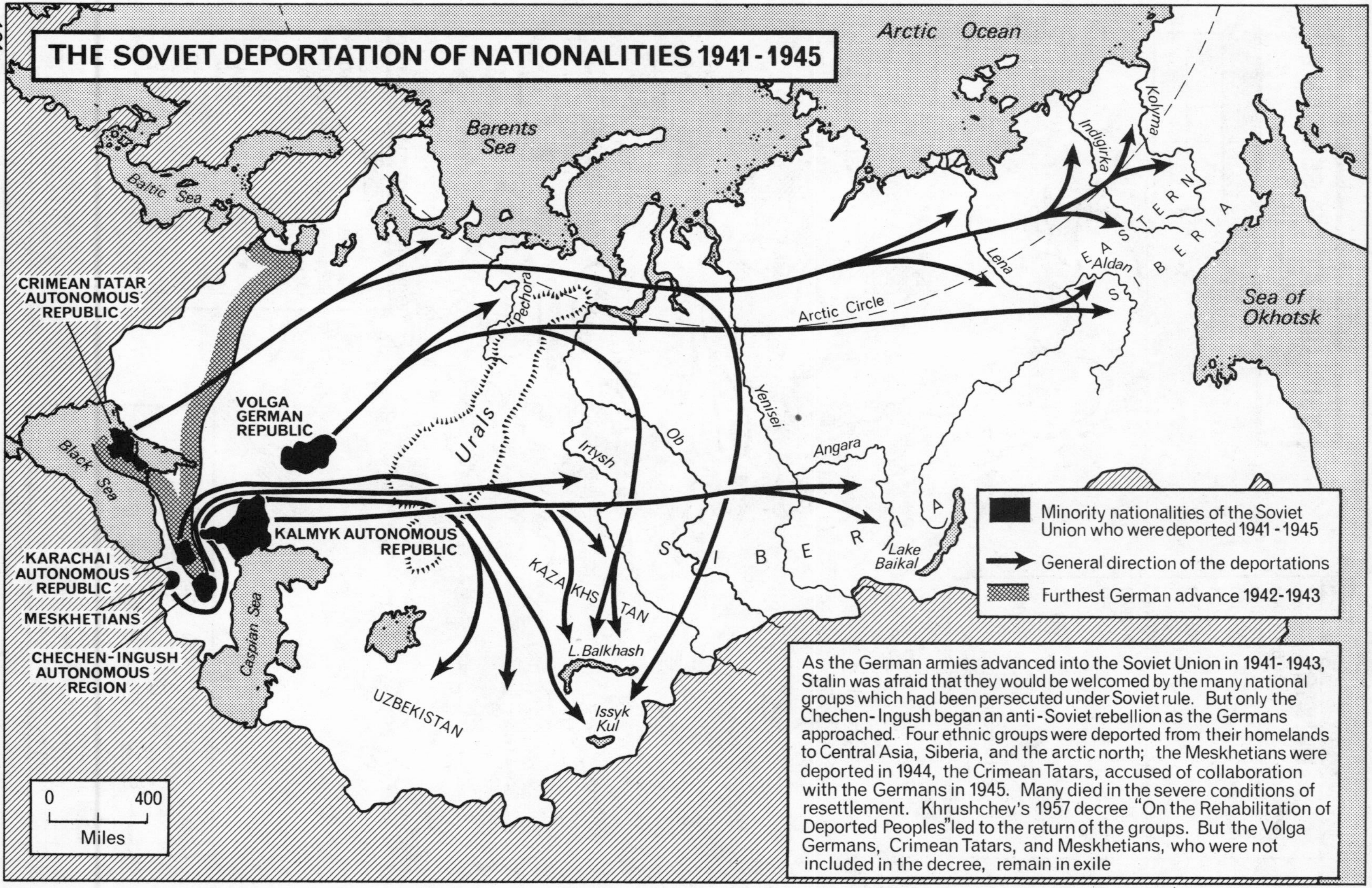
Arctic Ocean
Barents Sea
Baltic Sea
Black Sea
Caspian Sea
Sea of Okhotsk
CRIMEAN TATAR AUTONOMOUS REPUBLIC
VOLGA GERMAN REPUBLIC
KALMYK AUTONOMOUS REPUBLIC
KARACHAI AUTONOMOUS REPUBLIC
MESKHETIANS
CHECHEN-INGUSH AUTONOMOUS REGION
Urals
Pechora
Irtysh
Ob
Yenisei
Angara
Lena
Aldan
Indigirka
Kolyma
Arctic Circle
KAZAKHSTAN
UZBEKISTAN
L. Balkhash
Issyk Kul
Lake Baikal
SIBERIA
EASTERN SIBERIA
Minority nationalities of the Soviet Union who were deported 1941 - 1945
General direction of the deportations
Furthest German advance 1942-1943
0 400
Miles

As the German armies advanced into the Soviet Union in 1941-1943, Stalin was afraid that they would be welcomed by the many national groups which had been persecuted under Soviet rule. But only the Chechen-Ingush began an anti-Soviet rebellion as the Germans approached. Four ethnic groups were deported from their homelands to Central Asia, Siberia, and the arctic north; the Meskhetians were deported in 1944, the Crimean Tatars, accused of collaboration with the Germans in 1945. Many died in the severe conditions of resettlement. Khrushchev's 1957 decree "On the Rehabilitation of Deported Peoples" led to the return of the groups. But the Volga Germans, Crimean Tatars, and Meskhetians, who were not included in the decree, remain in exile

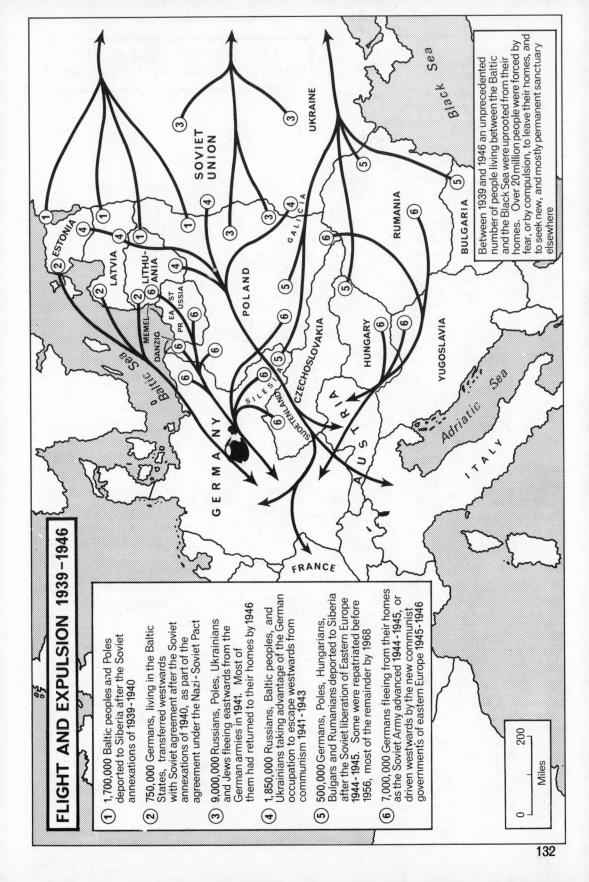

FLIGHT AND EXPULSION 1939–1946

Between 1939 and 1946 an unprecedented number of people living between the Baltic and the Black Sea were uprooted from their homes. Over 20 million people were forced by fear, or by compulsion, to leave their homes, and to seek new, and mostly permanent sanctuary elsewhere

① 1,700,000 Baltic peoples and Poles deported to Siberia after the Soviet annexations of 1939-1940

② 750,000 Germans, living in the Baltic States, transferred westwards with Soviet agreement after the Soviet annexations of 1940, as part of the agreement under the Nazi-Soviet Pact

③ 9,000,000 Russians, Poles, Ukrainians and Jews fleeing eastwards from the German armies in 1941. Most of them had returned to their homes by 1946

④ 1,850,000 Russians, Baltic peoples, and Ukrainians taking advantage of the German occupation to escape westwards from communism 1941-1943

⑤ 500,000 Germans, Poles, Hungarians, Bulgars and Rumanians deported to Siberia after the Soviet liberation of Eastern Europe 1944-1945. Some were repatriated before 1956, most of the remainder by 1968

⑥ 7,000,000 Germans fleeing from their homes as the Soviet Army advanced 1944-1945, or driven westwards by the new communist governments of eastern Europe 1945-1946

0 — 200 Miles

132

THE SOVIET UNION IN EASTERN EUROPE 1945 - 1948

Territory annexed by Russia 1939-1940, and re-incorporated in Russia in 1945

Former German and Czechoslovak territory annexed by Russia in 1945

States liberated by the Soviet army, and in which Communist regimes came to power between 1945 and 1948

Russian occupation zones in Austria (evacuated 1950) and Germany

British, French and American occupation zones

The 'Iron Curtain' in 1948

FINLAND

Vyborg

Leningrad

Reval

Pskov

North Sea

SWEDEN

Baltic Sea

ESTONIA

Riga

LATVIA

Memel

LITHUANIA

Kovno

Vilna

Minsk

Königsberg

EAST
PRUSSIA

S O V I E T

Bremen

Stettin

annexed
by Poland
from Germany

Bialystok

Berlin

Posnan

Warsaw

Pinsk

U N I O N

G E R M A N Y

Erfurt

POLAND

Bonn

Dresden

Breslau

SILESIA

Cracow

Nuremburg

Prague

Przemysl

Lvov

GALICIA

FRANCE

CZECHOSLOVAKIA

Munich

Vienna

Chernovtsy

A U S T R I A

Uzhgorod

Jassy

Kishinev

SWITZ.

Budapest

BESSARABIA

HUNGARY

RUMANIA

Trieste

ITALY

Belgrade

Bucharest

YUGOSLAVIA

Adriatic Sea

Black Sea

Sofia

BULGARIA

Tirana

ALBANIA

GREECE

Ægean
Sea

TURKEY

The Russian liberation of Eastern Europe was quickly followed by the establishment of communist regimes, and an 'Iron Curtain' from the Baltic to the Adriatic. Communist rule brought national subservience to Russian policy, and the subordination of personal liberty. The cities of Berlin and Vienna were divided into Russian, British, French and American sectors

0   200
Miles

133

THE SOVIET UNION IN EASTERN EUROPE 1949-1968

0   200
Miles

FINLAND

North Sea

SWEDEN

Baltic Sea

Vyborg

Leningrad

Tallin (Reval)

Riga

Klaypeda (Memel)

Kaliningrad

S O V I E T

U N I O N

Rostock

Gdansk

East Berlin

Szczecin

EAST GERMANY

POLAND

Posnan

Warsaw

Halle

Lodz

Dresden

Wroclaw

Lublin

Cracow

WEST GERMANY

Prague

CZECHOSLOVAKIA

Brno

Przemysl

Kiev

Lvov

Kosice

FRANCE

Bratislava

Debrecen

SWITZ.

AUSTRIA

Györ

Budapest

HUNGARY

Jassy

Cluj

Odessa

Zagreb

Pécs

RUMANIA

Rijeka

Arad

Constanza

Belgrade

Adriatic Sea

YUGOSLAVIA

Bucharest

Split

Nish

Varna

Black Sea

ITALY

Kotor

BULGARIA

Burgas

Tirana

Sofia

Durres

ALBANIA

Vlone

T U R K E Y

GREECE

Aegean Sea

— Frontiers of communist states since 1945

Only European communist state entirely free from Soviet direction of foreign, economic and domestic policy since 1949

Only communist state within the Soviet bloc pursuing a relatively independent foreign policy since 1968

Only communist state in Europe aligned with China and refusing all contact with the Soviet Union since 1961

Only European communist state to accept Soviet guidance with equanimity

Principal areas of anti-Soviet protest and revolt 1953-1968, crushed by Soviet military intervention (East Germany, Hungary, Czechoslovakia) and by strong political pressure (Poland)

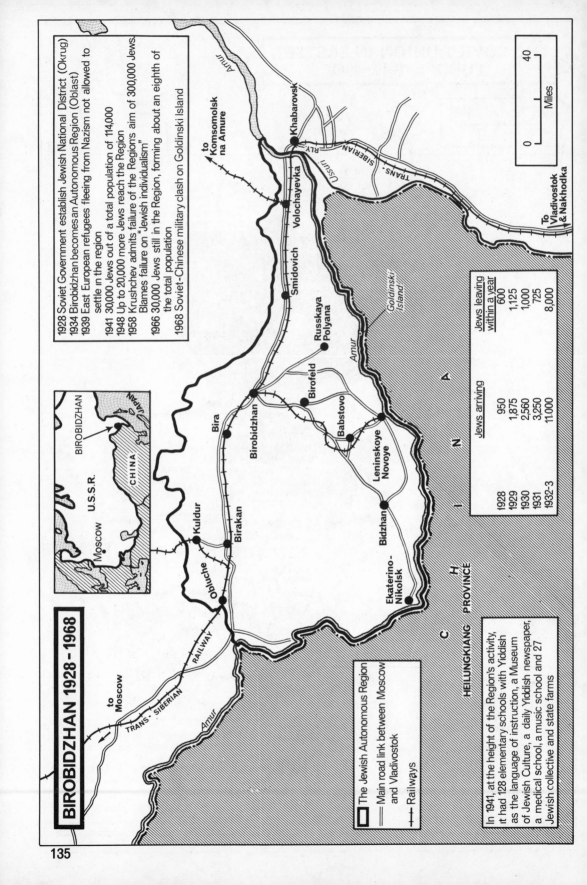

BIROBIDZHAN 1928-1968

BIROBIDZHAN

U.S.S.R.

Moscow

CHINA

1928 Soviet Government establish Jewish National District (Okrug)
1934 Birobidzhan becomes an Autonomous Region (Oblast)
1939 East European refugees fleeing from Nazism not allowed to settle in the region
1941 30,000 Jews out of a total population of 114,000
1948 Up to 20,000 more Jews reach the Region
1958 Krushchev admits failure of the Region's aim of 300,000 Jews. Blames failure on "Jewish individualism"
1966 30,000 Jews still in the Region, forming about an eighth of the total population
1968 Soviet-Chinese military clash on Goldinski Island

Amur

to Komsomolsk na Amure

Khabarovsk

Ussuri

TRANS - SIBERIAN RLY

To Vladivostok & Nakhodka

Volochayevka

Smidovich

Russkaya Polyana

Birofeld

Babstovo

Goldinski Island

Bira

Birobidzhan

Leninskoye Novoye

Bidzhan

Ekaterino-Nikolsk

Kuldur

Birakan

Obluche

Amur

to Moscow

TRANS - SIBERIAN RAILWAY

Amur

	Jews arriving	Jews leaving within a year
1928	950	600
1929	1,875	1,125
1930	2,560	1,000
1931	3,250	725
1932-3	11,000	8,000

C H I N A

HEILUNGKIANG PROVINCE

☐ The Jewish Autonomous Region
═══ Main road link between Moscow and Vladivostok
┼┼┼ Railways

In 1941, at the height of the Region's activity, it had 128 elementary schools with Yiddish as the language of instruction, a Museum of Jewish Culture, a daily Yiddish newspaper, a medical school, a music school and 27 Jewish collective and state farms

0   40

Miles

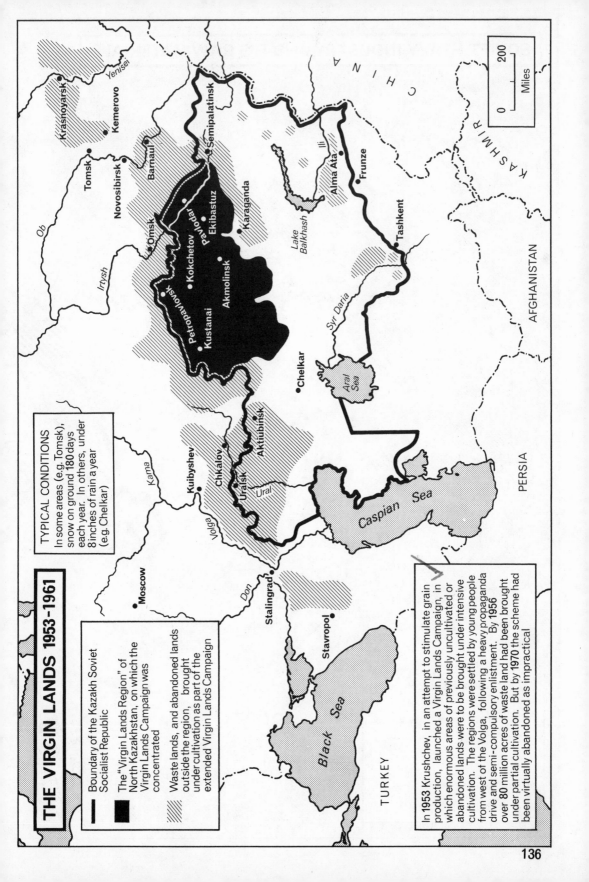

THE VIRGIN LANDS 1953-1961

TYPICAL CONDITIONS
In some areas (e.g. Tomsk), snow on ground 180 days each year. In others, under 8 inches of rain a year (e.g. Chelkar)

Boundary of the Kazakh Soviet Socialist Republic

The "Virgin Lands Region" of North Kazakhstan, on which the Virgin Lands Campaign was concentrated

Waste lands, and abandoned lands outside the region, brought under cultivation as part of the extended Virgin Lands Campaign

In 1953 Krushchev, in an attempt to stimulate grain production, launched a Virgin Lands Campaign, in which enormous areas of previously uncultivated or abandoned lands were to be brought under intensive cultivation. The regions were settled by young people from west of the Volga, following a heavy propaganda drive and semi-compulsory enlistment. By 1956 over 80 million acres of waste land had been brought under partial cultivation. But by 1970 the scheme had been virtually abandoned as impractical

Krasnoyarsk
Yenisei
Kemerovo
Tomsk
Novosibirsk
Ob
Barnaul
Semipalatinsk
Omsk
Irtysh
Ekibastuz
Pavlodar
Kokchetov
Karaganda
Petropavlovsk
Akmolinsk
Kustanai
Ili
Alma Ata
Frunze
Lake Balkhash
Tashkent
Syr Daria
Chelkar
Aral Sea
CHINA
KASHMIR
AFGHANISTAN
Aktiubinsk
Chkalov
Uralsk
Ural
Kuibyshev
Kama
Caspian Sea
PERSIA
Volga
Moscow
Don
Stalingrad
Stavropol
Black Sea
TURKEY

200
0
Miles

SOVIET HEAVY INDUSTRY AND ITS RAW MATERIALS

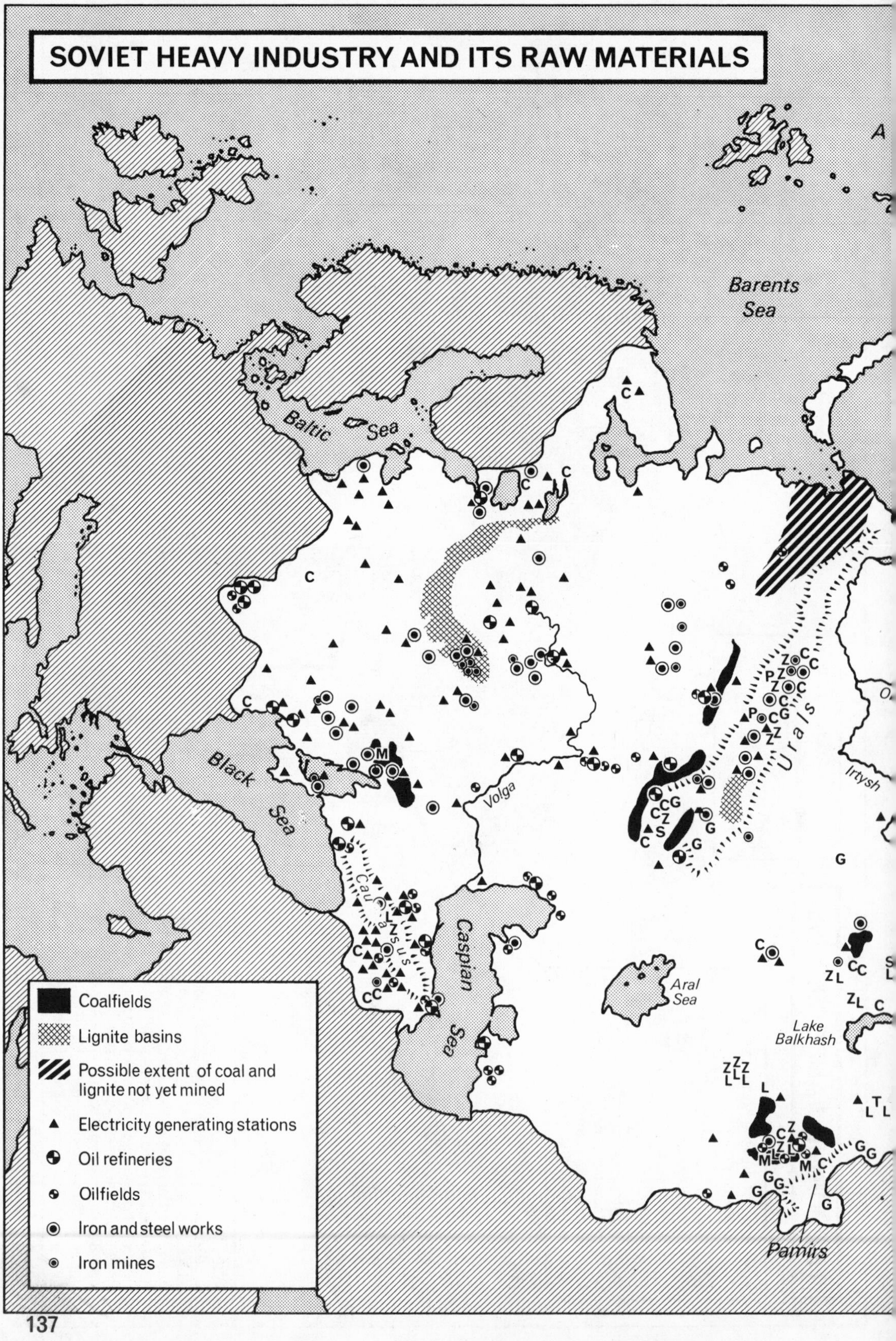

Barents Sea

Baltic Sea

Black Sea

Caspian Sea

Volga

Urals

Irtysh

Caucasus

Aral Sea

Lake Balkhash

Pamirs

Legend:

- ■ Coalfields
- ▦ Lignite basins
- ▨ Possible extent of coal and lignite not yet mined
- ▲ Electricity generating stations
- ⊕ Oil refineries
- ◕ Oilfields
- ◉ Iron and steel works
- ⊙ Iron mines

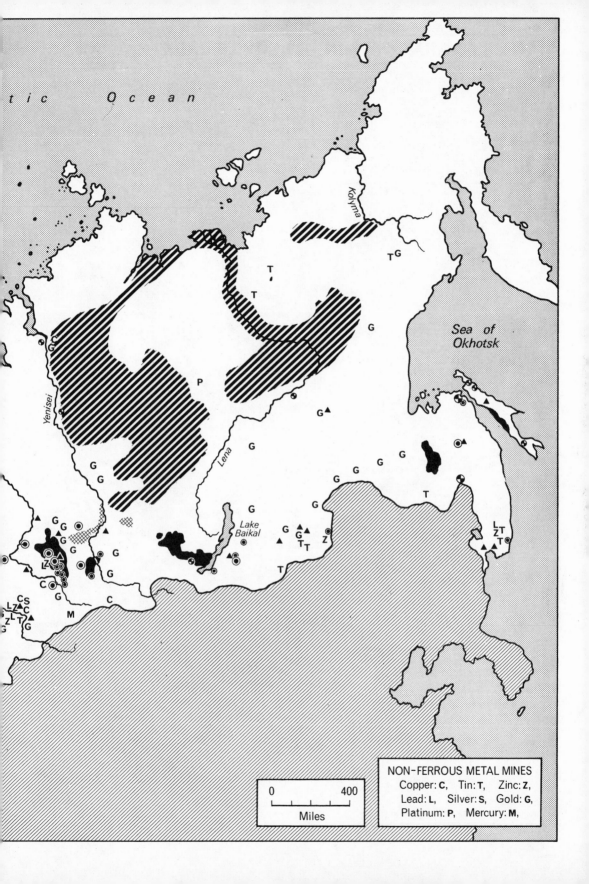

tic   O c e a n

Kolyma

T G

T

T

Sea   of
Okhotsk

G

G

P

G

G

Yenisei

Lena

G

G

G

G   G   G

T

G   G

G
G

Lake
Baikal

G   G

T

L T
Z T

G

G   ▲

G   ▲

T

▲

G   ▲   ▲

Z

G   T   T

T

▲

▲

G   G
G   G
G   G

G

C

G

Z

C

M

C S C
L Z L T
Z T G
G

NON-FERROUS METAL MINES
Copper: **C**,   Tin: **T**,   Zinc: **Z**,
Lead: **L**,   Silver: **S**,   Gold: **G**,
Platinum: **P**,   Mercury: **M**,

0   400

Miles

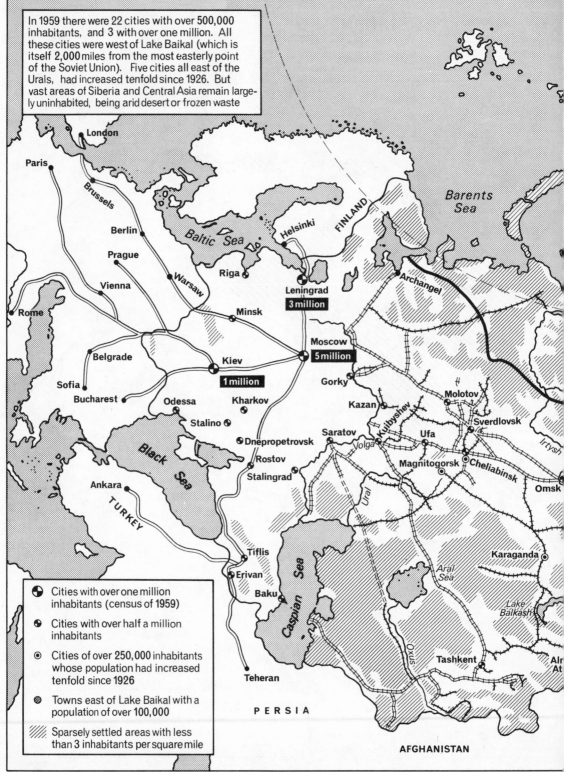

CITIES AND RAILWAYS IN THE SOVIET UNION 1917-1959

In 1959 there were 22 cities with over 500,000 inhabitants, and 3 with over one million. All these cities were west of Lake Baikal (which is itself 2,000 miles from the most easterly point of the Soviet Union). Five cities all east of the Urals, had increased tenfold since 1926. But vast areas of Siberia and Central Asia remain largely uninhabited, being arid desert or frozen waste

London

Paris

Brussels

Berlin

Prague

Vienna

Warsaw

Rome

Belgrade

Sofia

Bucharest

Baltic Sea

Helsinki

FINLAND

Riga

Leningrad
3 million

Minsk

Moscow
5 million

Kiev

1 million

Gorky

Kharkov

Kazan

Odessa

Stalino

Dnepropetrovsk

Rostov

Saratov

Kuibyshev

Ufa

Stalingrad

Magnitogorsk

Molotov

Sverdlovsk

Cheliabinsk

Volga

Ural

Irtysh

Omsk

Barents
Sea

Archangel

Ankara

TURKEY

Black Sea

Tiflis

Erivan

Baku

Caspian Sea

Aral
Sea

Lake
Balkash

Karaganda

Teheran

PERSIA

Oxus

Tashkent

Alm
At

AFGHANISTAN

Legend

⊕ Cities with over one million inhabitants (census of 1959)

⊖ Cities with over half a million inhabitants

⊙ Cities of over 250,000 inhabitants whose population had increased tenfold since 1926

⊗ Towns east of Lake Baikal with a population of over 100,000

▨ Sparsely settled areas with less than 3 inhabitants per square mile

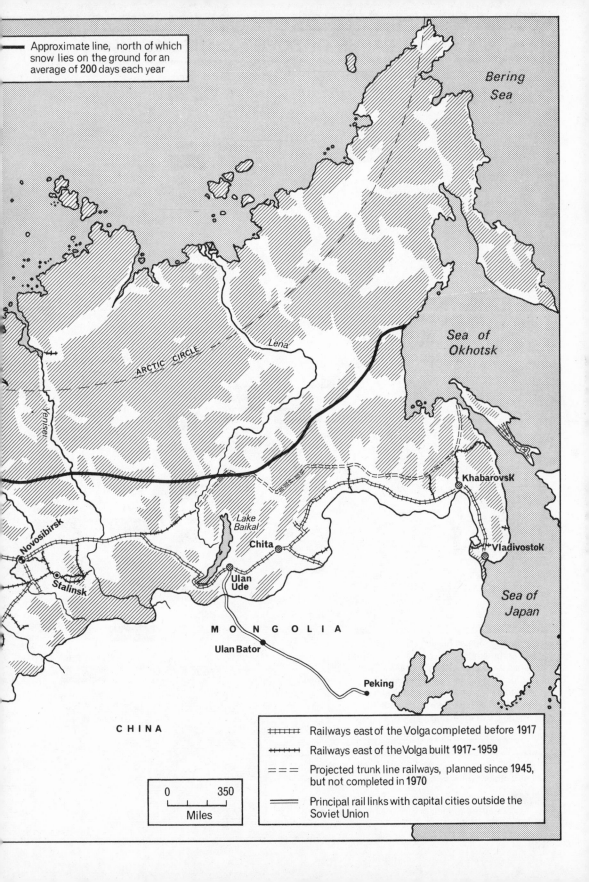

Approximate line, north of which
snow lies on the ground for an
average of 200 days each year

Bering Sea

Sea of Okhotsk

ARCTIC CIRCLE   *Lena*

Yenisei

Khabarovsk

Lake Baikal

Chita

Novosibirsk

Vladivostok

Ulan Ude

Stalinsk

Sea of Japan

M O N G O L I A

Ulan Bator

Peking

C H I N A

┼┼┼┼┼┼	Railways east of the Volga completed before 1917
┼┼┼┼┼┼	Railways east of the Volga built 1917-1959
= = =	Projected trunk line railways, planned since 1945, but not completed in 1970
═══	Principal rail links with capital cities outside the Soviet Union

0   350
Miles

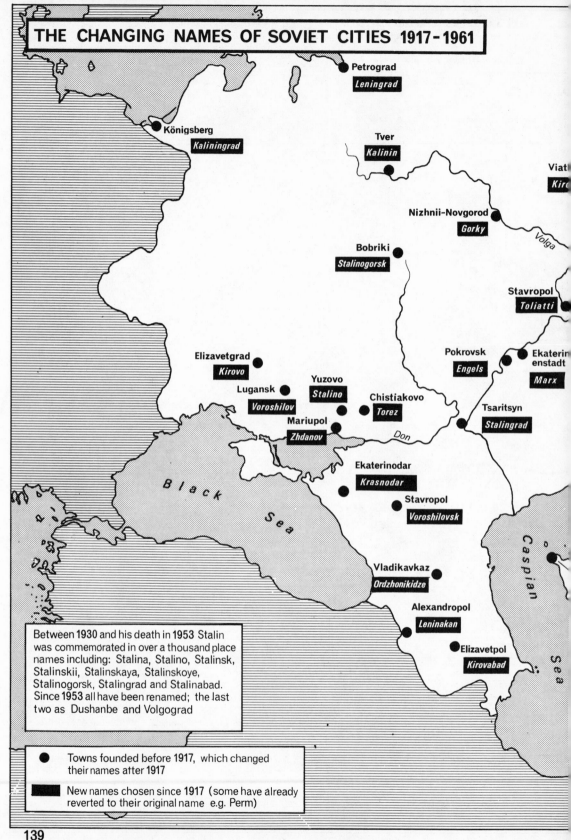

THE CHANGING NAMES OF SOVIET CITIES 1917-1961

Petrograd
Leningrad

Königsberg
Kaliningrad

Tver
Kalinin

Viat
Kiro

Nizhnii-Novgorod
Gorky

Volga

Bobriki
Stalinogorsk

Stavropol
Toliatti

Elizavetgrad
Kirovo

Pokrovsk
Engels

Ekaterin
enstadt
Marx

Yuzovo
Stalino

Lugansk
Voroshilov

Chistiakovo
Torez

Tsaritsyn
Stalingrad

Mariupol
Zhdanov

Don

Black

Sea

Ekaterinodar
Krasnodar

Stavropol
Voroshilovsk

Caspian

Vladikavkaz
Ordzhonikidze

Alexandropol
Leninakan

Sea

Elizavetpol
Kirovabad

Between **1930** and his death in **1953** Stalin
was commemorated in over a thousand place
names including: Stalina, Stalino, Stalinsk,
Stalinskii, Stalinskaya, Stalinskoye,
Stalinogorsk, Stalingrad and Stalinabad.
Since **1953** all have been renamed; the last
two as Dushanbe and Volgograd

●   Towns founded before **1917**, which changed
    their names after 1917

▬   New names chosen since **1917** (some have already
    reverted to their original name e.g. Perm)

Since 1917 many Soviet cities have changed their names, choosing new names connected with the revolution and its leaders. Many hundred villages and small towns adopted such names as Oktiabrskii (after the October revolution of 1917), Komsomolsk (after the Young Communist League), Pervomaiskoie (the first of May), Krasnoarmeisk (the Red Army), Krasnogvardeisk (the Red Guard), Krasnyi Oktyabr (Red October), Krasnye Barrikady (the Red barricades) and Komintern (the Communist International)

Among the towns and villages named after Lenin are; Lenina, Leninabad, Leninakan, Leningori, Leninka, Lenino, Leninogorsk, Leninskii and Leninizm

Perm
Molotov

Ekaterinburg
Sverdlovsk

Kuznetsk
Stalinsk

₁ara
ibyshev

Orenburg
Chkalov

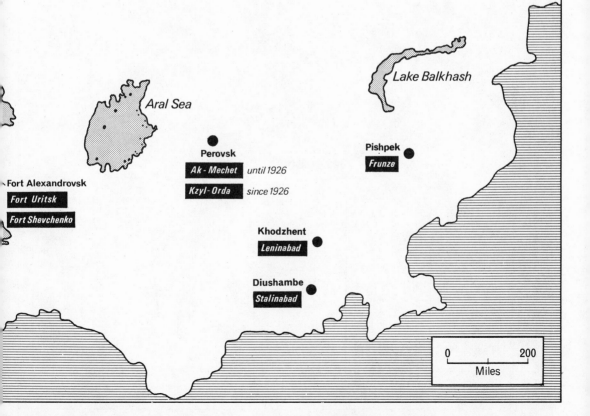

Lake Balkhash

Aral Sea

Perovsk
Ak - Mechet   until 1926
Kzyl- Orda   since 1926

Pishpek
Frunze

Fort Alexandrovsk
Fort Uritsk
Fort Shevchenko

Khodzhent
Leninabad

Diushambe
Stalinabad

0 ————— 200
Miles

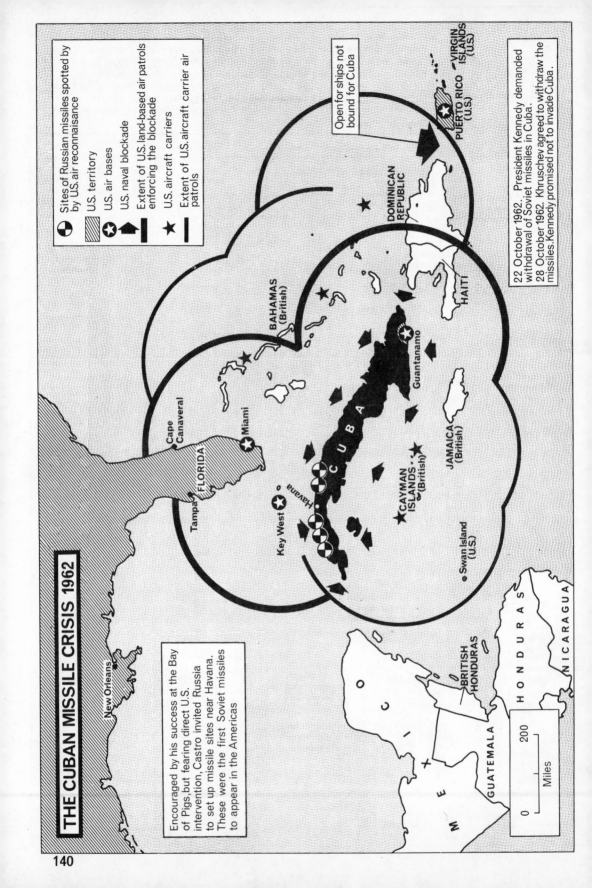

THE CUBAN MISSILE CRISIS 1962

Legend:

- ◔ Sites of Russian missiles spotted by U.S. air reconnaissance
- ▨ U.S. territory
- ✪ U.S. air bases
- ◆ U.S. naval blockade
- ▬ Extent of U.S. land-based air patrols enforcing the blockade
- ★ U.S. aircraft carriers
- | Extent of U.S. aircraft carrier air patrols

Encouraged by his success at the Bay of Pigs, but fearing direct U.S. intervention, Castro invited Russia to set up missile sites near Havana. These were the first Soviet missiles to appear in the Americas

Open for ships not bound for Cuba

22 October 1962. President Kennedy demanded withdrawal of Soviet missiles in Cuba.
28 October 1962. Khruschev agreed to withdraw the missiles. Kennedy promised not to invade Cuba.

New Orleans

FLORIDA

Tampa

Cape Canaveral

Miami

Key West

Havana

C U B A

Guantanamo

BAHAMAS (British)

CAYMAN ISLANDS (British)

JAMAICA (British)

Swan Island (U.S.)

DOMINICAN REPUBLIC

HAITI

PUERTO RICO (U.S.)

VIRGIN ISLANDS (U.S.)

M E X I C O

GUATEMALA

BRITISH HONDURAS

H O N D U R A S

N I C A R A G U A

0   200
Miles

140

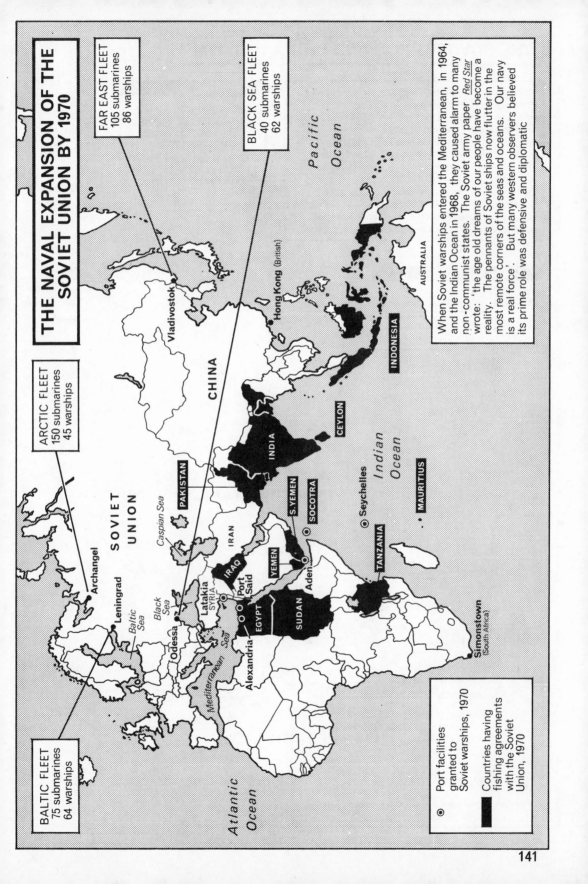

THE NAVAL EXPANSION OF THE SOVIET UNION BY 1970

FAR EAST FLEET
105 submarines
86 warships

BLACK SEA FLEET
40 submarines
62 warships

ARCTIC FLEET
150 submarines
45 warships

BALTIC FLEET
75 submarines
64 warships

Pacific
Ocean

AUSTRALIA

Hong Kong (British)

INDONESIA

CEYLON

INDIA

Indian
Ocean

Seychelles

SOCOTRA

S.YEMEN

MAURITIUS

PAKISTAN

TANZANIA

Vladivostok

CHINA

SOVIET UNION

Caspian Sea

IRAN

IRAQ

YEMEN

Aden

Port
Said

Latakia
SYRIA

EGYPT

SUDAN

Alexandria

Odessa

Black
Sea

Mediterranean Sea

Baltic
Sea

Leningrad

Archangel

Atlantic
Ocean

Simonstown
(South Africa)

When Soviet warships entered the Mediterranean, in 1964, and the Indian Ocean in 1968, they caused alarm to many non-communist states. The Soviet army paper *Red Star* wrote: 'the age old dreams of our people have become a reality. The pennants of Soviet ships now flutter in the most remote corners of the seas and oceans. Our navy is a real force'. But many western observers believed its prime role was defensive and diplomatic

◎ Port facilities granted to Soviet warships, 1970

■ Countries having fishing agreements with the Soviet Union, 1970

THE SOVIET UNION AND CHINA 1860-1970

The Chinese Communist Party was founded in 1921. But the Soviet Union preferred to support the Kuomintang under Chiang Kai Shek, to which it gave substantial military aid to establish its power 1923-1927, and to fight the Japanese 1937-1941 (when Stalin formed a Non-Aggression pact with Japan). In 1945 Soviet troops drove the Japanese from Northern China. In 1949 the Chinese Communists came to power. From a policy of considerable Soviet aid to China in the 1950's, the two nations became increasingly hostile. By 1960 the rift was open, and soon led to armed skirmishes on the frontier

TANNU TUVA

1914	Russian protectorate
1921	Independent "Peoples' Republic" allied with the Soviet Union
1944	Annexed by the Soviet Union

SINKIANG

1760-1920	Chinese
1921-1949	Under Soviet influence and partial occupation
Since 1949	Chinese. Heavily colonized by Chinese settlers

Territory annexed by Russia 1858-1860

Communist Party cells established under Moscow's instructions 1920-1924 and urged to collaborate with the Kuomintang (nationalists)

Soviet air units defending Kuomintang strongholds against Japan 1941

Soviet military advances across China in the war against Japan 1945

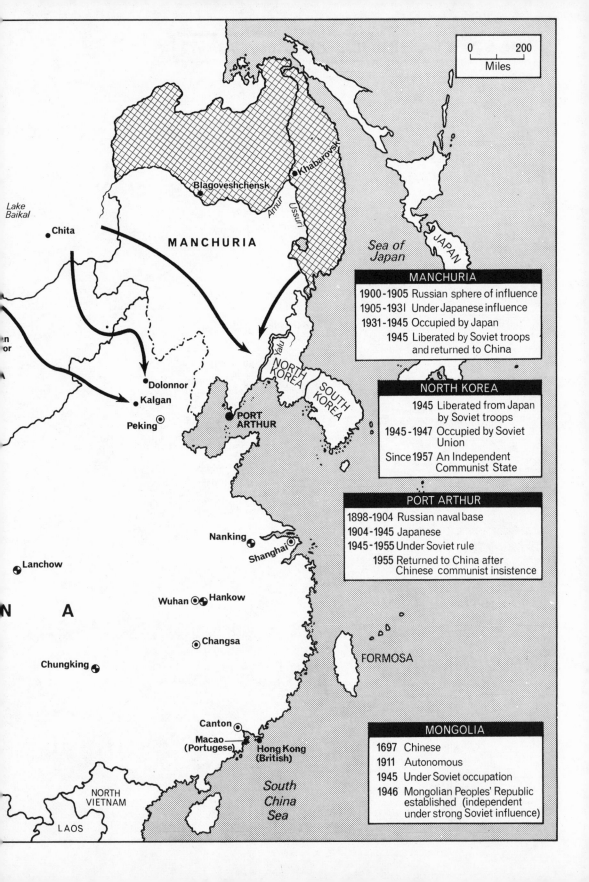

Lake
Baikal

● Chita

MANCHURIA

● Blagoveshchensk

Amur

Ussuri

● Khabarovsk

Sea of
Japan

JAPAN

n
or

● Dolonnor

Kalgan

Peking ◉

Yalu

NORTH
KOREA

SOUTH
KOREA

PORT
ARTHUR

● Lanchow

Wuhan ◉● Hankow

Nanking

Shanghai

Changsa ◉

Chungking ●

FORMOSA

N   A

Canton ◉

Macao
(Portugese)

Hong Kong
(British)

South
China
Sea

NORTH
VIETNAM

LAOS

0   200
Miles

MANCHURIA

1900-1905 Russian sphere of influence

1905-1931 Under Japanese influence

1931-1945 Occupied by Japan

1945 Liberated by Soviet troops
and returned to China

NORTH KOREA

1945 Liberated from Japan
by Soviet troops

1945-1947 Occupied by Soviet
Union

Since 1957 An Independent
Communist State

PORT ARTHUR

1898-1904 Russian naval base

1904-1945 Japanese

1945-1955 Under Soviet rule

1955 Returned to China after
Chinese communist insistence

MONGOLIA

1697 Chinese

1911 Autonomous

1945 Under Soviet occupation

1946 Mongolian Peoples' Republic
established (independent
under strong Soviet influence)

THE SOVIET-CHINESE BORDERLANDS 1970

──────────	The Soviet-Chinese border
─·─·─·─	Other international borders
┼┼┼┼┼┼┼	Soviet, Mongolian and Chinese railways in the border area
▨	Land over 2000 metres (6562 feet)
✛	Main airfields

Caspian Sea

Aral Sea

S O V I E

to Moscow

Omsk

TRANS - SIBERIAN RAILWAY

PERSIA

Novosibirsk ✛

Achinsk ✛

Karaganda ✛

Barnaul

Krasnoyarsk

Rubtsovsk

Semipalatinsk ✛

Biisk

Leninogorsk

Abakan

Lake Balkash

Aktogai

Tashkent ✛

Lake Zaisan

Lugovoi

Urdzhar

Lake Markakol

Samarkand

Zaisan

Panfilov

Diushambe

Frunze

L. Alakol

Tahcheng

Ulyungur Nor

Dzhalal Abad

Alma Ata ✛

Ebi Nor

Osh

Rybachiye

Issyk Kul

Kuldja

AFGHANISTAN

Urumchi ✛

Kashgar

Aksu

M

Lop Nor

PAKISTAN

KASHMIR

Lanchov

I N D I A

C H I

0	250

Miles

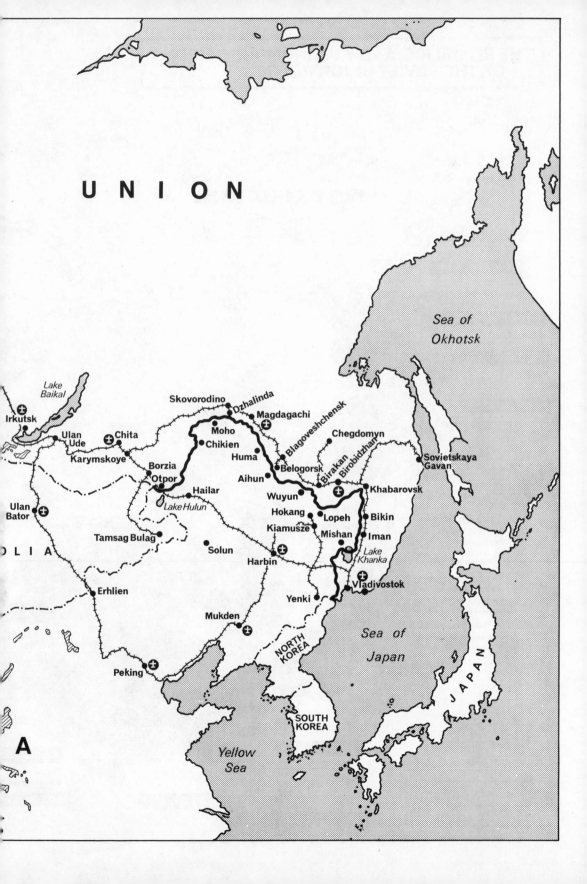

U N I O N

Lake
Baikal

Irkutsk

Ulan
Ude

Chita

Karymskoye

Skovorodino   Dzhalinda
                              Magdagachi
              Moho   Blagoveshchensk
              Chikien   Chegdomyn
                     Huma
Borzia   Belogorsk   Birakan
Otpor   Aihun   Birobidzhan
         Hailar   Wuyun   Khabarovsk
              Lake Hulun
Ulan   Hokang   Bikin
Bator   Lopeh
                                       Kiamusze   Mishan   Iman
         Tamsag Bulag   Lake
                          Solun   Khanka
O L I A   Harbin
                                                       Vladivostok
Erhlien
                                 Yenki

         Mukden

                         NORTH
                         KOREA

Peking

                                       SOUTH
                                       KOREA

Sea of
Okhotsk

Sovietskaya
Gavan

Sea of
Japan

J A P A N

Yellow
Sea

A

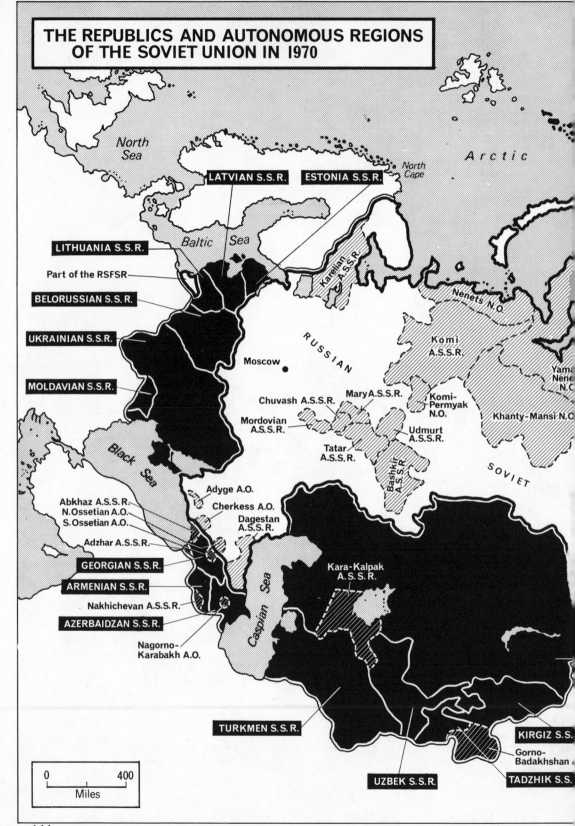

THE REPUBLICS AND AUTONOMOUS REGIONS OF THE SOVIET UNION IN 1970

North Sea

Arctic

North Cape

LATVIAN S.S.R.

ESTONIA S.S.R.

LITHUANIA S.S.R.

Baltic Sea

Karelian A.S.S.R.

Nenets N.O.

Part of the RSFSR

BELORUSSIAN S.S.R.

R U S S I A N

Komi A.S.S.R.

Yama Nene N.O

UKRAINIAN S.S.R.

Moscow

MOLDAVIAN S.S.R.

Chuvash A.S.S.R.

Mary A.S.S.R.

Komi-Permyak N.O.

Khanty - Mansi N.O

Mordovian A.S.S.R.

Udmurt A.S.S.R.

Black Sea

Tatar A.S.S.R.

Bashkir A.S.S.R.

S O V I E T

Adyge A.O.

Abkhaz A.S.S.R.
N.Ossetian A.O.
S.Ossetian A.O.

Cherkess A.O.

Dagestan A.S.S.R.

Adzhar A.S.S.R.

Kara-Kalpak A.S.S.R.

GEORGIAN S.S.R.

Caspian Sea

ARMENIAN S.S.R.

Nakhichevan A.S.S.R.

AZERBAIDZAN S.S.R.

Nagorno-Karabakh A.O.

KIRGIZ S.S.

Gorno-Badakhshan

TURKMEN S.S.R.

UZBEK S.S.R.

TADZHIK S.S.

```
0        400
      Miles
```

144

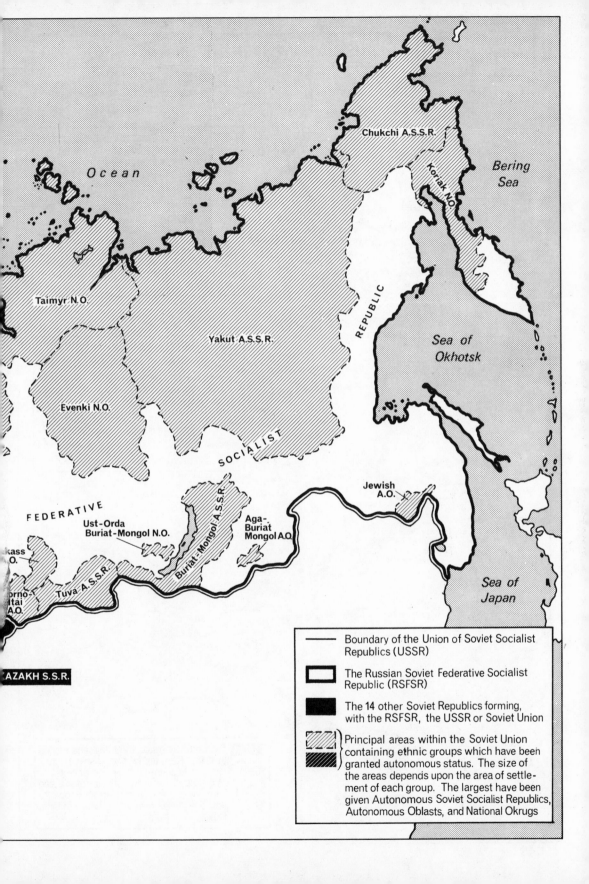

Ocean

Chukchi A.S.S.R.

Bering
Sea

Koriak N.O.

Taimyr N.O.

REPUBLIC

Sea of
Okhotsk

Yakut A.S.S.R.

Evenki N.O.

SOCIALIST

Jewish
A.O.

FEDERATIVE

Ust-Orda
Buriat-Mongol N.O.

Buriat-Mongol A.S.S.R.

Aga-
Buriat
Mongol A.O.

kass
O.

orno-
ltai
A.O.

Tuva A.S.S.R.

Sea of
Japan

AZAKH S.S.R.

———— Boundary of the Union of Soviet Socialist Republics (USSR)

▢ The Russian Soviet Federative Socialist Republic (RSFSR)

◼ The **14** other Soviet Republics forming, with the RSFSR, the USSR or Soviet Union

▨
▨ Principal areas within the Soviet Union containing ethnic groups which have been granted autonomous status. The size of the areas depends upon the area of settlement of each group. The largest have been given Autonomous Soviet Socialist Republics, Autonomous Oblasts, and National Okrugs

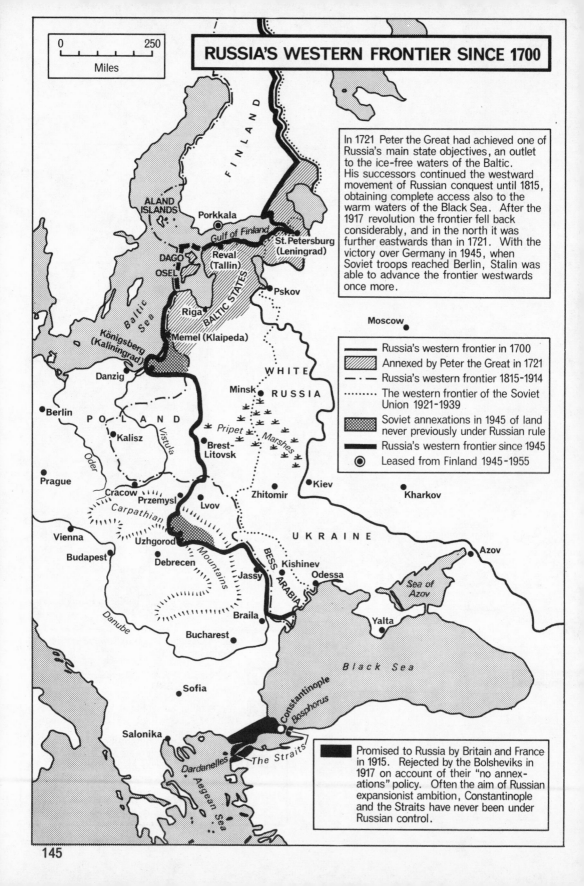

RUSSIA'S WESTERN FRONTIER SINCE 1700

0   250

Miles

In 1721 Peter the Great had achieved one of Russia's main state objectives, an outlet to the ice-free waters of the Baltic. His successors continued the westward movement of Russian conquest until 1815, obtaining complete access also to the warm waters of the Black Sea. After the 1917 revolution the frontier fell back considerably, and in the north it was further eastwards than in 1721. With the victory over Germany in 1945, when Soviet troops reached Berlin, Stalin was able to advance the frontier westwards once more.

FINLAND

ALAND ISLANDS

Porkkala

Gulf of Finland

St. Petersburg (Leningrad)

DAGO

Reval (Tallin)

OSEL

Pskov

Baltic Sea

Riga

BALTIC STATES

Moscow

Königsberg (Kaliningrad)

Memel (Klaipeda)

Danzig

WHITE

Minsk

RUSSIA

Berlin

P O L A N D

Vistula

Pripet

Marshes

Oder

Kalisz

Brest-Litovsk

Prague

Cracow

Przemysl

Lvov

Zhitomir

Kiev

Kharkov

Carpathian

U K R A I N E

Vienna

Uzhgorod

Mountains

Budapest

Debrecen

Jassy

BESS

ARABIA

Kishinev

Odessa

Azov

Sea of Azov

Braila

Yalta

Bucharest

Danube

Black Sea

Sofia

Constantinople

Bosphorus

Salonika

The Straits

Dardanelles

Aegean Sea

——————	Russia's western frontier in 1700
(hatched)	Annexed by Peter the Great in 1721
—·—·—	Russia's western frontier 1815-1914
··········	The western frontier of the Soviet Union 1921-1939
(stippled)	Soviet annexations in 1945 of land never previously under Russian rule
▬▬▬▬	Russia's western frontier since 1945
◉	Leased from Finland 1945-1955

Promised to Russia by Britain and France in 1915. Rejected by the Bolsheviks in 1917 on account of their "no annexations" policy. Often the aim of Russian expansionist ambition, Constantinople and the Straits have never been under Russian control.

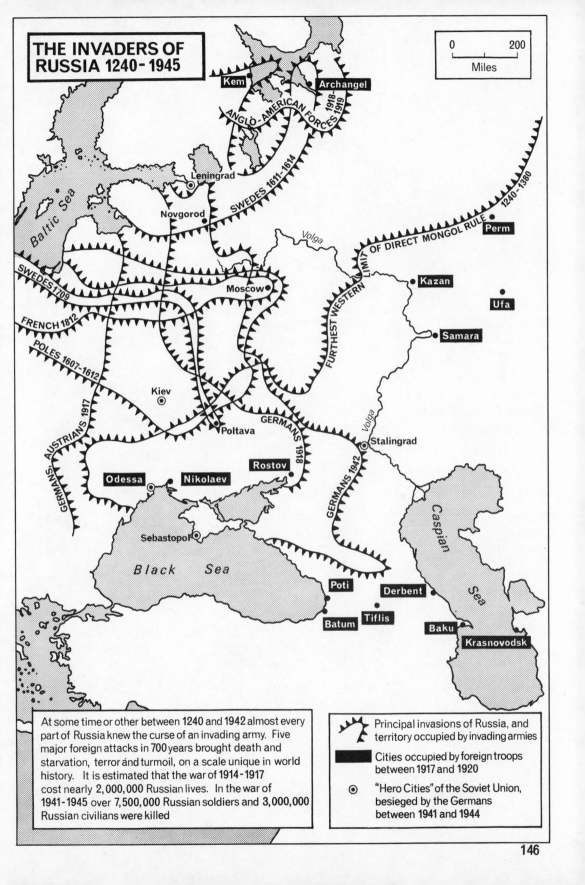

THE INVADERS OF RUSSIA 1240-1945

0   200
Miles

Kem   Archangel
1918-1919
ANGLO-AMERICAN FORCES

Leningrad
Novgorod
SWEDES 1611-1614
LIMIT OF DIRECT MONGOL RULE   1240-1380
Perm
Volga
SWEDES 1709
Moscow   Kazan
Ufa
FRENCH 1812
FURTHEST WESTERN
Samara
POLES 1607-1612
Kiev
Poltava
GERMANS 1918
Stalingrad
Volga
AUSTRIANS 1917
Odessa   Nikolaev   Rostov
GERMANS 1942
Caspian
Sebastopol
GERMANS,
Black   Sea   Sea
Poti   Derbent
Batum   Tiflis   Baku
Krasnovodsk

At some time or other between 1240 and 1942 almost every
part of Russia knew the curse of an invading army. Five
major foreign attacks in 700 years brought death and
starvation, terror and turmoil, on a scale unique in world
history. It is estimated that the war of 1914-1917
cost nearly 2,000,000 Russian lives. In the war of
1941-1945 over 7,500,000 Russian soldiers and 3,000,000
Russian civilians were killed

Principal invasions of Russia, and
territory occupied by invading armies

Cities occupied by foreign troops
between 1917 and 1920

"Hero Cities" of the Soviet Union,
besieged by the Germans
between 1941 and 1944

Bibliography of Works Consulted

(i) ATLASES

Baratov, R. B. (and others), *Atlas Tadzhikskoi Sovetskoi Sotsialisticheskoi Respubliki* (Dushanbe and Moscow, 1968)

Bartholomew, John (ed), *The Times Atlas of the World*, 5 vols (London, 1959)

Bazilevich, K. V., Golubtsov, I. A. and Zinoviev, M. A., *Atlas Istorii SSSR*, 3 vols (Moscow, 1949–54)

Beloglazova, O. A. (ed), *Atlas SSSR* (Moscow, 1954)

Czapliński, Wladislaw and Ladogórski, Tadeusz, *Atlas Historyczny Polski* (Warsaw, 1968)

Droysens, G., *Historischer Handatlas* (Bielefeld and Leipzig, 1886)

Durov, A. G. (General editor), *Atlas Leningradskoi Oblasti* (Moscow, 1967)

Engel, Joseph, *Grosser Historischer Weltatlas* (Munich, 1962)

Grosier, L'Abbé, *Atlas Générale de la Chine* (Paris 1785)

Hudson, G. F. and Rajchman, Marthe, *An Atlas of Far Eastern Politics* (London, 1938)

Kalesnik, S. V. (and others), *Peterburg–Leningrad* (Leningrad, 1957)

Kosev, Dimiter (and others), *Atlas Po Bulgarska Istoriya* (Sofia, 1963)

Kubijovýc, Volodymyr, *Atlas of Ukraine and Adjoining Countries* (Lvov, 1937)

Kudriàshov, K. V., *Russkii Istoricheskii Atlas* (Leningrad, 1928)

Kovalevsky, Pierre, *Atlas Historique et Culturel de la Russie et du Monde Slave* (Paris, 1961)

McEvedy, Colin, *The Penguin Atlas of Medieval History* (London, 1961)

Penkala, Maria, *A Correlated History of the Far East* (The Hague and Paris, 1966)

Oxford Regional Economic Atlas: The USSR and Eastern Europe (Oxford, 1956)

Sochava, V. B. (Principal ed), *Atlas Zabaikalia* (Moscow and Irkutsk, 1967)

Taaffe, Robert N. and Kingsbury, Robert C., *An Atlas of Soviet Affairs* (London, 1965)

Terekhov, N. M. (senior editor), *Atlas Volgogradskoi Oblasti* (Moscow, 1967)

Toynbee, Arnold J. and Myers, Edward D., *Historical Atlas and Gazetteer* (London, 1959)

Voznesenski (and others), *Atlas Razvitiya Khoziastva i Kultury SSSR* (Moscow, 1967)

Westermann, Georg, *Atlas zur Weltgeschichte* (Braunschweig, 1956)

Zamyslovski, Igor E., *Uchebnii Atlas po Russkoi Istorii* (St Petersburg, 1887)

(ii) MAPS

Atanasiu, A. D., *La Bessarabie* (Paris, 1919)

Bazewicz, J. M., *Polska w Trzech Zaborach* (Warsaw, n.d.)

Bazileva, Z. P., *Rossiiskaya Imperia 1801–1861* (Moscow, 1960)

British G.H.Q., Constantinople, *Ethnographical Map of Caucasus* (Constantinople, 1920)

Fedorovskaya, G. P. (publisher), *Promyshlennost Rossii 1913; Promyshlennost Soyuza SSR 1940* (Moscow, 1962)

Filonenko, W. J., *Volkstumkarte der Krim* (Vienna, 1932)

Kuchborskaya, E. P., *Rossiiskaya Imperia 1725–1801* (Moscow, 1959)

Stanford, Edward, *Sketch of the Acquisitions of Russia* (London, 1876)

Wyld, James, *Wyld's Military Staff Map of Central Asia, Turkistan and Afghanistan* (London, 1878)

(iii) ENCYCLOPAEDIAS, REFERENCE BOOKS AND GENERAL WORKS

Baedeker, Karl, *Russland* (Leipzig, 1912)
Cole, J. P., *Geography of the USSR* (London, 1967)
Florinsky, Michael T. (ed), *Encyclopaedia of Russia and the Soviet Union* (New York, 1961)
Katzenelson, Y. L. and Gintsburg, D. G. (eds), *Evreiskaya Entsiklopediya,* 16 vols (St Petersburg, 1906–13)
Kubijovyć, Volodymyr (ed), *Ukraine: A Concise Encyclopaedia* (Toronto, 1963)
Pares, Bernard, *A History of Russia* (London, 1926)
Parker, W. H., *An Historical Georgraphy of Russia* (London, 1968)
Sumner, B. H., *Survey of Russian History* (London, 1944)
Utechin, S. V., *Everyman's Concise Encyclopaedia of Russia* (London, 1961)
Zhukov, E. M. (ed), *Sovetskaya Istoricheskaya Entsiklopediya,* vols 1–12 (Moscow, 1961–69)

(iv) BOOKS ON SPECIAL TOPICS

Allen, W. E. D., *The Ukraine: A History* (Cambridge, 1940)
Allen, W. E. D. and Muratov, P., *Caucasian Battlefields: A History of the Wars on the Turco-Caucasian Border 1828–1921* (London, 1953)
Allilueva, A. S., *Iz Vospominanii* (Moscow, 1946)
Armstrong, John A. (ed), *Soviet Partisans in World War II* (Madison, 1964)
Armstrong, Terence E., *The Northern Sea Route* (Cambridge, 1952)
Avalishvili, Zourab, *The Independence of Georgia in International Politics 1918–1921* (London, 1940)
Baddeley, John F., *The Russian Conquest of the Caucasus* (London, 1908)
Baddeley, John F., *Russia, Mongolia, China,* 2 vols (London, 1919)
Caroe, Olaf, *Soviet Empire: The Turks of Central Asia and Stalinism* (London, 1953)
Chamberlin, William Henry, *The Russian Revolution 1917–1921,* 2 vols (New York, 1935)
Clark, Alan, *Barbarossa: The Russo-German Conflict 1941–1945* (London, 1965)
Conquest, Robert, *The Soviet Deportation of Nationalities* (London, 1960)
Cresson, W. P., *The Cossacks, their History and Country* (New York, 1919)
Dallin, Alexander, *German Rule in Russia 1941–1945* (London, 1957)
Dallin, David J., *The Rise of Russia in Asia* (London, 1950)
Dallin, David J. and Nicolaevsky, Boris I., *Forced Labour in Soviet Russia* (London, 1948)
Dixon, C. Aubrey and Heilbrunn, Otto, *Communist Guerilla Warfare* (London, 1954)
Dubnow, S. M., *History of the Jews in Russia and Poland* (Philadelphia, 1916–20)
Eudin, X. J. and Fisher, H. H., *Soviet Russia and the West 1920–1927: A Documentary Survey* (Stanford, 1957)
Fennell, J. L. I., *Ivan the Great of Moscow* (London, 1963)
Fennell, J. L. I., *The Emergence of Moscow 1304–1359* (London, 1968)
Fischer, Louis, *The Soviets in World Affairs,* 2 vols (London, 1930)
Fischer, Louis, *The Life of Lenin* (London, 1964)
Freund, Gerald, *Unholy Alliance: Russian-German relations from the Treaty of Brest-Litovsk to the Treaty of Berlin* (London, 1957)
Futrell, Michael, *Northern Underground: Episodes of Russian Revolutionary Transport and Communications through Scandinavia and Finland 1863–1917* (London, 1963)
Greenberg, Louis, *The Jews in Russia: The Struggle For Emancipation,* 2 vols (New Haven, 1944, 1951)

Höhne, Heinz, *The Order of the Death's Head: The Story of Hitler's S.S.* (London, 1969)

Indian Officer, An (anon), *Russia's March Towards India*, 2 vols (London, 1894)

Jackson, W. A. Douglas, *Russo-Chinese Borderlands* (Princeton, 1962)

Joll, James, *The Anarchists* (London, 1964)

Kamenetsky, Ihor, *Hitler's Occupation of Ukraine 1941–1944: A study of Totalitarian imperialism* (Milwaukee, 1956)

Kazemzadeh, F., *The Struggle for Transcaucasia* (New York, 1951)

Katkov, George, *Russia 1917: The February Revolution* (London, 1967)

Kennan, George, *Siberia and the Exile System* (New York, 1891)

Kerner, Robert J., *The Urge to the Sea: The Course of Russian History* (Berkeley and Los Angeles, 1946)

Kirchner, Walther, *Commercial Relations Between Russia and Europe 1400 to 1800* (Bloomington, Indiana, 1966)

Klyuchevskii, Vasilii Osipovich, *Peter the Great* (London, 1958)

Kochan, Lionel, *Russia in Revolution 1890–1918* (London, 1966)

Kolarz, Walter, *Russia and her Colonies* (London, 1952)

Krypton, Constantine, *The Northern Sea Route* (New York, 1953)

Lang, D. M., *A Modern History of Georgia* (London, 1962)

Leslie, R. F., *Reform and Insurrection in Russian Poland* (London, 1963)

Lias, Godfrey, *Kazak Exodus* (London, 1956)

Liubavskii, M. K., *Ocherk Istorii Litovsko-Russkovo Gosudarstva* (Moscow, 1910; Russian Reprint Series, The Hague, 1966)

Lorimer, F., *The Population of the Soviet Union: History and Prospects* (Geneva, 1946)

Lyashchenko, Peter I., *History of the National Economy of Russia to the 1917 Revolution* (New York, 1949)

Maksimov, S., *Sibir i Katorga*, 3 vols (St Petersburg, 1871)

Malozemoff, A., *Russian Far-Eastern Policy 1881–1904* (Los Angeles, 1958)

Manning, Clarence A., *Twentieth-Century Ukraine* (New York, 1951)

Mazour, Anatole G., *The First Russian Revolution, 1825: the Decembrist movement* (Stanford, 1961)

Mikhailov, V., *Pamiatnaya Knizhka Sotsialista-Revoliutsionera*, 2 vols (Paris, 1911, 1914)

Miller, Margaret, *The Economic Development of Russia 1905–1914* (London, 1926)

Mora, Sylvestre and Zwierniak, Pierre, *La Justice Sovietique* (Rome, 1945)

Nasonov, A. N., *Russkaya Zemlia* (Moscow, 1951)

Nikitin, M. N. and Vagin, P. I., *The Crimes of the German Fascists in the Leningrad Region: Materials and Documents* (London, 1947)

Nosenko, A. K. (ed), *V. I. Lenin 1870–1924* (Kiev, n.d.). A collection of photographs, with 2 maps

Obolenski, Prince Eugene, *Souvenirs D'Un Exilé en Sibérie* (Leipzig, 1862)

Owen, Launcelot A., *The Russian Peasant Movement 1906–17* (London, 1937)

Park, Alexander G., *Bolshevism in Turkestan 1917–1927* (New York, 1957)

Philippi, Alfred and Heim, Ferdinand, *Der Feldzug gegen Sowjetrussland 1941–1945* (Stuttgart, 1962)

Pierce, Richard A., *Russian Central Asia 1867–1917* (Berkeley and Los Angeles, 1960)

Pipes, Richard, *The Formation of the Soviet Union: Communism and Nationalism 1917–1923* (Cambridge, Massachusetts, 1954)

Platonov, S. F., *Ocherki Po Istorii Smuti v Moskovskom Gosudarstve* (Moscow, 1937)

Pospelov, P. N., *Istoriya Kommunisticheskoi Partii Sovetskovo Soyuza*, 6 vols (Moscow, 1964–68)

Pounds, Norman J. G., *Poland Between East and West* (Princeton, 1964)

Radkey, Oliver H., *The Agrarian Foes of Bolshevism* (New York, 1958)

Rapport du Parti Socialiste Revolutionnaire de Russie au Congres Socialiste International de Stuttgart (Ghent, 1907)

Reddaway, W. R., Penson, J. H., Halecki, O. and Dyboski, R. (eds), *Cambridge History of Poland*, 2 vols (Cambridge, 1941, 1950)

Reitlinger, Gerald, *The House Built on Sand: The Conflicts of German Policy in Russia 1939–1945* (London, 1960)

Riasanovsky, Nicholas V., *A History of Russia* (New York, 1963)

Rosen, Baron A., *Russian Conspirators in Siberia* (London, 1872)

Rostovtzeff, M., *The Iranians and Greeks in South Russia* (Oxford, 1922)

Salisbury, Harrison E., *The Siege of Leningrad* (London, 1969)

Schuyler, Eugene, *Peter the Great: Emperor of Russia,* 2 vols (London, 1844)

Schwarz, Solomon M., *The Russian Revolution of 1905* (Chicago, 1967)

Serge, Victor, *Memoirs of a Revolutionary 1901–1941* (London, 1963)

Seton-Watson, Hugh, *The Russian Empire 1801–1917* (London, 1967)

Shukman, Harold, *Lenin and the Russian Revolution* (London, 1966)

Simpson, Sir John Hope, *The Refugee Problem* (London, 1939)

Skazkin, S. D. (and others), *Istoriya Vizantii*, 3 vols (Moscow, 1967)

Slusser, Robert M. and Triska Jan F., *A Calendar of Soviet Treaties 1917–1957* (Stanford, 1959)

Squire, P. S., *The Third Department: The establishment and practices of the political police in the Russia of Nicholas I* (Cambridge, 1968)

Stephan, John J., *Sakhalin* (Oxford, 1971)

Sullivant, Robert S., *Soviet Politics and the Ukraine 1917–1957* (New York, 1962)

Sumner, B. H., *Peter the Great and the Ottoman Empire* (Oxford, 1949)

Sumner, B. H., *Peter the Great and the Emergence of Russia* (London, 1950)

Suprunenko, M. I. (and others), *Istoria Ukrainskoi RSR* (Kiev, 1958)

Tikhonov, Nikolai (and others), *The Defence of Leningrad: Eye-witness Accounts of the Siege* (London, 1944)

Treadgold, Donald W., *The Great Siberian Migration* (Princeton, 1957)

Trotsky, Leon, *My Life* (London, 1930)

Vernadsky, George, *The Mongols and Russia* (London, 1953)

Wheeler, G., *The Modern History of Soviet Central Asia* (London, 1964)

Woodward, David, *The Russians at Sea* (London, 1965)

Yarmolinski, Avram, *The Road to Revolution: A Century of Russian Radicalism* (London, 1957)

Yaroslavsky, E., *History of Anarchism in Russia* (London, 1937)

Zimin, A. A., *Reformy Ivana Groznovo* (Moscow, 1960)

(v) ARTICLES

Anon, 'How the Bear Learned to Swim', *The Economist* (London, 24–30 October 1970)

Bealby, John Thomas, Kropotkin, Prince Peter Alexeivitch, Philips, Walter Alison and Wallace, Sir Donald Mackenzie, 'Russia', *The Encyclopaedia Britannica* (Eleventh edition, London and New York, 1910)

Carsten, F. L., 'The Reichswehr and the Red Army 1920–1933', *Survey* (London, 1962)

Dziewanowski, M. K., 'Pilsudski's Federal Policy 1919–21', *Journal of Central European Affairs* (London, 1950)

Footman, David, 'Nestor Makno', *St Antony's Papers No. 6: Soviet Affairs No. 2* (Oxford, 1959)

Lobanov-Rostovsky, A., 'Anglo-Russian Relations through the Centuries', *Russian Review*, vol 7 (New York, 1948)

Parkes, Harry, 'Report on the Russian Caravan Trade with China', *Journal of the Royal Geographic Society*, vol 25 (London, 1854)

Stanhope, Henry, 'Soviet Strength at Sea', *The Times* (London, 25 January 1971)

Sullivan, Joseph L., 'Decembrists in Exile', *Harvard Slavic Studies,* vol 4 (The Hague, 1954)

Wildes, Harry Emerson, 'Russia's Attempts to Open Japan', *Russian Review,* vol 5 (New York, 1945)

Yakunskiy, V. K. 'La Révolution Industrielle en Russie', *Cahiers du Monde Russe et Sovietique* (The Hague, 1961)

Index

Compiled by the Author

83
88